NAIS

Journal of the NATIVE AMERICAN *and*
INDIGENOUS STUDIES ASSOCIATION

VOLUME 10.2

Fall 2023

NAIS (ISSN 2332-1261) is published two times a year in spring and fall (Northern Hemisphere) by the University of Minnesota Press, 111 Third Avenue South, Suite 290, Minneapolis, MN 55401-2520. http://www.upress.umn.edu

Postmaster: Send address changes to *NAIS*, University of Minnesota Press, 111 Third Avenue South, Suite 290, Minneapolis, MN 55401-2520.

Information about manuscript submissions can be found at naisa.org, or inquiries can be sent to journal@naisa.org.

Books for review should be addressed to *NAIS* Journal, The University of Texas at Austin, 150 W. 21st Street, Stop B3700, Austin, TX 78712-1155.

Address subscription orders, changes of address, and business correspondence (including requests for permission and advertising orders) to *NAIS*, University of Minnesota Press, 111 Third Avenue South, Suite 290, Minneapolis, MN 55401-2520.

SUBSCRIPTIONS
- **Individual subscriptions to *NAIS*** are a benefit of membership in the Native American and Indigenous Studies Association. NAISA's tiered membership ranges from $25 to $100 annually. To become a member, visit http://naisa.org/.
- For current **institutional subscriptions** and **back issue** prices, please visit: http://www.upress.umn.edu.
- **Digital subscriptions to *NAIS* for institutions** are now available online through Project MUSE at https://muse.jhu.edu.

NAIS

Journal of the NATIVE AMERICAN *and*
INDIGENOUS STUDIES ASSOCIATION

CONTENTS
VOLUME 10 ● ISSUE 2

Fall 2023

DEDICATION

The NAISA family
mourns the loss of NAISA Executive Assistant
Justin Hill

Tammy and Justin Hill
Photo by Tammy Hill.

NAISA depended on Justin's tremendous work ethic, his positive joy in doing a job well, and his ever-thoughtful, compassionate, and inquiring intellect. Humane and humorous, Justin was a staunch advocate for and ally with Indigenous peoples.

K. TSIANINA LOMAWAIMA *and* KELLY MCDONOUGH

WE WRITE THESE REMARKS in March 2023 as we near the end of our four-year term as *NAIS* journal coeditors; you will read these remarks when volume 10, no. 2 is published in the fall, after the journal's editorial offices have moved from the University of Texas at Austin to the University of Victoria in British Columbia. We are thrilled that the journal is moving into the capable hands of coeditors Heidi Kiiwetinepinesiik Stark and Gina Starblanket. We are confident that the journal will continue to excel and innovate under their exemplary leadership.

It has been an honor and a joy to help guide the journal through the last four years, from volume 7, no. 1 (2020) through volume 10, no. 2 (2023). We are grateful to the many committed members of the journal's editorial board who have supported and enhanced the work of the journal. Two developments in our term were sparked by editorial board conversations and could not have been accomplished without their labor. The first project was to revise the journal's peer review guidelines to reflect and embody Indigenous values of collegiality, kindness, generosity, and constructive encouragement to reach the highest levels of intellectual integrity and analysis. The second project began with conversations about how to support and encourage emerging and early-career scholars to publish and resulted in the establishment in 2021 of the journal's Writing Fellowship (see https://naisa.org /journal-nais/nais-fellowship/). Editorial board members oversee the application and selection process and work with the coeditors to recruit mentors for four to seven writing projects to support. Fellows are paired with mentors from the *NAIS* editorial board or NAISA membership, with whom they work for an academic year to move their writing project toward submission for publication. The coeditors arrange (virtual) gatherings to discuss issues such as vetting journals, submission guidelines, the peer-review process, and the journey of a manuscript through the editorial process from submission to publication. Our editorial term was interrupted by the COVID-19 pandemic and the movement of NAISA annual meetings to an online platform for two years, but it is the intention of the program to bring fellows and mentors together annually at the NAISA meeting.

During our term at the journal, we added the section "Teaching Native American and Indigenous Studies." This teaching category joins the journal's other categories of research articles: "Notes from the Field," "Intervention," and "Reviews." Whereas "Teaching" and "Notes from the Field" manuscripts are submitted by authors for consideration, "Intervention" consists of invited manuscripts, or sets of manuscripts, on issues of import to our readership. In volume 8, no. 1, working with prior *NAIS* editors Jean O'Brien and Robert Warrior, we recruited thirteen essays from a variety of perspectives for the "Intervention" section entitled "Indigenous Studies Reflections on the Land-Grab University Project" (for more on the project see https://www.landgrabu.org/ and https://github.com/HCN-Digital-Projects /landgrabu-data). In the same issue, as part of the transition from the editorial team of O'Brien and Warrior, they and we coauthored an editors' introduction, "*NAIS* Editorial Ethics, Principles, and Practices," to offer a brief history of the founding of the journal and to make transparent the journal's guiding ethical principles and editorial practices (see also: https://naisa .org/journal-nais/editorial-policies/).

One of the editorial practices we introduced into the peer review process of submitted manuscripts is the practice of developmental feedback. If we feel a submitted manuscript has great promise but is not ready to send out for peer review, we send a developmental feedback letter encouraging the author(s) to address issues—such as flow of narrative, technical aspects of the writing, methodology, theoretical framing, formatting, and so on— in the hopes of expediting the peer review process. We find this feedback has more productive results than a "decline with encouragement" letter, which—however encouraging—is still a decline. Two of the great joys of working as *NAIS* editors are to learn from the manuscripts submitted to the journal and to see how humane and constructive excellent peer reviews can be. As a whole, the constituencies we turn to in order to recruit peer reviewers—the membership of NAISA and scholars working in the international, interdisciplinary world of Indigenous studies—provide authors with reviews of great integrity and constructive help. They are detailed, kind, generous with assistance and suggestions, laudatory of the work already accomplished and the writers' strengths, and they motivate our authors to elevate fine work to excellent, deeply insightful work.

We owe many thanks to many constituencies, and we extend heartfelt thanks to the many reviewers who have materially contributed to the success and excellence of the *NAIS* journal. During our term, we were able to publish several hundred reviews of monographs, films, and websites. This means that several hundred scholars and community members in Indigenous studies—some of you more than once—contributed time, effort, and expertise to this meaningful service. O'Brien and Warrior continued to serve the journal throughout our term in what we came to call the "Review Collective": the four of us putting our heads together to choose works to review and the very best reviewers to do so. This puts O'Brien and Warrior's varied service to the journal at eleven years, for which we are immensely grateful.

We also owe immense gratitude to:

- The authors who submit their manuscripts to *NAIS*—in a very real sense, this is where it all begins.
- Our editorial team members, the graduate students working as managing editors over the years at the University of Texas at Austin who have handled the emails, reviews, manuscripts, correspondence with author and reviewers, submission of issues—all the myriad details that add up to a lot of work to keep the journal working. Thank you to Montserrat Madariaga-Caro, Alina Scott, Jessica L. Sánchez Flores, and Adam Martinez.
- Dr. Ann Huff Stevens, Dean of the College of Liberal Arts at the University of Texas at Austin for funding, and Dr. Jorge Pérez, chair of the Department of Spanish and Portuguese for course releases, managing editor tuition and health benefit support, and office space.
- The members of the journal's editorial board, who have offered innovative ideas, reviews, constructive criticism, labor, moral support, guidance on manuscripts, much-appreciated help in recruiting readers and reviewers, leadership in establishing the fellowship, and much more.
- Leadership and staff at the University of Minnesota Press (UMP), including Jason Weidemann, Susan Doerr, Jeff Moen, Daniel Ochsner, Rachel Moeller, Alicia Gomez, Diandra Coles, Anthony Silvestri, UMP's copy editors, and the talented members of the design team responsible for the journal's beautiful covers. UMP has been a staunch supporter of NAISA since the organizations' inception and a wonderful partner in producing the journal.
- NAISA Council for its financial support of the journal office and the writing fellowship, and for its unwavering respect for the editorial independence and integrity of the journal.
- Our readers, the membership of NAISA, committed to moving Indigenous studies forward in ethical, meaningful, innovative, and responsible ways.
- Jeani O'Brien and Robert Warrior, two of the cofounders of NAISA and inaugural coeditors of the journal (2013–2019), who built a rock-solid foundation for both NAISA and the *NAIS* journal.

- Heidi Kiiwetinepinesiik Stark and Gina Starblanket for their enthusiastic and joyful approach to taking over the editorship of *NAIS*—we look forward to seeing the fruits of your editorial labor and reading every issue cover to cover!

LIANNE C. LEDDY, BRITTANY LUBY, KIMBERLEY McLEOD, EMMA STELTER, *and* KIM ANDERSON

Refusing Confederation: Indigenous Feminist Performance as a Tool for Colonial Reckoning and Community (Re)Building

Abstract

In 2017, the Kika'ige Historical Society, an Indigenous women's performance troupe based in Guelph, Canada, created *Tabling 150* in response to celebrations of Canada's sesquicentennial. *Tabling 150* presented an opportunity for Indigenous women to engage in truth-telling amid celebrations of settler-colonial nationalism. By taking on personas of the "Grannies of Confederation," a play on the title of the well-known painting *The Fathers of Confederation,* the performers participated in Native feminist spatial practice, creating new orders through felt theory, presencing, and enacting refusals within their time and place in the academy. Drawing on interviews with the performers, we examine questions of the felt experience of doing Indigenous artivist resistance. Data from the participant performers was inductively coded, revealing four prominent themes: connecting with ancestors, taking space as resistance, community solidarity and empowerment, and Indigenous women's work in spatial practice while Indigenizing the academy. The analysis revealed that performance is an effective tool for calling out Canada's mistreatment of Indigenous Peoples at Confederation and the social inequities encoded into Canadian law during a period of settler-colonial celebration. The collective act of truth-telling by Indigenous performers strengthened a community through which it became safe to reflect upon and challenge colonial norms.

IN SUMMER 2021, Canadian nationalist pride hit a crisis flashpoint when news of uncovering thousands of unmarked graves of Indigenous children who attended Indian residential schools between 1831 and 1996 was published by mainstream media outlets, triggering expressions of shock, anger, and sadness.[1] As this reporting emerged in the weeks preceding the annual July 1 holiday that celebrates Canadian Confederation, Indigenous and allied communities called to cancel Canada Day, which a number of organizations and municipalities did. The news about children's graves also reinvigorated an uptake of decolonizing artivist practices, such as throwing red paint on statues of colonial figures or pulling them down. The statue head of Queen Victoria was tossed into the Assiniboine River in Manitoba and that of Egerton Ryerson (one of the architects of Indian residential schools in Canada) ended up on a spike at a Land Back Reclamation Camp in Southern Ontario. As in other locales and contexts, these practices were called out by some Canadians as an erasure of history. Conservative Party Members of Parliament representing Manitoba, along with the Conservative leader of the Canadian Senate, wrote a public letter calling the takedowns an attack on Canadian democracy and Canadian democratic institutions.[2] The federal Conservative leader Erin O'Toole indicated that Canada "should be proud to fly its flag even though it has a sad history of colonial abuse."[3]

The notion of "erasing history" by removing colonial markers from the landscape versus "truth-telling" by asserting Indigenous presence in Indigenous homelands engages the authors of this paper: three Indigenous historians/performers/artivists—Lianne Leddy, Brittany Luby, and Kim Anderson; settler artist/scholar Kimberley McLeod; and a student of Indigenous history, Emma Stelter.[4] We are practitioners and supporters of resistance and placemaking in response to settler nationalism in an era of truth and reconciliation. We explore the outcomes of a performance art piece that Anderson, Leddy, and Luby cocreated to respond to commemorations of Canada 150, focusing on the insights and feelings of the Indigenous women we recruited to perform by occupying a Canada 150 conference luncheon at the University of Guelph in 2017. We interviewed six participant performers about what the performance meant to them and found four prominent themes: connecting with ancestors, taking space as resistance, community solidarity and empowerment, and Indigenous women's work in spatial practice while Indigenizing the academy. As all the performers were Indigenous women working in the postsecondary sector, we were able to explore particular questions about how we Indigenous women negotiate space in mainstream institutions amid the discourse of national reconciliation and the connected project of "Indigenizing the Academy."[5]

We begin with how the Kika'ige Historical Society, a public history and performance art troupe formed by Anderson, Leddy, and Luby, responded to Canada 150, the celebration of 150 years since Canadian Confederation. Like other Indigenous individuals, communities, and allies, we felt the need to resist the extended Canada 150 celebrations that took place in 2017 for the same reasons that "Cancel Canada Day" was called for in 2021. From the standpoint of Indigenous truth-tellers, the year-long commemoration of Canada 150 erased the connection between nation building and broken treaties, forced removal from Indigenous lands, starvation, genocidal policies, Indian residential school atrocities, and the ongoing structural poverty among Indigenous Peoples within Canada who struggle for things as basic as clean drinking water.

In summer 2017, when Anderson was invited to speak at a Canada 150 symposium on her university campus, her response was to invite the Kika'ige Historical Society to reframe Canada's Confederation through Indigenous feminist performance art with a panel to follow.[6] The Kika'ige Historical Society's Canada 150 performance, entitled *Tabling 150,* created an opportunity to explore how Indigenous women take up space, combat erasure, and engage in truth-telling amid celebrations of settler-colonial nationalism. Our exploration was particularly focused on what it means to take up this practice within postsecondary institutions at a time when calls for truth and reconciliation by a national commission under the same name have resulted in negotiating Indigenous physical, relational, and epistemological space within such institutions.[7]

Such work was necessary and responsive to Indigenous demands for reckoning with settler colonialism. The Truth and Reconciliation Commission (TRC) of Canada (2015), a reckoning with Canada's residential school legacy, produced ninety-four calls to action, among them calls to Canadians and the institutions that serve them to better educate themselves and others on truths about the colonization of Indigenous Peoples.[8] Uptake of the recommendations has been limited and has thus elicited criticism.[9] Nevertheless, the TRC and, more recently, the National Inquiry into Missing and Murdered Indigenous Women and Girls (MMIWG) (2019) have opened a national dialogue and created a push for change in some sectors, including the postsecondary institutions where we work.[10] Many of these changes serve to counteract the erasure of Indigenous histories and contemporary experiences. Universities in Canada now routinely do land or territorial acknowledgments in advance of events, on syllabi or in faculty email signatures, to pay respect to the traditional Indigenous territories and the contemporary peoples of those places. Some institutions mandate courses or course credits for education about Indigenous Peoples as part of their degree programs. Most universities in Canada have developed (or are in the process of developing) some kind of Indigenous strategy to better serve Indigenous populations and better educate students, faculty, and staff. For example, at the University of Guelph, where three of the authors work, the Indigenous Initiatives strategy addresses matters of governance, curriculum, research, Indigenous student life and campus safety, security, and placemaking.[11]

Within this context of reckoning and reconciliation, Indigenous women find themselves engaged in truth-telling in postsecondary workplaces and fields of study. Our findings indicate that the performance allowed the Kika'ige Historical Society and the other performers to call on our grand-mothers and ancestors for guidance in order to occupy space as an act of resistance as we go about this work. By following the work of Indigenous women storytellers before us, we participated in what Indigenous feminists have articulated as Native feminist spatial practice, creating new orders through felt theory, presencing, and enacting refusals within our time and place in the academy.[12]

Placeholding and Indigenous Narration in a Time of Truth and Reconciliation

In collaboration with Indigenous feminists from other parts of the world, Anderson has described what Indigenous feminists bring to the process of "Indigenizing" the academy in settler-colonial states, including: taking up/ making space for Indigenous women and communities in postsecondary environments, engaging in community-based research, challenging colo-nial epistemologies, and introducing Indigenous knowledges and practices.[13] Anderson outlined how her Indigenous feminist work in the academy draws upon Mishuana Goeman's concept of "Native Feminism's Spatial Practice" to renarrate colonial histories and engage in Indigenous placemaking.[14] This Indigenous feminist work calls on us to teach and generate knowledge about the heteropatriarchal practices that have caused so much trauma to Indige-nous women and their communities—the dismantling of Indigenous kinship and gender relations through Indian residential schools and the systemic violence against women, girls, and queer/Two-Spirit peoples being two egre-gious examples, as the TRC and MMIWG have demonstrated. Our Indigenous feminist practice means advancing the narrative that nation building in Can-ada relied on the removal of Indigenous Peoples from their lands, a process that required dismantling the social relations that kept our nations strong.[15]

As Canada celebrated its sesquicentennial anniversary, members of the Kika'ige Historical Society felt that Indigenous perspectives were once again marginalized and ignored as the historical actions of exclusively white and male political leaders were celebrated across the country. Creating a performance art work in resistance to Canada 150 was conceived as an Indigenous feminist response to the "Fathers of Confederation" narrative that underpins Canadian Confederation, for, as Goeman says, "Native women's alternatives to heteropatriarchal representation of national space, referred to as traditional geography, are fundamental to understanding the ways in which nation-states in North America have built themselves through gendered spatial metaphors of dominance."[16] Our Indigenous feminist lens reminds us that when these "fathers" came to the table to negotiate the terms of a new nation during the Charlottetown conference of 1864 (Canada), the Indigenous matrilineal and matrifocal communities and the lands our ancestral grandmothers sustained were turned upside down with a violence that continues to this day. Indian residential schools, established shortly after Canadian Confederation and advocated for by some of these "fathers" and the colleagues who followed, were one of the key mechanisms designed to break down kinship, disrupt extended family systems governed by women, and instill heteropatriarchal systems of gender.[17] The ways in which Indigenous women take up, hold, and create space in the academy and elsewhere, the truths we tell today, are a response to that legacy of dispossession, offering practices of resistance.

Background to the Kika'ige Historical Society and Tabling 150

Anderson, Leddy, and Luby, three Indigenous women with doctorates in Canadian history, first formed the Kika'ige Historical Society in 2015 as Canada 150 plans were beginning across the country (well in advance of the 2017 sesquicentennial date). Their first act to challenge the Canadian nationalist narrative was a performance art piece in which Leddy and Anderson dressed up in jail uniforms and sat in chairs that were part of a newly erected statue of Canada's first prime minister, Sir John A. Macdonald.[18] After this performance, Anderson invoked Indigenous protocols by giving semma (tobacco) to Anishinaabe Elder Rene Meshake to request his help in finding an appropriate name for the troupe. Rene spoke about the role his father had in blazing a trail for the Ministry of Natural Resources crew to follow and gifted the following name in the spirit of trailblazing: "KIKA'IGE. It's in present tense. It means making marks on a tree by chipping off a piece of the bark. Like blazing a trail for students and travellers. I can see clearly that that's what you're doing in the academic world." The name itself has roots in the Anishinaabe culture of Leddy and Luby and also represents what the performance and public history troupe aims to accomplish: to interrupt settler narratives and to present Indigenous feminist ways of understanding history and heritage in what is now Canada, with a clear understanding of its meaning in Indigenous communities today.

Tabling 150 was Kika'ige's attempt to celebrate Indigenous womanhood and call attention to what settler nation-building projects have meant for Indigenous women. While Indigenous women holding leadership authorities among their own sovereign peoples might not have chosen a seat at settler nation-building tables, it is provocative to consider how Canada might have evolved under the imaginings of Indigenous women: or, more in line with Indigenous sovereignty, what Canada might have looked like had Indigenous women held authorities in negotiating treaties that were subsequently honored. Either way, we wanted to put our ancestral grandmothers at the table to provoke some thinking about what a nation that listened to Indigenous women might have looked like. The Kika'ige founders enlisted nine other Indigenous women with roots in various places in what is now Canada to help us perform and generate this discussion. All of us were employed at that time at one of three neighboring universities: University of Guelph, Wilfrid Laurier University, and the University of Waterloo.

We began by encouraging the performers to research what to wear in honor of how their grandmothers might have dressed had they been at the "Confederation table" or at the dinners and balls that took place during the 1864 Charlottetown conference discussing Canadian Confederation. The end result ranged from present-day regalia to borrowing from the theater

FIGURE 1. Lianne Leddy in front of Creelman Hall, University of Guelph, Ontario, Canada. Image by Tenille Campbell, sweetmoon photography.

FIGURE 2. Natasha Young as audience enters Creelman Hall, University of Guelph. Image by Tenille Campbell, sweetmoon photography.

department to dress as the "Grannies of Confederation," asserting our distinct ancestral identities through the visual aspects of the performance. As a group, we prepared the space for the banquet, with places for participants to write on the tables, and assisted each other as we dressed for the performance. Dene/Métis poet, author, scholar, and photographer Tenille Campbell of sweetmoon photography did individual portraits of each "Granny" and took pictures during our preparations and throughout the performance.

As conference participants entered the dining hall space where the luncheon was being served, the "Grannies" stood in quiet meditation throughout the room, our silence inviting participants to reflect on how they occupied space. Some performers stood in the room, others climbed on tables, some held specific items in their hands: but above all, no one spoke, even when we were approached by audience members. All of the tables had kitsch "Indian" souvenirs/figurines on them. Participants had to reckon with colonial reductions of Indigenous personhood before dynamic, living Indigenous women. It was a stark reminder that Confederation impacted human beings—not stock characters/figurines like Indian warriors and Indian princesses. Each place setting also had a table mat with an image of the "Fathers of Confederation" on the top side, and on the flip side, there was an excerpt from the *Constitution Act, 1867,* the legal foundation for Confederation. Canada's early objectification of Indigenous women can be linked to this document. In Section

91, Indigenous Peoples were and are categorized with things like "Beacons, Buoys, Lighthouses," "currency and coinage," and "Weights and Measures." Table settings reminded participants that people, law, and stereotypes constrained where and how Indigenous women could (and can) be in what is currently known as Canada despite their ability to hold space.

After the performance, we ate together at a large central table and Kawennakon Bonnie Whitlow opened with the Haudenosaunee Thanksgiving Address in Kanyen'kéha, or the words that come before all else. We feasted together as a group of performers, and then Anderson, Leddy, and Luby began a discussion that introduced the Kika'ige Historical Society, Indigenous views of Canadian history, and what reconciliation means to us as Indigenous women and scholars. McLeod acted as a discussant with a focus on performance art, drawing observations from having witnessed the performance unfold. Conference participants were invited to comment and ask questions of the panel and to reflect on the performance and what they were feeling afterward.[19] At this point some of the performers shared their own perspectives on the performance, as well as their experiences as Indigenous People living within Canada. At the end, after the audience left, all of the performers gathered onstage, and Campbell positioned us as the "Grannies of Confederation," a play on the title of the well-known painting featuring several politicians present at the Charlottetown Conference: *The Fathers of Confederation*.[20] With this act, we commemorated resistance.

Research Questions and Methods

In an effort to better understand the ways in which the performance was experienced and interpreted by both performers and audience members, we interviewed six performers and seven spectators.[21] While bigger questions of Canada 150, nation building, and the positioning of Indigenous women were discussed by the panelists at the event, we also wanted to explore the experience of placeholding, resistance, and truth-telling on the part of the performers—and as experienced by the attendees. We were interested in questions about what it means for Indigenous women to create and hold space in the university and amid celebrations and dialogue relating to settler nationalism. How do Indigenous women create counter-narratives, and what is their experience in doing so? What is the experience of settler subjects when they encounter Indigenous women in this practice? What are the costs and risks? Our interviews were open-ended but included broad questions ranging from asking participants to describe how they felt about the performance; what it prompted them to think about, learn, or reflect upon; and finally, how they would describe the experience to a friend.

This section focuses on the felt experiences of the performers, all of whom were academic staff members, examining questions of doing the work of artivist resistance from the inside. We analyzed their interviews as well as the speeches that some of them made during the debrief at the event. This data was coded using Braun and Clarke's reflexive thematic analysis, which is a method for identifying themes within qualitative data through data familiarization, data coding, theme development, and revision.[22] Four prominent themes were identified and are described here: connecting with ancestors, taking space as resistance, community solidarity and empowerment, and Indigenous women's work in spatial practice while Indigenizing the academy. The collective act of truth-telling by Indigenous performers strengthened a community through which it became safe to reflect upon and to challenge colonial norms—not only of the Dominion of Canada but of Canadian academic institutions. In solidarity, Indigenous women used performance to reject colonial power and to assert Indigenous feminist presence. Centering the embodied, performative storytelling experience of the women we interviewed brings us to the "felt theory" work of Indigenous feminist theorist Dian Million. Given that *Tabling 150* began as a project in which Indigenous women historians addressed settler nationalist commemoration, we appreciate Million's articulation of how we "seek to present our histories as affective, *felt*, intuited as well as thought."[23] In describing felt theory, Million honors the ancestral and living Indigenous women authors and truth-tellers who set the stage for us; those who have presented their lived, felt experiences versus the "objective accounts of Canadian (and U.S.) colonial histories."[24]

Findings: Felt Experiences of the Performers

Connecting with Ancestors

We learned from the interviews that the performance was significant to the performers from the outset as it encouraged them to learn about and make connections with their own ancestors prior to the performance. As noted earlier, each performer took care choosing their clothing for the event, thinking of their distinct ancestry as they did so. One woman (P10) described the involvement of family knowledge and her own learning journey through this preparation:

> I had been talking to one of my aunts who had collected some old photos of my family and we had been talking about it in the summer. It came full circle that I was able to pull those photos out and I really tried to sit with them, and think about how to embody my great great great grandmother. I had some self-learning, thinking about who my family was, who I am today, and how I wanted to represent my grannies.

For this performer, it was not simply a time to dress up. She planned her performance clothing in a way that would honor her ancestors and how they lived. The performer then identified the juxtaposition between the formality of the Charlottetown Conference and her own family's experiences in their territory:

> I think initially we talked about it being a bit like a formal ball, like the fathers of Confederation were all dressed up. But when I looked at those family photos, they were all women on the land, women wearing aprons, working hard with children mulling around. So instead of dressing up, I really wanted to live in that space, of someone of the land. It doesn't really matter if your skirt is perfectly clean. It's like choosing to be of true to that, and a lot of woolen blankets as shawls.

In her postperformance speech, another performer (P2) made note of the same connection to family history, stating: "Sitting there, I was representing what I thought that the women would have been doing back in those days . . . working on my moccasins, and thinking about my kokomish, my ancestors." These performers understood the importance of documenting Indigenous women's labor in their dress, as well as their relationship to land. This required attention to more than just details in the family photo; it is clear that P10 thought about her own family history, as well as a deep understanding of Indigenous women's history and responsibilities to the land. So instead of formal ball attire from the mid-nineteenth century, P10 and P2 chose clothing that represented women's contributions to community and territory.

References to Indigenous grannies as inspirations came up in other aspects of the performance as well. As one performer (P10) noted, the performance was an exercise in representation and revisioning the past in a very personal way. She remarked that, among the performers there were "a lot of people that you know and a few people you don't know but [we were] all coming together with that shared grounding of representing who we are, representing our grannies, or envisioning who our grannies might have been." Another performer (P7) remarked on the energy in the room and the impact of being surrounded by other Indigenous women, noting that "knowing who you are [is] amplified when you get to be around other Indigenous People and Indigenous women . . . your energies intermingle with each other." She noted the presence of her ancestors, as well as those of the other women in the room:

> I [generally] feel the support of my ancestors, but when you get in a room like that, it's like you have all these powerful women with all the powerfulness of their ancestral lines together. Physically, there was 15, 18 of us maybe there in the room . . . But spiritually it was like that room was so crowded that those white people had a hard time walking into [it].

P9 harnessed the image of a granny for strength and inspiration during the performance, when she was envisioning and staging her own comportment:

> Initially I chose a stern and challenging stance and a very stern and challenging type of way to use my rattle. So instead of a soft gentle calling in that I could have done, I hit it into the palm of my hand as if it were a war club. So when people were entering into the space, because I was facing that front door, people would smile. And being raised in this kind of [welcoming] environment, I wanted to smile back. But I had to remind myself of the fact that I wasn't being my smiley hospitable self. I was being that stern grandmother that had a very stern message to give my children.

The performer's use of the space in her strong stance and her taking on the spirit of a "stern granny" helped her draw out those parts of herself for the performance. She noted that because of the way she was raised, and due to our Indigenous responsibilities to show hospitality, her initial compulsion to smile was taken over by her granny persona. These guests were not ordinary guests, and this was no ordinary feast. The performer's use of the war rattle "as if it were a war club" made it clear that diplomacy in the context of Confederation was challenged; this particular performer thought this was no time for smiling and, thinking back to her matriarchal ancestors, issued a warning instead. To suppress the impulse to smile at one of the audience members, she said, "I had to consciously think about how Canada has treated Indigenous people across time. I started to think about all of the racist moments in my life that I've experienced. And then I was just like 'Nope. I'm not gonna smile at the man, I'm just going to maintain this.'" She summed it up with, "So I guess I was practicing my granny toughness."

Taking Space as Resistance

Some of the performers spoke about the experience as a chance to reverse the discomfort experienced in settler spaces throughout their lives. These reflections followed remarks by McLeod, who in her postperformance discussant role talked about the productive tentativeness as the settler audience entered the room and were faced with tough Indigenous women, unwilling to speak or provide comfort. One performer talked about her realization that the discomfort mirrored her own daily lived experience as an Indigenous woman:

> When Dr. McLeod was talking about watching people coming in; the experience, the tentativeness, the looking for a place. "Do I fit? Where do I go?" . . . It occurred to me: this is our experience of living in Canada our whole lives. My whole life. I remember going to school, in those early years, and feeling

like that. I remember when I left home, and I wasn't among the people that I had grown up with and knew. I grew up in a village of 600 people so I knew everybody and their entire family histories and all of that, and when I came out here it was years and years before I could teach myself to look at people. To meet their eyes. To talk to people. It's still difficult for me. After all these years, it's still not easy. And often I'm in environments where I feel that awkwardness and that not belonging feeling, and it was so profound for me.

This performer, who was in her late sixties, remarked that performing allowed her to experience, understand, and reflect on what it meant to be marginalized: "I articulated something that I hadn't been able to articulate in [number] years of living until that day. So for me it was really a transformative kind of experience."

The discomfort of finding oneself in an unwelcoming place does not abate for many Indigenous women. P7 articulated similar feelings of discomfort, stating, "Many times I'll walk into spaces and . . . they're white spaces . . . patriarchal spaces. Whether it be conferences or other things . . . it just feels like—like it's not really a space for you or don't have anything valuable, that you can contribute or whatever." She then described witnessing the temporary discomfort among the *Tabling 150* spectators:

> When we got to sit down [at] the centre table, and we had the nicest china and just got to have fun—that felt good 'cause I think people were still awkward around us. And not to be boastful or that I want people to feel bad, it's not about that. But . . . I liked creating a space that tried to have others feel like we may feel in most of our lives, in some small way.

This performer also noted an incredibly important distinction between the lived experience of pervasive racism as an Indigenous woman and a fleeting moment of discomfort for our settler audience members: "In getting that, they still know in any given moment, they can walk out the door and go back into their comfortable space. Whereas, you know, we walk out the door [and] we can't get out of our bodies, our space."

P6 also noticed audience members' discomfort and wondered if they were "feeling the way I have felt in these spaces." She noted this pertained to being "an Indigenous person walking into academic spaces specifically . . . it was a conference, but even just any spaces that aren't necessarily safe." She commented on how she felt watching the audience come into the performance space: "I found myself wondering *how are they doing?* but also *are they experiencing what I've experienced?—as an Indigenous person, as an Indigenous academic.*" This reversal of the gaze was rooted in empathy but also based on an understanding that it is not unusual for Indigenous faculty and staff to feel uncomfortable in university spaces.

FIGURE 3. Kim Anderson, Kathy Absolon, and Kawennakon Bonnie Whitlow preparing for the performance, Creelman Hall, University of Guelph. Image by Tenille Campbell, sweetmoon photography.

P7 linked taking up space in the performance setting to the same process in her academic workplace, moving from discomfort to empowerment through increased visibility:

> It's about just being present and visible and taking up space, instead of just staying in our own space. All space is our space. This is our space, this is our land—not my Cree land specifically, but you know, this is Indigenous land . . . Even my staff meeting the other day—we used to just meet in our student centre—and I was like . . . we're gonna go the boardroom where the big windows are and everybody sees us. Like this whole building, this is our space. We work here and we can take up space, and be visible, and other people need to see us in the space.

For this performer, taking up space is an act of ongoing resistance, one that she sees as being linked to decolonization of Indigenous lands generally, as well as in her workplace. It can also be a performative act, as the example she describes is one in which Indigenous staff deliberately position themselves in a boardroom with big windows "where everybody sees us."

Community Solidarity and Empowerment

One of the unexpected elements of the performance was that it created a space to foster community solidarity among Indigenous women in the region's urban communities. This sentiment was noted in participant remarks about how we called upon our ancestors for assistance but also in how the coming together of Indigenous women created a gathering space that involved kinship, community, and empowerment at its foundation. It also provided the opportunity for healing and to actively resist erasure. In the words of P10, "The coming together is also a form of ceremony."

Several performers invoked a kinship connection between women performers throughout this experience. As P1 said, "I felt almost a kinship because everyone was a woman. And so I felt that . . . I guess connection in that we are able to claim space in the same way that men do in our society." P11 noted the community connections that helped her overcome her nervousness to perform: "I was nervous initially. And then I realized as people started to enter what a powerful feeling it was to be amongst other Indigenous women, especially, and two-spirit folks, and just those that were trying to emphasize the feeling of what it is that we feel on a day-to-day basis. So it was really powerful." P7 commented: "I just felt strong. And I felt in control. And I felt supported by the Indigenous sisters that were there and so it didn't really matter what people did when they came in . . . I was safe in that space and not just safe but like, we owned that space." P7 went on to explain how the women-centred performance was significant in making "the connections to matriarchal societies, the connections to the specific erasure, the violent erasure of Indigenous women." She made the connection to contemporary times "where we're still at with missing and murdered Indigenous women."

One performer (P8) saw the experience as a micro-expression of her own life, noting that "what the performance changed for me was my understanding of some of the challenges that I've overcome in my life. . . . but it doesn't just apply to me, it applies to all Indigenous people." She emphasized the work that Indigenous Peoples undertake to contribute to community healing, stating: "I think that it makes me even stronger in recognizing the importance of the work that we do as people . . . actually it's the women, working in the front lines, in the universities, in the social services and all over the place." She made the strong connection between her own convictions and the resurgence of Indigenous ways of being:

> I guess [performing] made me feel even stronger in what I already believed in, which is the work and the value and the fundamental beauty of Indigenous people. And it made me even more committed to the work that I do. Even more committed to never stopping. This is not going to be corrected in a hurry.

The performance allowed for a reimagining, a renarrating of kinship and in so doing offered an opportunity for one participant to resist the erasure of queer/Two-Spirit identities. P7 talked about the importance of kinship and support in making sure her identity was visible and how she asserted her identity when she was first invited to participate, saying "I'm two-spirit and . . . even back then, I'm pretty sure I would not have been wearing a dress or certain attire or whatever, and Kim was like 'yeah, yeah, just go with what feels strong and powerful for you.'" It was important for this performer to authentically represent her identity:

> Being in that historical context that we were in, being visibly centred in my two-spiritedness [and] being within that circle was also really cool and empowering for me because many of us in this conversation—it's still occurring today, on pretty much a daily basis in my life—you know . . . that erasure of the two-spirited people within the circle. And uh, there was no judgment; I was just within the circle with, with my sisters and my relatives there and it was good. Like it never came up in conversation or anything after, [about] why this granny was wearing pants.

As we came together to assert ourselves as grannies, many performers voiced how the experience of togetherness and visible identity reclamation was empowering. This was encapsulated by P9's reaction to seeing herself in a mirror: "In the moment—I had put on some face paint—and I looked at my face paint and it was pretty badass." Whether it was with face paint, regalia, or an apron in "country" dress, the performers felt good about doing embodied resistance to interrupt a nationalist narrative and claim their rightful place at the table.

Indigenous Women's Work in Spatial Practice while Indigenizing the Academy

All of the performers were faculty and/or had backgrounds in student support roles in the university setting. In several of the interviews, participants noted the themes of Indigenous labor and Indigenization, making particular reference to the labor of Indigenous women. Some performers made the connection between the performance and Indigenizing spaces more generally; as one participant argued, "It's the women working in the front lines, in the universities, in the social services and all over the place, trying to [make] change, [it's the women] that are so entrenched." Another performer (P6) noted the importance of Indigenous women's leadership in the performance: "Of course the leadership of that event was the Indigenous women and academics and researchers . . . we kind of reclaimed . . . to make it an Indigenized a space." P6 also noted that the postperformance discussion was led by women.

P6 went on to describe how Indigenizing the hall by taking up space could allow spectators to empathize and grow:

> There's lots of ways you can Indigenize a space . . . At the beginning . . . entering into that space with the grannies really intentionally positioned throughout the room, . . . doing things that felt right to them, whether that was drumming or reading or [acting] stoic or, and I think definitely an opportunity to learn.

Another performer (P10) remarked that holding that space was significant for her in terms of highlighting Indigenous women's strength and agency, stating: "I appreciated the idea that we would hold some space as Indigenous women in a time when we don't always have the opportunities to be portrayed, and be portrayed as strong individuals."

While the performance was meant to unsettle non-Indigenous conference participants and privilege Indigenous bodies and voices in the conference luncheon and panel, a number of the performers also experienced it as unsettling. As none of the women had done performance art previously, it is not surprising that some talked about their initial discomfort. P6 said:

> I felt very much on display, which I was. And so for me that was uncomfortable. I'm not an attention person; it makes me really nervous and so as soon as people started coming in, I started to wonder why I stood up on a chair

and made myself so high, when everyone else was either sitting at tables, sitting on tables or standing, like at sort of ground level.

The same performer went on to explain how her experience changed as the event unfolded and how it pushed her beyond her normal comfort level: "As people started coming in, I got used to it. But I still look back on that and think like, *whoa me standing on a chair is very not like me.* But I think that's also important—to push myself, you know, a little bit out of my comfort zone."

Like P6, many had been encouraged to participate by the Kika'ige founding members, and they noted the challenge of pushing themselves to participate in discussions of the legacies of Confederation as Indigenous women. P10 noted that she overcame her introverted nature and pushed herself to take up more space through what became an empowering experience for her:

> Although the performance put me in an awkward position 'cause I'm shy in those environments, I learned how to be in that space and thrive, to be okay with the discomfort, and really appreciate the gentle nudge Kim offered to encourage me to step into that role. To take a responsibility to be there because at first I was like *Nahhhh . . . that doesn't sound like me. The dressing up doesn't sound like me.* The holding space.

This participant remarked on the portraits that Campbell had taken of each "granny" outside the banquet hall, where she worked with participants one by one: "Thinking about the picture Tenille took of me—she got me to stand with my feet really broad because she said 'You're not taking up enough space!' Even thinking about that; how we can impact how people perceive us, by what we're wearing and how we're standing."

In addition to contemplating their own unease, some performers talked about actively resisting the need to make the settler audience comfortable, remarking on how this differed from the expectations in their workplaces. P11 reflected on her positionality as a university employee, saying, "My first instinct is to comfort someone who is feeling uncomfortable as a means to . . . form a relationship and discuss some of those important things, like the impact of colonization, decolonization in the education system, ways that they can learn, or unlearn, what they know about Canadian history— and I wasn't able to do any of that in that space." She went on to comment on our refusal to speak as performers, admitting that "being still and being silent was difficult in that process. It just kind of went against the nature of the work that we often do." She noted that this was made even more difficult because she knew some of the audience members. She remembered thinking at the time, "I've got to stop holding other's people guilt" when she realized this was one of her responses. P11 realized that we "are undergoing our own healing process ourselves, and too often I tend to want to take care of people's emotions or hold that space for them; I think that this performance really allowed me time to reflect on how it is that I feel day to day." She added, "I felt that it was a healing practice," bringing that idea of providing comfort full circle.

P11 had a follow-up conversation with one of the audience members after the event and reflected on the latter's learning experience. She felt empowered by their discussion:

> I ended up talking to a friend who participated who isn't Indigenous, and she was saying she felt very uncomfortable and was talking to me about what she had learned throughout . . . and while I understood her discomfort I also felt that it was great to finally talk about [the discomfort]; for her to finally feel that lived experience of what is felt so often day to day, and so it was empowering through that conversation.

P11 found it a positive and empowering experience to make the audience member aware of the reversal of the colonial gaze and thus also make them aware of the constant discomfort Indigenous People often feel in public spaces. She was able to turn the awkwardness into a teachable moment, as well as a productive moment of reflection for both of them.

Not all performers felt uncomfortable. P7 said she didn't feel awkward, which was a reversal of what she felt in her day job at the university. She described universities as often unwelcoming for Indigenous People and talked about having to hold uncomfortable conversations at work in order to encourage change. Again, this performer emphasized her role at her postsecondary institution, describing what that work entails: "The type of work that I do at the university, like 95% of the time I'm awkward and uncomfortable, going into these spaces and you know, having to try and engage non-Indigenous people in the conversations, and answer questions, and things like that." Her day-to-day experience in the university workplace, therefore, mitigated her own discomfort in this particular performance setting. She remarked: "People looked really awkward and uncomfortable coming in. I liked that."

When expanding on her feelings, P7 noted that awkwardness can be productive, especially since it was a reversal of the colonial gaze. She pointed out that Indigenous Peoples are "under the colonial gaze and interpreted under the colonial gaze." She saw the performance as a "kind of flipping that back on itself because I think they would see glimpses of colonialism but it was like reflected back with the Indigenous [women] in power."

Another performer (P2) talked about her childhood and being marginalized in a racist community:

I grew up in the bush I was bussed in half an hour every day to go to the public school . . . I grew up in a very Ojibway centred world . . . and I also grew up in a place where there was a lot of racism, around—people who judged us, people who rejected us, outward hostility, outward name calling, outward bullying. That was what I experienced in my education. From the teachers, and from the kids in the playground.

While P2 overcame these experiences, she worried that those same feelings would resurface at the time of the performance. She drew strength from the clothing she had chosen, as it allowed her to counteract "walking around in the world feeling invisible, being invisible." She pointed out that "the discomfort is in the silence. The discomfort is in the not making eye contact. The discomfort is in the just avoidance." Because this has been a strategy for survival in the past, the first part of the performance, where she was required to sit silently and not look at people, allowed her to reflect on other instances in which she had employed this behavior.

Discussion and Conclusion

The Kika'ige Historical Society had intended *Tabling 150* to be an educational performance for a largely settler audience, taking place in a university setting mostly populated by settler Canadians. We hoped to provoke discussion about nation building, the disempowerment of Indigenous women, and the strength they have demonstrated in resisting erasure and sustaining Indigenous families to the present day. We refused to celebrate Canada 150 but honored instead 150 years of survival against incredible odds. We did not anticipate that it would open up so many feelings and revelations in the performers themselves. Once we saw the response in the postperformance speeches, we were curious to further explore the felt experience of *Tabling 150*, which we did by inviting performers and audience members to interviews. In this discussion about the findings of our conversations, we draw upon the work of Indigenous and feminist theorists to deepen our understanding of the performers' accounts of their experience.

We began by referring to Goeman's concept of "Native feminism's spatial practice," which calls attention to the gendered ordering of space through colonialism and the possibilities that arise when Indigenous women engage in renarrating and (re)mapping through literary work.[25] Focusing on performer interviews allows us to center felt experiences of the renarrating and (re)mapping that occurred in *Tabling 150*. In her description of felt theory, Million highlights the trailblazing work of Indigenous women authors of the 1970s and 1980s. Our focus on felt theory acknowledges the ongoing legacy and impact of this work, both in relation to Canada 150 and more recent events. After a heated 2021 summer of statue takedowns, embodied protests, responses, and arguments among Canadian historians about the genocidal intent of Indian residential schools, Million's words are prescient:

> Because the affective knowledge of our experience informs alternative productions of truth, it is challenged ferociously. History is a site where founding narratives of nations are contested and legitimated. History as a discipline became challenged by changes in theories of knowledge as well as political orders outside of any one nation as those "without history" were called to witness. Indigenous women's voices became important to founding moments of these new orders.[26]

While the audience at *Tabling 150,* largely open to learning, did not ferociously challenge our alternative productions of settler-colonial historical "truths," our performance still led to discomfort on all sides and, as McLeod observed, "a productive tentativeness." It is possible that the willingness to listen may have allowed space for the performers' voices to be heard—perhaps more so than had we been in a more challenging public space. While we can't say what the long-term impact might be for those who attended, at least the audience was confronted with some of the "truths" about nation building in Canada at a time of settler-nationalist commemoration. McLeod's observations of the productive tentativeness speak to the possibilities of creating "new orders" through Indigenous feminist public history and performance.[27]

One significant finding from the interviews was that our use of performance art to create affective knowledge and alternative productions of truth opened up truths among the performers themselves. *Tabling 150* created an unanticipated collective, embodied experience for the performers that brought many of them to the borders of their own comfort zone, while producing feelings of empowerment. The affective nature of knowledge production that Million refers to was enhanced through the embodied, deliberately performative experience of the women who participated.

The embodied, ceremonial, and performative nature of the work also came together in what Leanne Simpson has described as "presencing." Simpson theorizes that Indigenous Peoples come from "societies of presence" that generated meaning through action, creative process, and ceremony.[28] She draws from the work of Anishinaabe curator and artist Wanda Nanibush:

> Wanda [Nanibush] writes that performance art, because it is based on process, contradiction, action and connection, is closer to Indigenous ideas of art and resistance. The meaning of both performance art and Indigenous thought is obtained through collective truths that are derived from the

experience of individuals, relationships and connections (to the non-human world, the land and each other) through action or "presencing" and through creative process.[29]

Through the performance, participants were able to express collective truths of what Canada has meant to Indigenous Peoples. As an act of presencing, this involved both physical and metaphysical elements and also a strengthening of kinship.

Presencing involves taking and making space, which can be seen in the example provided by the participant who decided to have Indigenous meetings in a very public and central boardroom at her university. While we did not set out with theoretical elements of presencing in mind, the empowerment of Indigenous women to take up space was one of the outcomes the Kika'ige Historical Society wanted to achieve through the performance. The example of the photographer encouraging one performer to embody power by physically taking up more space with her stance was a metaphor for the entire exercise: to unsettle the settler luncheon with our very presence and invite participants to see us as Indigenous women with agency—women with pasts and futures—and not as objects of the state as the underside of the placemats suggested. In the process, however, and with Campbell's encouragement and skill as the photographer, it became an embodied validation of power for the performers themselves.

Presencing is also an act of resistance to erasure and displacement, which came up in the interviews. Within the context of the postsecondary institutions where we work and where the performance took place, the performers' descriptions of discomfort and feeling displaced align with what Sara Ahmed has described as a reaction to "institutional whiteness."[30] While not an Indigenous feminist based in North America like the other theorists we draw from here, Ahmed's work validates the out-of-place experiences the performers described as Indigenous women working in the academy. Ahmed has written about how academic spaces are "shaped by the proximity of some bodies and not others: white bodies gather, and cohere to form the edges of such spaces."[31] The result of this "institutional whiteness" is that nonwhite bodies feel "uncomfortable, exposed, visible, different, when they take up this space."[32] The expressions of discomfort and empowerment expressed by the participants offer further evidence of what Ahmed has articulated about nonwhite bodies in the academy:

> Such bodies are made invisible when we see spaces as being white, at the same time as they become hyper-visible when they do not pass, which means they 'stand out' and 'stand apart'. You learn to fade into the

background, but sometimes you can't or you don't. The moments when the body appears 'out of place' are moments of political and personal trouble.[33]

Ahmed wrote this passage in 2007, drawing from her experiences as a woman of color working in Australia and the United Kingdom. But the descriptions of discomfort from the performers indicate that nonwhite bodies—even in the presumably welcoming context of Indigenizing the academy—experience embodied discord. This results, as the performers described, in feelings of wanting to "fade into the background" while also feeling drawn to embodied resistance.

Our findings reminded us that there is felt labor involved in renarrating and placeholding, and in the university contexts this is often done by women. As we grapple with reconciliation and Indigenization, we are reminded that this leadership has an often hidden cost, even to ourselves, as one of the participants pointed out. Across Canada, Indigenous women scholars have been vocal about the burden of making space for Indigenous Peoples and ways of knowing in the academy, which often leads to burnout.[34] Drawing on the work of Simpson, Tuck and Yang, and Grande, Candace Brunette-Debassige has documented Indigenous female administrators' practice of enacting "Indigenous refusals" in Canadian universities by "not lending their labour to certain projects, proactively creating and changing policies, and addressing colonial assumptions as they arose in their day-to-day encounters."[35] Brunette-Debassige also draws on Anzaldúa's borderlands theory to demonstrate how "women in the academy confront and negotiate complex spatial and epistemic borders in their leadership work."[36] Performing provided the Indigenous women involved a new felt avenue into their everyday experiences of doing Indigenous women's work in spatial practice and Indigenizing the academy. It raises feminist questions of why, as Indigenous women, we feel so responsible for educating others and making them comfortable with the unfolding Indigenization process—but also why we feel so tired. The performers' expressions of relief and guilty pleasure for stepping out of those roles exposed an invisible labor that, as one participant expressed, "is our experience of living in Canada our whole lives."

As Indigenous Peoples "living in Canada our whole lives," we were ultimately reminded by the participants that kinship among women, grounded in our matriarchal or matrilineal cultures, is one of the things that helped our peoples survive 150 years of Canada. We say this, mindful of the terrible and ongoing consequences of colonization, including the rampant violence against women and families so thoroughly documented in the Truth and Reconciliation Commission of Canada and the National Inquiry on Missing and Murdered Indigenous Women and Girls. In spite of this attack on

Indigenous kinship, grandmothers maintain their significance, as defined by distinct Indigenous cultures in which older women hold authority. The performers demonstrated their understanding of this with their immediate decision to perform as "grannies." They embraced the opportunity to learn more about their own grandmothers and reflect on ancestral histories while also bringing the past into the present. Our interviews with the women also thus reinforced that in practices of affective knowledge production and the creation of alternative truths, connecting with ancestral and spirit relations matters. "Dressing up" allowed the performers to bring their Indigenous ancestors along, at least how they imagined them to be: to be present where they had always been erased, while making the statement that we are still here and carry our relatives with us. This was a spiritual and ceremonial act, grounded in the kinship of women.

While Indigenous responses to settler nationalist commemoration in Canada have a rich history that has been documented elsewhere, this paper has offered insights into Indigenous feminist artivist storytelling/new ordering at a time of sesquicentennial settler narratives, calls for national reconciliation, and Indigenizing the academy.[37] What we learned from the performers was that they were able to voice their truths in a way that was unfamiliar to them, and this had the effect of opening up new truths and personal revelations. *Tabling 150* gave us the opportunity to join other Indigenous women who are practicing Native feminist spatial practice, presencing, enacting refusals, creating new orders, and engaging felt theory in keeping with the theories of Indigenous feminist scholars like Mishuana Goeman, Leanne Simpson, Wanda Nanibush, Audra Simpson, Sandy Grande, Eve Tuck, Candace Brunette-Debassige, and Dian Million. Summer 2021 amplified the pressing need to engage in such acts across the nation; flashpoints such as settler national commemorations, national holidays, and news of terrible histories invite such practice. For the Indigenous folks who perform alternative histories and truths, there is felt experience that involves kinship, ceremony, ancestral connections, and building new communities, as the performers so generously demonstrated.

LIANNE C. LEDDY (Anishinaabe, Serpent River First Nation) is associate professor in the Department of History at Wilfrid Laurier University.

BRITTANY LUBY (Anishinaabe descent) is associate professor in the Department of History at the University of Guelph.

KIMBERLEY McLEOD is assistant professor in the School of English & Theatre Studies at the University of Guelph.

EMMA STELTER is an independent scholar specializing in the treaties between the Mississauga and the Crown.

KIM ANDERSON (Métis) is a Canada Research Chair in Indigenous Relationships at the University of Guelph.

References

Ahmed, Sara. "The Phenomenology of Whiteness." *Feminist Theory* 8, no. 2 (2007): 149–68.

Anderson, Kim. "Kika'ige Historical Society." Shekon Neechie: An Indigenous History Site. June 21, 2018. https://shekonneechie.ca/category/videos.

Anderson, Kim, Elena Flores Ruiz, Georgina Tuari Stewart, and Madina Tlostanova. "What Can Indigenous Feminist Knowledges and Practices Bring to Indigenizing the Academy?" *Journal of World Philosophies* 4, no. 1 (2019): 121–55.

Anzaldúa, Gloria E. *Borderlands/La Frontera: The New Mestiza.* 4th ed. San Francisco: Aunt Lute, 2012.

Arvin, Maile, Eve Tuck, and Angie Morrill. "Decolonizing Feminism: Challenging Connections Between Settler Colonialism and Heteropatriarchy." *Feminist Formations* 25, no. 1 (2013): 8–34.

Austen, Ian. "The Indigenous Archaeologist Tracking Down the Missing Residential Children." *New York Times.* July 30, 2021. https://www.nytimes .com/2021/07/30/world/canada/indigenous-archaeologist-graves-school -children.html.

Bedard, R. E. Mznegiizhigo-kwe. "'Indian in the Cupboard': Lateral Violence and Indigenization of the Academy." In *Exploring the Toxicity of Lateral Violence and Microaggressions: Poison in the Water Cooler,* edited by C. L. Cho, J. K. Corkett, and A. Steele, 75–101. London: Palgrave Macmillan, 2018.

Bergen, Rachel. "Pallister '50 Years Out of Date,' Professor Says After Premier's Comment on Colonial History of Manitoba." *CBC News,* July 10, 2021. https:// www.cbc.ca/news/canada/manitoba/brian-pallister-manitoba-chiefs -colonialism-first-nations-1.6094834.

Braun, Virginia, and Victoria Clarke. *Successful Qualitative Research: A Practical Guide for Beginners.* Thousand Oaks, CA: SAGE, 2013.

Brunette-Debassige, Candace. "The Trickiness of Settler Colonialism: Indigenous Women Administrators' Experiences of Policy in Canadian Universities." Ph.D. diss., University of Western Ontario, 2021.

Canadian Historical Association. "Canada Day Statement: The History of Violence against Indigenous Peoples Fully Warrants the Use of the Word 'Genocide'." June 30, 2021. https://cha-shc.ca/news/canada-day-statement -the-history-of-violence-against-indigenous-peoples-fully-warrants-the -use-of-the-word-genocide-2021-06-30.

Cote-Meek, S. *Colonized Classrooms: Racism, Trauma and Resistance in Postsecondary Education.* Halifax: Fernwood, 2014.

Dummitt, Christopher. "The Canadian Historical Associations' Fake 'consensus' on Canadian Genocide." *National Post,* August 13, 2021. https://nationalpost .com/opinion/christopher-dummitt-the-canadian-historical-associations -fake-consensus-on-canadian-genocide.

"Fate of Toppled Statues Unclear, Federal Conservatives Want Them Restored." *CBC News,* July 5, 2021. https://www.cbc.ca/news/canada/manitoba /manitoba-legislature-toppled-statues-conservative-letter-1.6090840.

Gaudry, Adam, and Danielle Lorenz. "Indigenization as Inclusion, Reconciliation, and Decolonization: Navigating the Different Visions for Indigenizing the Academy." *AlterNative* 14, no. 3 (2018): 218–27.

Goeman, Mishuana. "Notes Toward a Native Feminism's Spatial Practice." *Wicazo Sa Review* 24, no. 2 (2009): 169–87.

Goeman, Mishuana. *Mark My Words: Native Women Mapping our Nations.* Minneapolis: University of Minnesota Press, 2013.

Grande, Sandy. "Refusing the University." In *Dissident Knowledge in Higher Education,* edited by M. Spooner and J. McNinch, 168–85. Regina: University of Regina Press, 2018.

Groat, Cody, and Kim Anderson. "Holding Place: Resistance, Reframing, and Relationality in the Representation of Indigenous History." *Canadian Historical Review* 102, no. 3 (2021): 465–84.

"Historians Rally vs. 'Genocide' Myth." *Dorchester Review,* August 12, 2021. https:// www.dorchesterreview.ca/blogs/news/historians-rally-vs-genocide-myth.

Honderich, Holly. "Why Canada is Mourning the Deaths of Hundreds of Children." *BBC.* July 15, 2021. https://www.bbc.com/news/world-us-canada-57325653.

Hopper, Tristin. "How Canada Forgot about More Than 1,308 Graves at Former Residential Schools. *National Post,* July 13, 2021. https://nationalpost.com /news/canada/how-canada-forgot-about-more-than-1308-graves-at -former-residential-schools.

Huhndorf, Shari M., and Cheryl Suzack. "Theorizing the Issues." In *Indigenous Women and Feminism: Politics, Activism, Culture,* edited by Cheryl Suzack, 1–17. Vancouver: University of British Columbia Press, 2010.

Indigenous Initiatives. *Bi-naagwad, It Comes into View: Indigenous Initiatives Strategy Summary Report.* University of Guelph, 2021. Accessed December 9, 2022. https://indigenous.uoguelph.ca/system/files/Indigenous-Initiatives -Strategy-Summary-Report.pdf.

Jewell, Eva, and Ian Mosby. "Calls to Action Accountability: A Status Update on Reconciliation." Yellowhead Institute, December 17, 2019. https:// yellowheadinstitute.org/2019/12/17/calls-to-action-accountability-a -status-update-on-reconciliation/.

Lavallee, L. "Resisting Exotic Puppetry: Experiences of Indigenous Women Leadership in the Academy." In *Critical Reflections and Politics on Advancing Women in the Academy,* edited by T. Moeke-Pickering, S. Cote-Meek, and A. Pegoraro, 21–32. Hershey, PA: IGI Global Publishing, 2020.

MacDonald, David. *The Sleeping Giant Awakens: Genocide, Indian Residential Schools, and the Challenge of Conciliation.* Toronto: University of Toronto Press, 2019.

McKegney, Sam. "'Pain, Pleasure, Shame. Shame': Masculine Embodiment, Kinship, and Indigenous Reterritorialization." *Canadian Literature,* no. 216 (Spring 2013): 12–33.

McLeod, Kimberley, Lianne C. Leddy, Brittany Luby, Emma Stelter, and Kim Anderson. "'I Guess it was Unsettling': Indigenous Performance, Nationalist Narratives, and Conciliation." *Theatre Research in Canada,* 44, no. 1 (2023): 55-81.

Million, Dian. *Therapeutic Nations: Healing in an Age of Indigenous Human Rights.* Tucson: University of Arizona Press, 2013.

Monaghan, David. "The Fathers of Confederation." History, Arts and Architecture, House of Commons. October 2007. https://www.ourcommons.ca/About/HistoryArtsArchitecture/collection_profiles/CP_Fathers_of_Confederation-e.htm.

National Inquiry into Missing and Murdered Indigenous Women and Girls. *Reclaiming Power and Place: The Final Report of the National Inquiry into Missing and Murdered Indigenous Women and Girls.* Vols. 1A and 1B. Ottawa: Privy Council Office, 2019.

Simpson, Audra. *Mohawk Interruptus: Political Life across the Borders of Settler States.* Durham, NC: Duke University Press, 2014.

———. "On Ethnographic Refusal: Indigeneity, 'Voice' and Colonial Citizenship." *Junctures* 9, no. 1 (2007): 67–80.

Simpson, Leanne. *Dancing on Turtle's Back: Stories of Nishnaabeg Re-Creation, Resurgence, and a New Emergence.* Winnipeg: ARP Books, 2011.

Tasker, John Paul. "Flags Lowered After Reports of Residential School Graves Should be Raised Now, O'Toole Says." *CBC News,* August 26, 2021. https://www.cbc.ca/news/politics/erin-otoole-flags-half-mast-1.6154417.

Truth and Reconciliation Commission of Canada. *Truth and Reconciliation Commission of Canada: Calls to Action.* Winnipeg: Truth and Reconciliation Commission of Canada, 2015a.

Truth and Reconciliation Commission of Canada. *Honouring the Truth, Reconciling for the Future: Summary of the Final Report of the Truth and Reconciliation Commission of Canada.* Winnipeg: Truth and Reconciliation Commission of Canada, 2015b.

Tuck, Eve. "Biting the University that Feeds Us." In *Dissident Knowledge in Higher Education,* edited by M. Spooner and J. McNinch, 149–68. Regina: University of Regina Press, 2018.

Woods, Rex. *The Fathers of Confederation,* 1968. Oil on canvas, 213.36 x 365.72 cm. House of Commons, Ottawa. Accessed October 28, 2020. https://www.ourcommons.ca/About/HistoryArtsArchitecture/collection_profiles/CP_Fathers_of_Confederation-e.htm.

Notes

1. Contrary to reports of "discovery" of the graves, we have chosen to frame it as mainstream Canadian news, as the Truth and Reconciliation Commission

of Canada (Vol. 4) called for investigation into the graves based on testimony of survivors, and Indigenous communities across the country have long known about these graves based on the oral histories of survivors among them. Mainstream outlets publicized mass graves at Canadian residential schools. See, for example, Holly Honderich, "Why Canada is Mourning the Deaths of Hundreds of Children," *BBC,* July 15, 2021, https://www.bbc.com/news/world-us-canada-57325653; Tristin Hopper, "How Canada Forgot About More than 1,308 Graves at Former Residential Schools," *The National Post,* July 13, 2021, https://nationalpost.com/news/canada/how-canada-forgot-about-more-than-1308-graves-at-former-residential-schools; and Ian Austen, "The Indigenous Archaeologist Tracking Down the Missing Residential Children, *The New York Times,* July 30, 2021, https://www.nytimes.com/2021/07/30/world/canada/indigenous-archaeologist-graves-school-children.html. These schools—framed by some as institutions of genocide—were mandated by the Canadian State and run by Catholic, Anglican, and United Churches who interned multiple generations of Indigenous children and subjected them to physical, emotional, mental, spiritual, and sexual abuse. Many died and were buried in unmarked graves, their families never to hear of them again. See David MacDonald, *The Sleeping Giant Awakens: Genocide, Indian Residential Schools, and the Challenge of Conciliation* (Toronto: University of Toronto Press, 2019), 133—45.

2. Rachel Bergen, "Pallister '50 Years Out of Date,' Professor Says After Premier's Comment on Colonial History of Manitoba," *CBC News,* July 10, 2021, https://www.cbc.ca/news/canada/manitoba/brian-pallister-manitoba-chiefs-colonialism-first-nations-1.6094834; and Christopher Dummitt, "The Canadian Historical Associations' Fake 'Consensus' on Canadian Genocide," *National Post,* August 13, 2021, https://nationalpost.com/opinion/christopher-dummitt-the-canadian-historical-associations-fake-consensus-on-canadian-genocide. Christopher Dummitt wrote: "The campaign to label Canada a genocide state isn't an isolated phenomenon, but is playing out as part of a larger effort to destroy any publicly displayed symbol of national pride." See also, "Fate of Toppled Statues Unclear, Federal Conservatives Want Them Restored," *CBC News,* July 5, 2021, https://www.cbc.ca/news/canada/manitoba/manitoba-legislature-toppled-statues-conservative-letter-1.6090840.

3. John Paul Tasker, "Flags Lowered After Reports of Residential School Graves Should Be Raised Now, O'Toole Says," *CBC News,* August 26, 2021, https://www.cbc.ca/news/politics/erin-otoole-flags-half-mast-1.6154417.

4. The authors define truth-telling as challenging colonial narratives which erase Indigenous presence, histories, and cultures.

5. Many scholars debate whether the current work within the academy is a process of "Indigenizing the academy" or "decolonizing the academy." We appreciate the framing offered by Adam Gaudry and Danielle Lorenz in "Indigenization as inclusion, reconciliation, and decolonization; navigating the different versions for indigenizing the Canadian academy," *AlterNative* 14, no. 3 (2018): 218—27. Gaudry and Lorenz identify a continuum of "Indigenization" work, which can include decolonization as an end point. In this paper we have chosen to use the unqualified term "Indigenizing" to situate ourselves in the

broader continuum of the work Gaudry and Lorenz describe and to note that "decolonizing" university spaces remains an enormous challenge.

6. The authors acknowledge the diversity of ways that Indigenous feminists define their theoretical practices and positionalities. Kim Anderson's Indigenous feminist approach is useful in understanding the perspective of the authors and performers in that it "necessitates learning how the Indigenous women of Turtle Island (North America) historically had political, economic, social, and spiritual authority, and how this authority came under attack." See Kim Anderson, Elena Flores Ruiz, Georgina Tuari Stewart, and Madina Tlostanova, "What can Indigenous Feminist Knowledges and Practices Bring to Indigenizing the Academy?" *Journal of World Philosophies* 4, no. 1 (2019): 123. For how Indigenous feminism challenges settler colonialism, heteropatriarchy, and heteropaternalism, see Maile Arvin, Eve Tuck, and Angie Morrill, "Decolonizing Feminism: Challenging Connections between Settler Colonialism and Heteropatriarchy" *Feminist Formations* 25, no. 1 (2013): 8—34.

7. Truth and Reconciliation Commission of Canada, *Honouring the Truth, Reconciling for the Future: Summary of the Final Report of the Truth and Reconciliation Commission of Canada* (Winnipeg: Truth and Reconciliation Commission of Canada, 2015b), 151; 157; 234—42.

8. Truth and Reconciliation Commission of Canada, *Truth and Reconciliation Commission of Canada: Calls to Action* (Winnipeg: Truth and Reconciliation Commission of Canada, 2015a), 1—11.

9. Eva Jewell and Ian Mosby, "Calls to Action Accountability: A Status Update on Reconciliation," Yellowhead Institute, December 17, 2019, https://yellowheadinstitute.org/2019/12/17/calls-to-action-accountability-a-status-update-on-reconciliation/.

10. Canada, National Inquiry into Missing and Murdered Indigenous Women and Girls, *Reclaiming Power and Place: The Final Report of the National Inquiry into Missing and Murdered Indigenous Women and Girls,* Volume 1B (Ottawa: Privy Council Office, 2019), 179, 193, 195, 206. See also National Inquiry into Missing and Murdered Indigenous Women and Girls, *Reclaiming Power and Place: The Final Report of the National Inquiry into Missing and Murdered Indigenous Women and Girls,* Volume 1A (Ottawa: Privy Council Office, 2019), 546—50.

11. Indigenous Initiatives, "Bi-naagwad, It Comes into View: Indigenous Initiatives Strategy Summary Report," University of Guelph, 2021, https://indigenous.uoguelph.ca/strategy.

12. For Native Feminist spatial practice, see Mishuana Goeman, "Notes toward a Native Feminism's Spatial Practice," *Wicazo Sa Review* 24, no. 2 (2009): 169—87; and Mishuana Goeman, *Mark My Words: Native Women Mapping our Nations* (Minneapolis: University of Minnesota Press, 2013), 1—39. For felt theory, see Dian Million, *Therapeutic Nations: Healing in an Age of Indigenous Human Rights* (Tucson: University of Arizona Press, 2013), 56—77. For presencing, see Leanne Simpson, *Dancing on Turtle's Back: Stories of Nishnaabeg Re-Creation, Resurgence, and a New Emergence* (Winnipeg: ARP Books, 2011), 93—96. Simpson reminds us that Indigenous societies generated meaning "through

engagement, presence and process—storytelling, ceremony, singing, dancing, doing." Performance art is one way to embody this creative process and take up space. Audra Simpson writes that in their assertions of sovereignty, people at Kahnawake "refused the authority of the state at almost every turn." They enacted this refusal through the research relationship, when participants chose not to answer questions directly or asked her to turn off the recorder. Simpson, "On Ethnographic Refusal: Indigeneity, 'Voice' and Colonial Citizenship," *Junctures* 9, no. 1 (2007): 67–80 (quote on page 73). Simpson grounds this in the "labor of principle and sovereignty, labor that begins with refusal." Audra Simpson, *Mohawk Interruptus: Political Life across the Borders of Settler States* (Durham: Duke University Press, 2014), 22. For Indigenous refusals in the university context, see S. Grande, "Refusing the University," in *Dissident Knowledge in Higher Education,* ed. M. Spooner and J. McNinch (Regina: University of Regina Press, 2018), 168–89; Audra Simpson, "On Ethnographic Refusal: Indigeneity, 'Voice' and Colonial Citizenship," *Junctures* 9, no. 1 (2007): 67–80; and Eve Tuck, "Biting the University that Feeds Us," in *Dissident Knowledge in Higher Education,* ed. M. Spooner and J. McNinch (Regina: University of Regina Press, 2018), 149–67. For Indigenous women's experiences in the academy, see Candace Brunette-Debassige, "The Trickiness of Settler Colonialism: Indigenous Women Administrators' Experiences of Policy in Canadian Universities" (Ph.D. diss., University of Western Ontario, 2021).

13. Kim Anderson, Elena Flores Ruiz, Georgina Tuari Stewart, and Madina Tlostanova, "What Can Indigenous Feminist Knowledges and Practices Bring to Indigenizing the Academy?" *Journal of World Philosophies* 4, no. 1 (2019): 121–55.

14. Goeman, "Notes toward a Native Feminism's Spatial Practice," 171.

15. Shari M. Huhndorf and Cheryl Suzack, "Theorizing the Issues," in *Indigenous Women and Feminism: Politics, Activism, Culture,* ed. Cheryl Suzack (Vancouver: University of British Columbia Press, 2010), 2.

16. Goeman, *Mark My Words,* 14.

17. Sam McKegney, "'Pain, Pleasure, Shame, Shame': Masculine Embodiment, Kinship, and Indigenous Reterritorialization," *Canadian Literature,* no. 216 (Spring 2013): 12; and Million, *Therapeutic Nations,* 41–42.

18. Links to the Kika'ige Historical Society's digital stories, as well as an overview of our purpose, can be found here: Kim Anderson, "Kika'ige Historical Society," Shekon Neechie: An Indigenous History Site. June 21, 2018, https:// shekonneechie.ca/category/videos.

19. The authors have written a separate paper to examine audience members' perspectives on this event. Kimberley McLeod, Lianne C. Leddy, Brittany Luby, Emma Stelter, and Kim Anderson, "'I Guess It Was Unsettling': Indigenous Performance, Nationalist Narratives, and Conciliation," *Theatre Research in Canada,* 44, no. 1 (2023): 55-81.

20. Rex Woods, *The Fathers of Confederation,* 1968, oil on canvas, 213.36 x 365.72 cm, Ottawa. This was a recreation of Robert Harris's painting, which was destroyed in 1916. For more information about the painting, see David Monaghan, "The Fathers of Confederation" History, Arts and Architecture,

Our Commons, 2007 (accessed October 28, 2020) https://www.ourcommons.ca/About/HistoryArtsArchitecture/collection_profiles/CP_Fathers_of_Confederation-e.htm.

21. This project received ethics clearance through the University of Guelph Research Ethics Board, a process that includes filling out a cross-cultural supplement for projects involving Indigenous Peoples.

22. Virginia Braun and Victoria Clarke, *Successful Qualitative Research: A Practical Guide for Beginners* (Thousand Oaks, CA: SAGE, 2013).

23. Million, *Therapeutic Nations,* 57. Italics in original.

24. Million, *Therapeutic Nations,* 56.

25. Goeman, "Notes toward a Native Feminism's Spatial Practice," 169–87; and Goeman, *Mark My Words,* 36–39.

26. See the Canadian Historical Association (CHA), "Canada Day Statement: The History of Violence Against Indigenous Peoples Fully Warrants the Use of the Word 'Genocide'," June 30, 2021, https://cha-shc.ca/news/canada-day-statement-the-history-of-violence-against-indigenous-peoples-fully-warrants-the-use-of-the-word-genocide-2021-06-30. The following month, fifty-three historians penned an open letter to express their "grave disappointment" with the CHA's statement, denying genocide in Canada. See "Historians Rally vs. 'Genocide' Myth," *Dorchester Review,* August 12, 2021, https://www.dorchesterreview.ca/blogs/news/historians-rally-vs-genocide-myth. For quotation, see Million, *Therapeutic Nations,* 68.

27. Million, *Therapeutic Nations,* 27.

28. Leanne Simpson, *Dancing on Turtle's Back,* 93.

29. Simpson, *Dancing on Turtle's Back,* 96.

30. Sara Ahmed, "The Phenomenology of Whiteness," *Feminist Theory* 8, no. 2 (2007): 149–86.

31. Ahmed, "The Phenomenology of Whiteness," 157.

32. Ahmed, "The Phenomenology of Whiteness," 157.

33. Ahmed, "The Phenomenology of Whiteness," 159.

34. R. E. Mznegiizhigo-kwe Bedard, "'Indian in the Cupboard': Lateral Violence and Indigenization of the Academy," in *Exploring the Toxicity of Lateral Violence and Microaggressions: Poison in the Water Cooler,* ed. C. L. Cho, J. K. Corkett, and A. Steele (London: Palgrave Macmillan, 2018), 75–101; L. Lavallee, "Resisting Exotic Puppetry: Experiences of Indigenous Women Leadership in the Academy," in *Critical Reflections and Politics on Advancing Women in the Academy,* ed. T. Moeke-Pickering, S. Cote-Meek, and A. Pegoraro (Hershey, PA: IGI Global, 2020), 21–32; and S. Cote-Meek, *Colonized Classrooms: Racism, Trauma and Resistance in Post-secondary Education* (Halifax: Fernwood, 2014), 46–86.

35. Brunette-Debassige, "The Trickiness of Settler Colonialism," 205; Simpson, "On Ethnographic Refusal," 67–80; Tuck, "Biting the University," 149–68; and Grande, "Refusing the University," 168–85.

36. Brunette-Debassige, "The Trickiness of Settler Colonialism," 68. Gloria E. Anzaldúa, *Borderlands/La Frontera: The New Mestiza,* 4th ed. (San Francisco: Aunt Lute, 2012), 67–68.

37. Cody Groat and Kim Anderson, "Holding Place: Resistance, Reframing, and Relationality in the Representation of Indigenous History," *Canadian Historical Review* 102, no. 3 (2021): 465–84.

DANE ALLARD

Kitchen Table Politics: Bannock and Métis Common Sense in an Era of Nascent Recognition Politics

Abstract

Bannock, a simple bread made of water, flour, and lard—fried or baked—is a staple of Indigenous diets across what is now called Canada. A pan-Indigenous symbol, bannock is a historically dynamic food grounded in both European and Indigenous origins. On both counts, it presents a paradox to the settler imagination, which clings to fixed definitions of Indigenous Peoplehood essentialized in precontact traditions. For Métis, however, bannock is no paradox. Neither its European origins nor its diverse forms and composition across time and place cause confusion. Rather, in oral history interviews Métis positioned bannock as a critical component that sustained a Métis identity through the twentieth century. Bannock offers important lessons for understanding the place of Métis within Canadian history and reveals how Métis mediated state interventions into Indigeneity in the 1980s. Tracing this historical trajectory, I suggest a useful inversion of Mark Rifkin's concept of settler common sense to focus on what I call a Métis common sense; that is, those aspects of a Métis livedness that were obvious for Métis. I follow other Métis writers who have proposed the kitchen table as a site of Métis identity survivance that functions as an alternative to public, androcentric expressions of Métis-ness legible to Canadian recognition politics. Métis interviewees negotiated with, and simultaneously rejected, essentialist assumptions of their Indigeneity. Interviewees understood bannock as a key marker of kinship sustained through female labor and activism within a matrilocal Métis Peoplehood.

> *If kokum's table could talk, it would hold all our family's secrets in its fibers . . . if her table could talk, it would tell you all the unwritten rules of visiting.*
> —SAMANTHA NOCK (MÉTIS POET), MAMAWI PROJECT

> *Mix the dry ingredients together. Rub the lard into flour mixture and then add the liquids. Make a very soft dough. Pat into a pie plate about 3/4" thick. Prick all over with fork. Cut in wedges as for pie. Bake at 350F.*
> —MANITOBA HERITAGE COOKERY

BANNOCK, A SIMPLE MIX OF WATER, FLOUR, AND LARD, is a hypervisible centerpiece of a pan-Indigenous culinary tradition in Canada today. In Vancouver, Salmon N'Bannock serves up a tasty west-coast-style bannock. You can visit Tea-N-Bannock in Toronto for a local slice of frybread.[1] And the Bannock Factory in Winnipeg advertises a premade, frozen line of Bannock-in-a-box products, bearing the slogan "no need to panic, we have bannock . . . & now you can too!"[2] But bannock is so much more than a delicious treat. For Métis, and many other Indigenous Peoples throughout Canada, bannock is a common-sense cornerstone of our collective Peoplehood. From a historical perspective, bannock offers important lessons for understanding the place of Métis within Canadian history and reveals how Métis mediated state interventions into Indigeneity in the 1980s through food culture. Canada constitutionally recognized Métis as an Aboriginal people in 1982 under Section 35 of the Canadian *Constitution Act*. Since that time, Métis political organizations have championed externally visible symbols of Métis identity in their pursuit of government fiduciary support. Bannock's widespread consumption by multiple Indigenous Peoples and its origins in colonial contact made it a poor fit for the demands of this recognition politics. Yet bannock has endured—not despite and even perhaps because of this—as an integral part of a lived Métis identity. Métis positioned bannock as critical for their self and collective identification because Métis women within matrilocal Métis society kneaded kinship into the dough.

I trace a historical arc of bannock's meaning to Métis Peoplehood between the mid- to late twentieth century. While bannock is a popular topic in popular Indigenous writing, and Indigenous academics in the United States have explored the meanings of bannock's cousin, frybread, bannock in the Canadian context has received scant academic consideration.[3] Bannock is hypervisible—on the powwow circuit and at community celebrations—but the lessons it stands to teach have remained unacknowledged by historians writing about Métis people. The lack of academic material on bannock is not apolitical; rather, it emerges from enduring colonial binary assumptions about authenticity that remain rooted in the historical discipline.

These binaries produce and sustain the issue of silence in Métis historiography. During an era of explicit colonial oppression between 1885 and 1982 Métis made conscious decisions when and how to articulate their Métis-ness. Following historian Michel Hogue, these strategic choices do not constitute a silence per se but indicate that settler academics were not attuned to listen; nor did Métis necessarily want to openly discuss their Indigeneity with outsiders.[4] Colonial oppression coupled with settler interest in the sociopolitical conflicts between Métis and the Canadian state structured an archive largely based in fur trade documents and the lives of nineteenth-century male political leaders such as Louis Riel and Gabriel Dumont. Writing Métis history in the twentieth century thus requires that we engage a different source base and employ Indigenous-centric methodologies. To this end, I turn to bannock, oral history, and the concept of livedness as defined by scholars such as Métis sociologist Chris Andersen. These threads weave together to ground Métis survivance within kitchen table politics.[5]

I begin by elaborating the methodological considerations necessary for writing a Métis history from a Métis perspective, and then I locate my oral history archive in its historical context and articulate the concept of what I call "Métis common sense." In defining and confronting the Bannock paradox, I explore how Métis rejected the cultural essentialism that the supposed Bannock paradox assumed. "Bannock conversations" elaborate the relationship between bannock and Métis common sense, accessing and assessing historiographical silences that have distorted scholarly understandings of Métis history and Peoplehood. Finally, the gendered nature of these distortions is explored. Métis perceived female labor as central to sustaining bannock as a Métis practice. Androcentric recognition politics, and the historiography that has followed in its wake, have obfuscated on-the-ground, female-centric livedness of kinship, expressed through baking bannock.[6] Ultimately, for Métis interviewees in the 1990s, kitchen table politics rather than recognition politics had more daily relevance to their sense of Métis Peoplehood.

Oral History, Métis Common Sense, and Gender

Métis voices preserved in the Métis Women of Manitoba Inc. Oral History Project (OHP) were consulted in this study. In 1993, Doreen Breland-Fines and Lorraine Freeman, two Métis codirectors of Métis Women of Manitoba Inc. (MWM), traveled across Manitoba interviewing Métis elders on their lived experiences during the twentieth century. Interviewees were selected from communities in southern and northern Manitoba including Selkirk, Camp Morton, Riverton, Matheson Island, Eriksdale, St. Laurent, Bacon Ridge, Crane River, St. Rose, Erickson, Binscarth, Ste. Lazare, The Pas, Wabowden, Churchill, South Indian Lake, Norway House, Powerview, Pine Falls, Winnipeg, and St. Francois Xavier. The result was an archival collection composed of 38 interview sessions with 44 elders and nearly 60 hours of tape. Breland-Fines and Freeman produced the OHP in partnership with the Provincial Archives of Manitoba, which houses the physical and digital material. As a public archive, the OHP did not require an ethics review. Rather, the OHP sought to make its collection widely available. To do so, the OHP engaged a distinct form of Métis nationalism resurgent in the early 1990s that sought enhanced visibility.

The 1990s were critical for Métis Peoplehood.[7] A decade of change wrought by shifts in government policy toward Indigenous Peoples in Canada encouraged increasing Métis engagement with a nascent recognition politics.[8] In 1982 Section 35 of the *Constitution Act* enshrined "Aboriginal and treaty" rights within Canada's legal framework and recognized Métis as an Aboriginal people. Métis organizations subsequently mobilized recognition to increase Métis visibility within the settler state, resulting in a resurgence of Métis nationalism and pride. Then in 1985, Bill C-31 allowed for the reinstatement of (some) Indigenous women denied "Indian status" through egregiously gendered amendments to the *Indian Act*. Both policy changes came in the wake of sustained and major Indigenous protest.[9] In this historical context MWM rationalized the OHP as a project to "capture and preserve a record of Metis traditional methods of imparting history and culture" and "educate Metis and others on the essence of being Metis."[10] This schema sutured the OHP to prevailing state-centric Aboriginal rights discourses. Partnering with the Manitoba Archives, where the OHP is now housed, MWM sought to gather information that would ensure state recognition of Métis communities. In so doing, it privileged Canadian expectations of preservation ethnography. The questions asked by interviewers reveal an implicit view that cultural expressions were legitimate only when disconnected from their roots in collective political sovereignty.

Dene scholar Glen Coulthard argues that recognition politics maintain Canadian colonial authority to determine Indigenous belonging.[11] Appeals to state institutions entrapped Métis organizations in state-centric discourses on Métis Indigeneity.[12] Despite the best intentions of Métis politicians, recognition politics caught Métis, like other Indigenous nations, in the need "to account for native particularity as a means to argue for increased recognition."[13] In this context, the "essence of being Metis" or Métis authenticity that the OHP sought to capture was not apolitical but was instead a conscious aspect of Métis organizations' attempts to turn the nascent recognition from federal and provincial governments into tangible outcomes, often through the Canadian legal system.[14] Though Freeman and Breland-Fines, both Métis themselves, had direct experience in the world that interviewees articulated, the confines of the project limited their field of vision. The questions Freeman and Breland-Fines posed reflected their interest in a concise articulation of Métis cultural difference: "I want to ask you about Métis women, if they dress different than other women, years ago?"[15] The OHP was primarily concerned with the visible ways that interviewees set themselves apart from other groups.

Interviewees repeatedly refused these parameters and instead leaned on elusive traits to articulate their Métis-ness. For interviewees, affective relationships—not externally legible symbolics—formed the heart of Métis Peoplehood. In these assertions we can perceive the contours of a Métis common sense. For instance, many interviewees centered their Métis-ness on humor. For Bernice Potoski, Métis were "humorous and they're happy-go-lucky. . . . Sometimes things aren't even funny, but they like to laugh a lot and make jokes."[16] Merrymaking was vital to Bella Morrisseau's community of Crane River; when asked "how long would a dance go on" Morrisseau laughed and responded, "Two or three days. As long as it had to!"[17] In an interview with Jules Chartrand, Freeman mused, "It seems that only Métis people laugh at Métis jokes." Chartrand retorted, "Well they would naturally understand them better."[18] There was nothing particular about humor that made it Métis. Joking and gaiety are affective traits across human societies. Humor, however, was a key identity marker that interviewees used to express a distinct Métis-ness.

Freeman and Breland-Fines struggled to make sense of these moments. Instead of engaging deeper, they promptly moved on. Métis could not use humor to articulate difference: everybody laughs! Humor would not help Métis in Canadian courts, which, as Andersen argues, are "fixated on finding the 'essence' of Indigenous difference."[19] In moments such as these, interviewees expressed a Métis common sense that went unappreciated by the interviewers. Nonetheless, the OHP recorded a Métis common sense that resisted attempts by the OHP to discipline it into terms legible to the settler state.

Interviewees emphasized humor because it linked their webs of kinship. At the end of a long genealogical story, Rose LaFreniere concluded, "That's all about the LaLibertés. It's a long story. But that's what I say, and my mom is related with the Allards. And my mom is a pure Métis like me."[20] Pushed to articulate what constituted a pure Métis, Rose LaFreniere responded that "it's the one that tells good jokes!"[21] Laughter held together the webs of kinship articulated by LaFreniere.[22] Humor in itself did not set Métis apart; rather, the intimate knowledge of knowing what was funny and how to laugh were intrinsic to Métis kinship. At first LaFreniere was formal and standoffish. She insisted on reading from a historical text in response to questions. However, once LaFreniere was able to situate Breland-Fines and Freeman into a familiar kinship network she relaxed and cracked jokes.[23]

In a similar vein, the gendered dynamics within the OHP speak to a dissonance between Métis on-the-ground and settler-colonial categories. Despite leading an organization built to advance Métis women, Breland-Fines and Freeman sought out both female and male perspectives. While the archival descriptions do record that most interviewees identified as female (30 of 44), nearly a third of interviewees identified as male. The significance of the gendered assumptions at play in the OHP is critical yet difficult to parse. Recent work from Métis scholars Allyson Stevenson and Cheryl Troupe suggest that in Saskatchewan, female-led activism was at the core of twentieth-century Métis political organizing.[24] "Whether around kitchen tables and by acts of everyday resistance, or through the creation of formal social and political organizations," Stevenson and Troupe argue, "Saskatchewan First Nations, Métis, and non-status women have attempted to prevent the settler colonial elimination of all Indigenous peoples by grounding themselves in their roles and responsibilities as mothers, aunties, and grandmothers."[25] In this construction, female labor at the kitchen table nourished Métis political movements physically and by sustaining the kinship connections critical to Métis resurgence into the 1990s. As Stevenson and Troupe state, "Activism that begins in the home should be seen as starting from a place of strength and support based on kinship, family and community structures."[26] Interviewees in the OHP demonstrated a similar understanding of female labor that ultimately tied baking bannock into a tradition of female-led community work. The relationship between humor, bannock, kinship, and female labor was common sense. Yet these activities were hardly unique to Métis peoples. At the same time, interviewees repeatedly invoked both humor and bannock as evidence of a distinctive Métis-ness. Situating the bannock paradox in its historical and legal context demonstrates the ways in which Métis in the OHP rejected binary expectations that conflicted with what they held to be common sense.

Confronting the Bannock Paradox: Methodologies in (Re)writing Métis History

Like many aspects of Métis society, bannock traces its roots to Scotland, arriving in North America during the eighteenth-century fur trade.[27] Scots employed with the Hudson's Bay Company imported culinary traditions, embedding bannock as a staple within proto-Métis communities. As Métis chef Shane Chartrand argues, "We inherited bannock from the British. We've also made it part of our culture, so is it part of our culture? Of course, it is. We've made it our own. When you're gifted something, it's yours."[28] As Chartrand knows, for Métis, bannock is not complicated. Settler colonial logics, however, cannot account for how a food that emerged in Europe, made of ingredients not native to North America and beloved in many countries around the world, can also be central to a distinct Métis Indigeneity. This is the bannock paradox.

The bannock paradox emerges from a praxis of settler thinking that positions culture as static. Literary scholar Mark Rifkin articulates this colonial ideology as settler common sense: the legal and political structures that frame everyday lived perceptions of Indigeneity and empower the assumptions through which "nonnative access to Indigenous territories come to be lived as given."[29] The obviousness of settler common sense maintains binary conditions that snare all Indigenous Peoples within settler expectations of static Indigeneity.[30] Settler-colonial logic posits that only pure, traditional practices determine Indigeneity and rejects anything that demonstrates modernity or adaptation as inauthentic. In this construction, Indigenous Peoples enter the conversation in terms that reenforce cultural essentialism: the rigid dichotomy between tradition and modernity. Historians such as Paige Raibmon and Philip Deloria have shown how colonial systems rely on binaries that exclude Indigenous Peoples from modernity.[31] Ultimately, settler common sense fails to account for what Métis sociologist Chris Andersen terms the livedness of Indigenous Peoples.[32] What seems paradoxical from a settler perspective is, from a Métis point of view, common sense. Here I flip Rifkin's concept to explore the particularities of what I term a Métis common sense: the lived experiences that inform our own Métis understandings of our identity and collective Peoplehood. Food culture, from this vantage, is a lived process grounded in social and political choices, what Ojibwe/Dakota scholar Scott Richard Lyons envisions as the "scraps, patches, and rags of everyday life."[33] Livedness challenges settler assumptions about the criteria of Indigeneity and asserts Indigenous priorities. Métis oral histories from the 1990s reveal the livedness of bannock, shifting the conversation to the terrain of a Métis common sense. Although framed by recognition politics, these oral histories capture a moment of Métis identity construction on Métis terms. Carefully read, they show that what interviewees understood as common sense represented a category failure for settler-colonial taxonomies.

Public and private conceptions of Metis-ness worked themselves out through intersecting arenas in the second half of the twentieth century. Settler-colonial politics figured largely in the public, while bannock was central to the private. In seeking to shift the spotlight from public-facing top-down political interventions into Métis identity, I follow Métis poet Samantha Nock and center the kitchen table as a critical site where Métis enacted their Peoplehood.[34] Food is historically conditional and nevertheless authentic; this is true of foreign foods adopted into distinct national cultures—think pasta in Italy or dumplings in Mongolia.[35] In the Canadian context, assumptions about the stasis of Indigenous traditional diets reflect colonial expectations of authenticity, such as the infamous Pizza Test in *Delgamuukw*.[36] Exhorted to identify traditional Métis foods, interviewees chose bannock, doing so with the full recognition that other distinct peoples, both Indigenous and European, also ate bannock. In centering bannock, these

Métis engaged with, and simultaneously rejected, essentialist assumptions of Indigeneity. In their choice of bannock as a distinct Métis food, the interviewees refused the false colonial binaries between traditional and modern, stasis and change, assimilation and adaptation. They took for granted that everybody ate bannock *and* that bannock was also distinctively Métis.

Rejecting the Bannock Paradox

When the Government talks about Aboriginal Rights it means no more than our cultural rights to perform Indian dances and songs, and to make bannock.
—CHIEF GEORGE MANUEL, QUOTED IN JENSON, POLLETTA, RAIBMON

In 1981 former president of the Union of British Columbia Indian Chiefs and the National Indian Brotherhood Chief George Manuel articulated that pervasive ideas of cultural essentialism and tradition embedded in binaries frame colonial discourses on Aboriginal rights. When it comes to Indigenous issues, Canadian institutions such as the courts have privileged a concept of cultural difference that assumes adaptation to be the same as assimilation.[37] As Andersen argues, "The fundamental assumption lying at the heart of these discussions is that real Indigeneity *was* rather than *is*—the more modern we appear, the manifestly less Indigenous we must be."[38] Thus, constitutionally protected Aboriginal rights rest on cultural practices of premodern traditions, not on continued collective sovereignty.[39] This praxis envelopes Canadian jurisprudence on Aboriginal rights and has informed the development of critical rulings on Métis Indigeneity. What I term the "bannock paradox" emerges from these binary structures, which in the late twentieth century impacted perceptions of Métis authenticity.

Prior to 1982 the Canadian state refused to recognize Métis as an extant Indigenous people. After the Red River Resistance of 1869–70, John A. Macdonald's government issued Scrip title for Métis in Manitoba, in what Métis understood as recognition of our inherent Aboriginal rights but what the Macdonald government saw as an extinguishment of Métis territorial claims. The Scrip system was a purposeful debacle that served to fracture communities, dispossess Métis from land and, above all, profit Canadian speculators.[40] Scrip functioned to individualize Métis and destabilize our collective Peoplehood. During the long century between the Riel Resistance and the *Constitution Act* the Canadian state pursued a policy of intentional neglect of Métis people, choosing to ignore our collective existence and rights. In 1982, under increased pressure from Indigenous organizations, the government of Canada recognized Métis as an Aboriginal people under Section 35 of the *Constitution Act, 1982*.[41] Pierre Trudeau's Liberal government did not expand on how to determine Métis-ness nor on what this recognition entailed. Trudeau had intended to iron out these "details" in a series of postconstitutional conferences; however, the conferences failed to achieve a conclusive result.[42]

Left with state recognition of a vague Métis-ness but nothing tangible, Métis organizations turned to the Canadian legal system to negotiate our collective relationship with the state.[43] In 1993, the same year that Freeman and Breland-Fines produced the OHP, Ontario Provincial Police charged two Métis men from Sault Ste. Marie, Ontario, for illegally hunting moose. Steve and Roddy Powley, backed by Métis organizations, fought their conviction by claiming Section 35 harvesting rights. Eventually, in 2003 the Supreme Court of Canada (SCC) agreed that the Powleys possessed, through their Métis identity, an Aboriginal harvesting right to hunt moose out of season. In doing so, the SCC established the *Powley* Test for locating eligible Métis rights claims. The *Powley* Test remains the legal standard for locating Métis people across Canada. As Andersen has argued, "The *Powley* decision is problematic not for the fact that it recognizes [Métis] but for how it does so."[44] *Powley* sets out three key criteria for determining valid Métis claims: self-identification, ancestral connection, and community acceptance. These three criteria appear to empower Indigenous self-recognition. As Andersen charts, however, the logic of the *Powley* Test stems from precedent set by the 1996 *R. v. Van der Peet* decision.[45] In *Van der Peet*, the SCC articulated Indigenous difference through an essentialist culturalist framework that froze "identities in time and space."[46] Legal scholar John Borrows has argued that Aboriginal rights jurisprudence in Canada follows an "originalist" interpretation at odds with the more common "living tree" framework in Canadian law. An originalist approach views cultural practices as static; the courts left no room for the living nature of Indigenous Peoplehood.[47] While *Powley* advanced the accepted time scale from precontact to preeffective European control, it nonetheless continued to "locate authentic Aboriginality historically rather than contemporarily."[48]

In this context, food is profoundly political. As historian Coll Thrush argues, food and eating traditions shaped the development of "complex and often contradictory understandings of difference" at the root of Canadian society.[49] The problem with food tradition is that, as Thrush writes, "Present-day essentialist ideas about 'traditional' diets . . . assume static ecological contexts, static networks of exchange, and static palates."[50] As Canadian courts have positioned themselves as arbiters of Indigeneity, these cultural discourses are apparent in the settler common sense that underpins Canadian legal thought. Here Métis are trapped in a double bind: our identity is assumed to be based in our supposed hybridity. As historians Gerhard Ens and Joe Sawchuk argue, "Certain symbols used by the Métis . . . demonstrate a mixed heritage. This often leads to accusations of their somehow being 'inauthentic.'"[51] Métis identity is mixed, thus it can never be authentic.[52] Food tradition, as an expression of authenticity, represents a category failure, yet these assumptions remain embedded in colonial legalese. As Chief George Manuel intuited, bannock sat, and continues to sit, at the crossroads of these tensions.

Despite their pretense, Canadian courts are not the arbiters of Indigeneity; Indigenous Peoples are the arbiters of their Indigeneity. Métis interviewed in the OHP chose bannock as representative of their Métis-ness and they did so with the full knowledge of the complex history of bannock. In the words of Kenneth McLeod, bannock is "a white man's recipe. Scotsmen brought it. They called it scones, they used to cook it on the wood stove . . . the Scots brought it eh, the Indians didn't have no bannock."[53] McLeod appreciated the European origins of bannock yet still maintained that bannock was a quintessential Métis food. Jules Chartrand elaborated a similar history; the Scots brought bannock and it was "quickly picked up by the voyageurs and then the Indians."[54] OHP conversations did not occur in a vacuum; they reveal the fundamental discord between Métis and settler common senses percolating in political and legal discourses in the late twentieth century.

As a pan-Indigenous food, bannock's widespread appeal distorts notions of distinctiveness expected in settler common sense. Interviewees such as Jules Chartrand openly acknowledged bannock's cultural fluidity. Doing so did not preclude bannock's ability to function as a critical marker of Métis identity. Asked about popular foods, Chartrand elaborated:

> One thing that was popular was boiling beef stew eh. And I still make that myself, eh. And having visitors I've noticed a lot of native people do exactly the same and they make exactly the same as the Métis people do. They boil this boiling beef and, you know, when it's boiled for a while, they add a can of tomatoes and either some rice or macaroni and that's exactly what we used to do at home . . . and they had exactly the same thing with bannock. Well, I felt pretty well at home.[55]

That Métis food practices were remarkably similar to those of other Indigenous Peoples is unsurprising considering close geographic, cultural, and kin connections. For Chartrand, bannock was Métis, and it was also pan-Indigenous; the two were not mutually exclusive. Chartrand applied a Métis common sense to make intelligible these overlapping food practices. The logics at work here fall apart when judged by settler common sense. If Canadian Aboriginal rights jurisprudence operates on clear distinctions between settlers and Indigenous Peoples, it also presupposes easily delineated boundaries between Indigenous nations. *Van der Peet* recognized those Indigenous cultural practices "of central significance to the aboriginal society in question—one of the things which made the culture of the society distinctive."[56] Bannock cannot be distinctive if it is a staple of numerous nations. Thus, bannock, like many aspects of pan-Indigenous Peoplehood, represents a category failure in colonial taxonomy.[57] Bannock fails both the specifics of the *Van der Peet* and *Powley* tests because it is both pan-Indigenous and a postcontact acculturation.

What matters here is that for those Métis interviewed, the well-known European origins of bannock and the fact that bannock was pan-Indigenous did not impact its importance for Métis Peoplehood. Bannock's boundary crossing was not just an Indigenous phenomenon; as Ernst Mohr knew, "All the white people eat that [too]."[58] A wide range of contemporary communities ate bannock, and interviewees like Mohr, McLeod, and Chartrand appreciated how bannock crossed cultural lines. In selecting bannock, interviewees, whether consciously or not, rejected a recognition politics grounded in settler common sense. Interviewees refused the binaries that produced the bannock paradox. In doing so, interviewees challenged not only the historical narrative that assumed Métis assimilation but also the historiography that reinforced this colonial perspective. Interviewees' rejection of the bannock paradox can be connected to the ways in which twentieth-century Métis history has been written.

The Importance of Twentieth-Century Métis History

I don't know, nothing Métis about it, unless there's my bannock of course.
—MARY POTTINGER, METIS WOMEN OF MANITOBA ORAL HISTORY PROJECT

Métis are not surprised that interviewees selected bannock as a distinctive Métis food. How they made this selection speaks to the inner workings of Métis common sense. As Mary Pottinger demonstrated, the OHP produced a formulaic pattern: interrogated on traditional Métis foods, interviewees often insisted that there was nothing particularly Métis about their diets. Pressed further, interviewees invariably realized bannock fit Freeman and Breland-Fines's criteria. Incomprehension punctuated these moments of realization, as if interviewees could not understand the need to articulate something considered common sense. Sensing interviewees' incredulity, Freeman and Breland-Fines took great pains to assert their own cultural knowledge of bannock. These fraught bannock moments illustrate how the on-the-ground experience of being Métis in the twentieth century challenges colonial assumptions about Métis history.

Food was a contested ground on which Freeman and Breland-Fines encountered interviewees. That few interviewees initially selected bannock as a distinct Métis food poses an interesting conundrum: if bannock was so important why did only one interviewee, Rose LaFreniere, begin with bannock? Many began like Kathleen Delaronde, stating that they didn't know of any traditional Métis foods.[59] Instead of an easily identifiable dish, most then emphasized the commonness of their diets. Interviewees insisted their diets did not differ from those of other people.[60] For Agnes Bell, Métis "eat all kinds of things, whatever they find out to eat."[61] This sentiment was echoed by Joe Bell: "Like in them days they used to eat anything."[62] What Métis like Bell did remember eating consisted predominately of local, seasonal foods. This was especially true of more remote northern communities, while southern Métis discussed the availability of store-bought food.[63] A listing of Métis game included gophers, "deer meat, moose meat, elk meat," in addition to "lots of jumper, and rabbits, prairie chicken."[64] Seasonal options included "muskrats . . . geese and ducks in the spring."[65] Northern communities also included caribou,[66] while Interlake communities, such as St. Laurent, relied on fisheries: "That's why the people are so brainy there eh, fish brain food, eh."[67] According to Ernest Mohr, European-style husbandry also supplemented local game: "There was a lot of meat, wild meat. My dad was a good hunter. That and a big garden, and they had a few head of cattle. Kill a cow in the fall, and a pig, and you're set for the winter. We milked cows all winter."[68] Locality and survival were more important than culinary nationalism; Métis recalled eating what was available.

Food represented a pragmatic choice. When asked about traditional Métis food, Therese Breland exclaimed gleefully, "Oh well, god . . . baloney?! *laughter*"[69] Made in jest, the connection of Métis with baloney demonstrates an important pattern. Jules Chartrand also emphasized baloney:

> Well, at St. Laurent, when I was young the people was poor so they used to, the store keeper used to order a lot of baloney eh. 'Course he was selling what was, he was ordering what was selling, eh. So, the items that were selling were baloney, a lot of beans . . .[70]

Chartrand connected Métis eating habits with economic necessity; baloney was a critical component of Chartrand's childhood because of availability and affordability. Though presented in jest, we cannot discount the fact that Métis, like Chartrand and Breland, asserted baloney as a distinctive Métis food. That Chartrand and Breland made affective connections with baloney is unsurprising given its prominence in their childhoods and reminds us that food tradition includes the foods that people actually eat. Store-bought baloney, though, is an even more inaccuarate measure of Métis authenticity than bannock in the logics of settler colonialism.

Searching for the "essence" of Métis-ness Breland-Fines and Freeman turned to the food that settler academics associate with Métis history: pemmican—bison meat pounded and dried into a jerky and usually supplemented with berries such as saskatoons. The standard historical narrative holds that the Métis nation emerged from its economic niche as pemmican purveyors for fur trade operations.[71] This historical interpretation privileges the androcentric aspects of the hunt and trade, obfuscating the critical role women played in pemmican production.[72] The historiographical weight of pemmican also serves to center the nineteenth century in Métis history at the expense of the twentieth century. Turning to oral sources helps to correct these biases. Métis interviewees in the twentieth century did not discuss pemmican. As interviewee Ernest Mohr recalled, "Oh, that's way before our day. We never seen that. I never tasted any of it."[73] While Mohr recognized the importance of pemmican, he asserted that pemmican was not a twentieth-century Métis experience for the simple fact that bison hunting was no longer viable. Instead, interviewees suggested bannock.

When interviewees eventually turned to bannock, they emphasized the same basic concerns that motivated their discussion of other foods. Métis ate bannock because it was cheap, pragmatic, and tasted good.[74] Whether baked in an oven, fried on a stove, or cooked over an open fire, bannock was quick and easy to make. Though, for Minnie Anderson, "that bannock's really good on the open fire."[75] Agnes Bell agreed: "Make a big fire . . . that's the best way."[76] For both, an open fire outside remained the preferred cooking method. However, bannock's simplicity does not capture its full appeal. Taste mattered too. Just discussing the baking process made Agnes Bell's mouth water: "I wish I'd have some of that right now. I would eat half a bannock right now! *laughter*"[77] Taste was obviously important, but on a basic level, interviewees recognized bannock's caloric importance. Bannock satiated the needs of marginalized and impoverished Métis. As Delia Allard stated, "Sometimes all we had to eat was bannock and lard."[78] Here, the similarities between baloney and bannock are striking. Like baloney, bannock was a pragmatic choice that could easily maintain a household. Bannock was cheap and filling, packing a lot of dense calories into an affordable and tasty product. As Joe Bell put it, "Bannock you eat that, [it] sticks with you."[79] Interviewees' identification of economic necessity as integral to their Peoplehood rejects culinary essentialism. However, this analysis falls short of articulating the full picture.

A prominent trope of Métis history—the inaccessibility of the twentieth century—seems to be supported by the interviewees minimizing the distinctiveness of bannock and discussing it in practical terms. Academic scholarship struggles to locate Métis in the twentieth century because of how historians perceived the supposed "silences" of the documentary record. These biases are deeply embedded in historical understandings of the Métis past. Throughout the twentieth century, colonial society enforced significant stigmas on openly expressing a Métis identity; in the words of one of historian Nicole St-Onge's interlocutors, "C'est pas beau être Métis. [It is not good to be Métis.]"[80] These stigmas are not easy to think or write about; the shame my relatives endured still lingers. For feminist Métis filmmaker Christine Welsh, "Amnesia, and silence, and a haunting sense of loss . . . [were her] inheritances."[81] The marginalization of Métis made for real experiences and are explored with true sensitivity by artists and scholars like Welsh.

The reality is that the settler state and society forced Métis peoples to make strategic choices about how they lived as Métis. In his 1978 ethnographic study, Joe Sawchuk argued that among Métis "there [was] a tendency . . . to suppress cultural differences that might precipitate further discrimination."[82] Sawchuk's assessment was accurate; however, the prognosis that this suppression amounted to silence is a mischaracterization. As historian Michel Hogue argues, the perceived archival barriers produced a historiographical tradition focused on the nineteenth century. The lack of historical work on the twentieth century, Hogue continues, has tangible consequences: "The troubling phenomenon of 'settler self-indigenization' takes advantage of the limited understanding of Métis history and culture and allows non-Indigenous people to lay claim to being Métis on the basis of their ability to trace descent from a (distant) Indigenous ancestor."[83] This historiographical gap reinforces a perceived disconnect between the past and contemporary issues of identity. Being Métis, however, is fundamentally grounded in the connections between the past and the present; it is not based in blood or DNA transmitted by a long-dead Indigenous ancestor but is an ongoing lived experience.

Understood through Métis common sense, it is clear that Métis in the twentieth century were not silent. Interviewees who may not have outwardly advertised their identity were willing to articulate their Métis-ness for a Métis audience. When asked about when she knew she was Métis, Rose LaFreniere responded, "Well, for gosh sake my parents were so I couldn't deny it."[84] Mary Pottinger simply stated, "I don't know, I never thought of that . . . you are what you are."[85] Therese Breland echoed her sentiment: "We didn't really beat it over the head. We knew who we were and that was it . . . We just knew who we were, but we didn't need to hear it every day."[86] Many interviewees might have only advertised their Métis-ness inwardly, and with kin, those interviewed expressed the feeling that they knew who they were and did not need anyone else telling them. These reactions reminded me of my own grandpère's enigmatic refusal to enroll in the Manitoba Metis Federation, claiming that he "did not need a card to tell him who he was."[87] He knew who he was; a piece of paper would not change that fact. Throughout the twentieth century, Canadians refused to hear this continued presence, rendering Métis identity invisible in a settler-colonial system that privileged racial and cultural whiteness. Coercive government policies, compounded by violent social and cultural pressure, shaped how Métis practiced their Peoplehood. Many held on to those practices that they could shield from a public gaze. This does not mean that Métis stopped being Métis or that they were hiding. It means that to understand how Métis identity survived the twentieth century, we must turn inward, and as Samantha Nock gestures, toward the kitchen table.

The attraction of bannock was not just one of necessity or taste. Métis expressed strong affective attachments to bannock because it was a fundamental part of being Métis in the twentieth century beyond the colonial gaze. Their initial refusal to select a distinctive Métis food was not a form of silence but evidenced Métis common sense. Bannock was self-evident; if you were Métis, you knew how to make it, and you knew the social customs that were rolled into the dough. Interviewees' treatment of bannock as self-evident created conflict with Freeman and Breland-Fines. The attempts of Freeman and Breland-Fines to elicit elaborations on something that interviewees took for granted resulted in humorous encounters. For example, an exchange with Minnie Anderson:

> FREEMAN: When you say bannock, can you tell me what that is?
>
> MINNIE ANDERSON: What do you mean?
>
> FREEMAN: Like . . . the reason I ask, I should have explained this before, to most people it sounds like a stupid question . . .[88]

Or, an exchange with Kenneth McLeod:

> FREEMAN: We were talking Mr. Mcleod about bannock a few minutes ago, and I was telling you that a lot of young people don't know what that is, can you tell me what that is?
>
> KENNETH McLEOD: What is it?
>
> FREEMAN: Bannock.
>
> KENNETH McLEOD: Bannock?!
>
> FREEMAN: Yeah.[89]

Asked to explain bannock, both Anderson and McLeod responded with incomprehension. Why should they articulate something so obvious? Trapped and frustrated, Freeman resorted to explaining the reasoning behind the question: the preservation of cultural knowledge for Métis youth disconnected from kin networks. In doing so, Freeman leaned on the geographic divide between northern and southern Métis communities, emphasizing the apparent lack of cultural knowledge for Métis youth living in southern Manitoba among a larger and more developed settler population. Real differences existed between the concerns of northern and southern interviewees, yet bannock transcended the divide in ways that other concerns could not.

Freeman's questions about bannock were at odds with the world envisioned by interviewees such as Anderson and McLeod. Both saw the knowledge of bannock as common sense and responded incredulously to questioning. That Freeman and Breland-Fines had to ask for specific detail provoked strong reactions that often led to ridicule:

FREEMAN: What is bannock?

LIONEL ALLARD: You don't know what bannock is?!

DELIA ALLARD: You're not a Michif then!

FREEMAN: I know what Bannock is, I just want you to describe it for our kids is all . . .[90]

Delia and Lionel Allard made a direct connection between being Métis and the knowledge of bannock. For Allard, bannock was an obvious part of being Métis. Challenged to articulate something Allard took as common sense, he responded by teasing Freeman, implying that she was not Métis for asking such a ridiculous question. Freeman responded defensively, demonstrating that she too knew that her question was simplistic. In posing the question, Freeman and Breland-Fines opened themselves to teasing from their subjects. Bannock became a way for interviewees to assert the priorities of a Métis common sense and to discipline Freeman and Breland-Fines into that worldview.

Rose LaFreniere of St. François-Xavier, Manitoba provided a compelling example of a Métis common sense. Unlike the pattern that most interviewees followed, LaFreniere immediately asserted "bannock of course" as a traditional Métis food.[91] After listing a number of other items including tourtière and boulettes, LaFreniere then turned the interview back on Freeman and Breland-Fines. LaFreniere chided them: "You know how to make bannock?!" Reluctant and embarrassed, Freeman responded, "I'm going to say no because it usually ends up like a rock" before trailing off that "my mom and my sisters have the knack."[92] Freeman's inadequate response set LaFreniere off on a long monologue:

Well, you know some people are so stupid, they phone me and they ask "how many cups of flour do you use to make bannock" I say "how stupid can you be!" Come here and I'll teach you how to make bannock. "You don't measure?" Like in school there this lady wanted to know how many cups I use you know, well "you stand there, and you'll see how many cups I use." *laughter* I have a big bowl, and I fill it with flour and then I make a bird's nest in the middle . . . I put my baking powder, a little bit salt. I prepare margarine and then the lard to make the bannock. It tastes a lot better. And I take half a pound of margarine and I melt it and I put cold water on it. You don't put it hot in there . . . And then I roll my bannock and I take my fork and I pick, pick, pick . . . There's a woman and she makes it and one day she says she'll send me a bannock . . . so she sends me a bannock and she had used a knife to poke holes in her bannock you know, I never said nothing but I thought you're wrong lady.[93]

The anthropologist Brigitte Sebastia describes traditional food as evoking "cultural heritage, the know-how shared and transmitted, quite often by word of mouth, amongst a more or less wide group of people."[94] Small details mattered in LaFreniere's account, like her insistence on using a fork to pick the bannock. That one would use a fork *and not a knife* at this critical stage was common sense to her. LaFreniere insisted that making bannock was the most obvious act. Not knowing how much flour to use elicited derision: "How stupid can you be!"[95] It was critical to add the margarine and lard at the right temperature and consistency. The addition of margarine itself was a modern adaptation yet, for LaFreniere, was also a precise measure of genuine bannock. Recipes may change, but at the same time some baking methods were simply either right or wrong. As Ernest Mohr argued, "Well if you didn't cook your bannock right then that'll be hard tack."[96] Proper baking techniques mattered.

LaFreniere directed the underlying message of her outburst at Freeman, who bore the brunt of LaFreniere's teasing. The humor of the interaction reverberated. After all, for LaFreniere, a pure Métis "was the one that told good jokes."[97] The network of humor and bannock was thus integral to Métis conceptions of themselves. Lionel and Delia Allard displayed a similar affect when they taunted Freeman for asking simple questions about bannock: "You're not Michif then!"[98] Humor around bannock was integral to Métis sociability. LaFreniere enforced social expectations that tied together humor, common sense, and bannock. In this formula, bannock helped sustain a Métis identity. Outward symbols were impossible to maintain; it was dangerous to be Métis in the twentieth century. Why would people choose to expose themselves to violent ridicule from a broader Canadian public? Hence the critical importance of bannock and its associated foodways. Métis common sense placed bannock as an integral link in a chain of kinship that bound individuals, families, and communities together. Bannock knowledge was common sense to those embedded in interviewee kin networks. Kinship is the common ingredient that makes bannock Métis. To outsiders, bannock does not make sense precisely because the kinship is an invisible ingredient. Rose LaFreniere and other interviewees were acutely aware of bannock's continued importance to the livedness of Métis.

Seen this way, the kitchen table was a key site at which Métis enacted their Peoplehood in the twentieth century. Settler historians have tended to miss this fact because of their inclination to privilege androcentric political moments that produced accessible written documents.[99] Métis historiography clusters around political moments such as the Red River Resistance that produced a rich documentary archive.[100] Scholars have tended to write off the rest as untraceable because of the lack of a sufficient archival record. In engaging with Canadian recognition politics, Métis political organizations in turn perpetuated the privileging of androcentric history. Gender must be deployed as a necessary correction to challenge the priorities of androcentric political organizations and their political priorities.

Bannock, Gender, and Recognition Politics

> *Any old Métis girl that has anything to do with them can make bannock.*
> —FRANK WALTER, METIS WOMEN OF MANITOBA ORAL HISTORY PROJECT

Steeped in misogynist assumptions, interviewee Frank Walter nonetheless demonstrated the deep connection between bannock and female labor. Situating Walter's recognition with Métis scholar Adam Gaudry's call to "reconceptualize Métis-ness as a process of everyday life arising from the relationships between Métis people rather than between Métis individuals and a bureaucratic body," I explore the dissonance between the OHP and Métis organizations that emerged in reaction to another state intervention into Indigeneity: Bill C-31. The on-the-ground Métis experiences expressed in the OHP were at odds with the nationalism promulgated by Métis organizations subsequent to Bill C-31. Embedded in colonial recognition politics, Métis political organizations privileged expressions of identity that emerged from androcentric perspectives. Consciously or not, interviewees in the OHP distorted these associations. Interviewees spoke affectionately of bannock and its implied gendered relationships—and in so doing, centered kitchen table politics over recognition politics.

In 1985, pressured by a vociferous Indigenous women's movement, Canada unilaterally enacted an amendment to the Indian Act: Bill C-31. Intended to relieve the most egregious gendered discriminations of the Indian Act, Bill C-31 provided a mechanism for disenrolled Indigenous women and their children to regain status.[101] In so doing, Bill C-31 engineered new faults within status, nonstatus, and Métis communities. The experiences of Bill C-31 are impossible to encapsulate in this article. Suffice it to say, for Métis organizations in the 1990s Bill C-31 was a direct threat to their political power, while individual, on-the-ground experiences varied. In sum, Métis organizations faced the prospect of losing potential citizens. For example, in South Indian Lake, Hilda Dysart recounted how the community once had a large Métis population that dwindled in the wake of "Bill C-31 coming in and a lot people applying to have their status."[102] Bill C-31 pushed Métis organizations to reevaluate their purpose. Through the early to mid-twentieth century most Métis organizations included nonstatus peoples. Bill C-31 coupled with Section 35 impelled Métis organizations to rearticulate their mandate through an exclusive Métis nationalism.[103]

Bill C-31 was a profoundly affective state intervention into Indigeneity, in which interviewees, such as Chris Baker, positioned Métis as uniquely challenged by federal and provincial policies:

> If I went to the hospital, they would recognize me as a Native right away because my skin is dark and my hair is dark and my eyes are brown, and I'll go to the reserve and they'll say no you're a white man, we can't help you. You get shuffled around. Nobody wants to be responsible for you. And that's not fair.[104]

Interviewees frequently invoked ideals of fairness. As Kathleen Delaronde framed it, "I paid my way this long I'm gonna keep paying it."[105] Bill C-31 exacerbated tensions that interviewees read around a narrative of Métis marginalization. Denied the (meager) benefits of status, interviewees understood being Métis as having to work harder. For Rebecca McIvor the difference between women with status and Métis women was "the treaties . . . they can get free help. But Métis, I guess, women have never had anything to fall back on for help. They've had to do that on their own."[106] Resentment was a powerful script; the tensions aroused by Bill C-31 were deeply personal, often pitting kin against kin. While Delaronde refused to take Bill C-31, she noted that "some of my brothers and sisters have."[107] Asked if she would consider taking Bill C-31, Delaronde snapped back "no."[108]

Others, such as Baker, expressed little concern about identity boundary crossing. Baker opined "that, like, I'm glad that the women fought for their rights."[109] Baker positioned Bill C-31 in a gendered political analysis that emphasized the hard-fought political campaigns waged by Indigenous women. While lauding this female victory, Baker also expressed apprehensions about the sincerity of the Canadian government, arguing that "the government is just playing a bunch of silly games with us folks."[110] Hilda Dysart also questioned the benefits of Bill C-31: "I don't know if at this point, they've found that they've really gained anything from going under the Bill C-31."[111]

Bill C-31 is a testament to the ways that government interventions sow confusion among communities, while simultaneously revealing the ways that Indigenous Peoples negotiate and challenge colonial taxonomies. Interviewees acknowledged divisions between First Nations and Métis communities but the boundaries they emphasized were porous and not the same boundaries that the state enforced. Individuals such as Baker projected a nonchalance incommensurate with government policy: "Well like I can get my status if I want. But I prefer not. Because I'm more a halfbreed than a treaty Indian. And maybe someday I'll decide to get my status, I don't know."[112] In the end though it mattered little to him: "All my friends know [I'm] Métis but they [also] know that I'm an Indian."[113] Baker rooted his identity in his community belonging, not government interventions. Interviewing Eve Carpick, Freeman enquired, "Will you be what you called yourselves earlier, half-breeds or Métis, will you be that if you get [Bill C-31]? To which Carpick responded, "Well, I don't know. I still feel that I'm [Métis] whether I get my treaty rights or not."[114] In the bipolar colonial order one can only be First Nations or Métis; there is no room for a hyphenated identity in the way that Canada affords settlers (i.e., Ukrainian-Canadian). It was a balancing act Hilda Dysart understood: "Like the way I thought about it was that you know like, well, gee, you know, I'm Métis and if I get a treaty number than I'm still Métis but it doesn't work that way *laughter*"[115] Whether interviewees could claim Bill C-31 status or not, they still chose to assert their Métis-ness on their own terms through their own Métis common sense. In the same way that Jules Chartrand could acknowledge familiarity with bannock from First Nations communities and still maintain bannock as distinctly Métis, interviewees reacted to Bill C-31 in ways that emphasized a distinctive Métis identity—just not in the dichotomous way the state enforced.

The kitchen table was the site of these gendered political conversations, and thus, my invocation of kitchen table politics necessitates an engagement with gender. The gendered dynamics of bannock apparent within the OHP archive reveal the centrality of female labor in sustaining Métis social and political activism through the twentieth century. Historically, though, men baked bannock as often as women did. As a staple of the fur trade, bannock was a convenient food that men on the canoe routes could easily prepare.[116] This tradition carried through to the twentieth century. For example, George La Fleur of Sled Lake, Saskatchewan, took home first prize at the bannock-baking contest during the annual Back to Batoche celebrations in 1978.[117]

But for Métis interviewed in the OHP, baking bannock was strongly associated with female labor in the home, thus tying together bannock, gender, and Métis Peoplehood.

Métis political scientist Daniel Voth argues that we must center the lived experiences of Métis women to understand Métis Peoplehood.[118] Voth's argument builds on the significant contributions of Métis scholar Brenda Macdougall whose work on Métis ethnogenesis at Île-à-la-Crosse, Saskatchewan, notes that Métis society in Saskatchewan emerged through matrilocal patterns.[119] Crucially, "the notion of matrilocal residency," Métis historian Gabrielle Legault argues, "contradicts historical writing that regards historic Métis society as transient and unstable."[120] Further, Voth and Jesse Loyer contend that as a matrilocal society, Métis communities are grounded by "women [who] are instructors, carrying cultural values and educating others about Métis values."[121]

While the OHP never explicitly engaged a gendered analysis, gender was intrinsic within these interviews. Here a simple exchange between Freeman and Henry Garrick is revealing. Discussing Métis foods, Freeman asked, "Did the women bake much back then?" to which Garrick responded, "bannock yeah. Mostly bannock."[122] Freeman linked baking with female labor, and Garrick added bannock into the mix. While some interviewees, like Jules Chartrand, articulated bannock as something anyone could bake, most associated bannock with women's work.[123] Both Freeman's questions and interviewee responses reflected these assumptions. As a site of Métis survivance, the kitchen table represented the private and domestic, constructed as female space. Métis women exploited Eurocentric patriarchal expectations of the role of women in society to practice a Métis Peoplehood beyond the colonial gaze. Métis survivance in the twentieth century centered on female labor in the kitchen, including baking bannock. Shifting toward the domestic terrain of bannock entails moving away from androcentric political organizations.

Bannock was a key link in the chain of Métis female kinship and knowledge production. Agnes Bell and Hilda Dysart both associated bannock with maternal labor. When asked about traditional bannock practices Bell stated that "mother used to . . . used to bake bannock."[124] It was from their mothers that interviewees learned the proper ways of baking bannock. Freeman also structured bannock in a network of female kinship and knowledge. Justifying her questions about bannock to Minnie Anderson, Freeman emphasized the connections between bannock and maternal labor: "Métis kids, who don't have a grandma and all that, they don't understand what bannock is . . ."[125] Here Freeman linked bannock to Métis kin networks and asserted it within a system of generational knowledge transfer inherently tied to women's work.

Baking bannock as female labor held tangible significance for Métis. When asked about bannock, Frank Walter responded that "any old Métis girl that has anything to do with them can make bannock and that's why I married a 15-year-old girl because she could cook bannock."[126] Walter chose to emphasize bannock as a key factor in his marriage. This was not a flippant comment but a declaration steeped in meaning. For Walter, bannock was central to a life-altering decision. Walter acknowledged the gendered labor of bannock and emphasized its importance. Kitchen table politics were tangible; bannock directly impacted everyday life for Métis interviewees.

I am not the first scholar to note the connections between Métis identity, bannock, and female labor. In the early feminist Métis film *Women in the Shadows*, Cree/Métis scholar Emma Larocque, tongue firmly in cheek, presents Métis filmmaker Christine Welsh with a store-bought bannock mix as a (satirized) symbol of Welsh's reestablished connection with the Métis Nation. This comedic moment operates on a few critical gestures. For one, it acknowledged the gap in Welsh's cultural knowledge; she did not grow up learning her family's traditions. That Larocque chose to use bannock to symbolize Welsh's reconnection was no accident. This act acknowledged the centrality of bannock to Indigenous—and in this case a distinctive Métis—Peoplehood while playing with the tropes of cultural essentialism. Store-bought, premixed bannock was a modern interpretation of traditional food that was available to anyone for purchase. It was a purposeful stretch of the meaning of tradition and an intentional disregard of colonial binaries. It was also what connected Welsh to her Métis heritage. This "modern" bannock was an invitation back into Welsh's Métis kin networks; it connected Welsh with her ancestors, the women in the shadows. Bannock—even store-bought, premixed bannock—as female labor practiced in the kitchen survived both colonial assimilation and the disciplinary misperceptions of recognition politics.

The webs of kinship emanating from private, female labor bound Métis Peoplehood tightly. I have dealt primarily with how individual Métis claimed a national belonging structured around bannock. The inversion would be: "Who claims you?" Here, Therese Breland revealed another way that gendered bannock performances were central to Métis identity:

> Remember I told you about Aunty Mary, the one who didn't want to be a Métis. Well, she may have not wanted to be a Métis but boy she could make Red River twists. She made good Red River twists . . . A sort of a variation on, I guess a bannock but not exactly. They have something that I've had at the Métis pavilion, it's kind of a long, fat thing . . . it's like bannock only it's fried . . . c'est ci bon [it's good]. I can give you the recipe . . .[127]

The tensions embedded in this quote are fraught, and it is by no means my intention to refute anyone's personal identity, but this moment demonstrates a number of important aspects of Métis identity construction. For one, it emphasizes the centrality of bannock to Métis identity. Aunty Mary, despite the obviousness of her kin connections and the common sense of her baking, rejected this identity. Breland clearly found Aunty Mary's rejection amusing, which led to frequent teasing.[128] From Breland's perspective Aunty Mary's knowledge and prowess in the kitchen—her labor—bound her in web of kinship that was unmistakably Métis. Baking was an enactment of this identity, legible to all those in the know. Subsequently, that Breland was willing to pass on the recipe to Freeman and Breland-Fines was a clear indication of her recognition of Freeman and Breland-Fines's own Métisness and an assertion of Métis survivance. Métis would continue to exist as a collective people because of the women who baked in spite of Canada's assimilatory practices.

My work consciously responds to Voth's call "to build a Métis nationalism that is explicitly oriented towards defying structures of gendered violence."[129] In "'Descendants of the Original Lords of the Soil': Indignation, Disobedience, and Women Who Jig on Sundays" Voth employs a favorite Métis story connecting jigging and resistance to colonialism. In Voth's version, jiggers resist the strict orders of the local priest. I have heard other versions that mock the RCMP. Whatever the colonial authority, the gist of the story is the same. The priest/police drives by to check on the Métis families. He sees them through their windows standing around at home not doing much of anything. Satisfied, he drives on. Beyond his gaze, however, below the window the Métis are jigging. Voth extends this story as metaphor to articulate what he calls "indignant disobedience," the conscious resistance to colonial and patriarchal authority. I extend the metaphor in a slightly different direction; I use it to describe how both Canadian historiography and Métis organizations have focused on what is legible in settler common sense. By appealing to the state for recognition, Métis organizations have taken on these perspectives. From such a perspective, Métis appear motionless, but we miss what their feet are doing; we are missing the on-the-ground experience. When we get closer, however, and focus on Métis experiences, our perception of Métis history shifts—Métis action is apparent. Bannock provided such an opportunity to shift scales. Thinking through bannock reveals the critical female labor that sustained a Métis identity at the kitchen table. These are the histories that matter for an inclusive, anti-colonial Métis Peoplehood.

Conclusion

Baking bannock does not make you Métis. Bannock, however, as practiced kinship, is at the heart of Métis Peoplehood. In this article I have used bannock to center the kitchen table as a critical site of Métis survivance during the twentieth century. Thanks to the dedicated labor of Lorraine Freeman and Doreen Breland-Fines, who engaged Métis elders at a critical historical moment, I have been able to articulate a Métis common sense that rejects the binary assumptions of Canadian settler colonialism. Interviewees asserted bannock as a distinctive component of a Métis identity but in a way that cannot function within the tests of Indigeneity expected in settler common sense. Embedded in colonial perspectives is the still lingering assumption of the inevitability of Indigenous assimilation. The bannock paradox is symptomatic of this organizing principle. The Canadian state perpetually presumes our disappearance into the white settler population. Métis understandings of bannock complicated this narrative; bannock demonstrated the inedibility of assimilation. Throughout the twentieth century, Métis continued to consume bannock as both a necessity and as a choice. Either way, interviewees linked it to their identity as Métis. Interviewees did not care about cultural essentialism or about measures of authentic tradition; they did not see themselves along a spectrum of assimilation. One could add margarine, and still the bannock would be bannock and the Métis a Métis.[130] Métis knew that bannock came from Scotland and that people in other nations ate it; however, what mattered for them was how bannock linked them through kinship with their ancestors, their past, and their future. For interviewees in 1993, kitchen table politics superseded nascent recognition politics.

I do not intend to endorse a rose-colored vision of either tradition or adaptation. Scholars such as Devon Mihesuah force us to grapple with the serious health implications of Indigenous dietary decisions and the colonial forces that impinge on those choices.[131] Dismissing bannock (even with the best intentions) as unhealthy or nontraditional obfuscates its critical role in Métis survivance in the twentieth century and gives credence to the binary assumptions embedded in colonial jurisprudence. The health implications of eating bannock are our issues to deal with, not the issues of the settler state. If Métis choose to no longer bake bannock as a cultural practice then so be it, but this should be a decision based on our collective political sovereignty not on the logics of settler colonialism.

To come full circle, the epigraphical recipe that opened this article belonged to my great-grandmère Josephine Allard and great-aunt Marie-Rose Lavallee. Without fail, that bannock was at the center of any family meal. However, we always used the term *galet*. Later in life I learned that galet is the Michif word for bannock. Despite two generations removed from fluency in Michif, the language lived on in our food practices structured around bannock and the female labor that sustained it at our kitchen table.

DANE ALLARD (Métis/Settler) is a Ph.D. candidate at the University of British Columbia on the unceded territories of the Musqueam Nation. Born in Winnipeg, Manitoba in Treaty 1 territory, his familial ties are linked to the Red River Métis community of St. François-Xavier, Manitoba.

References

Archival Material

Metis Women of Manitoba Inc. "Oral History Project." Archives of Manitoba. Accession No. 1997—44, Location Codes C2397—C2456. Accessed July 24, 2019, http://pam.minisisinc.com/SCRIPTS/MWIMAIN.DLL/122896985/1/1/1267?RECORD&DATABASE=DESCRIPTION_WEB_INT.

Allard, Lionel, and Delia Allard. Oral History interview with Lionel and Delia Allard of St. Laurent, Manitoba. June 22, 1993. Accession No. 1997—44, Location Code C2408. Métis Women of Manitoba Inc. oral history project records, Archives of Manitoba.

Baker, Chris. Oral History interview with Chris Baker of South Indian Lake, Manitoba. May 17, 1993. Accession No. 1997—44, Location Code C2434. Métis Women of Manitoba Inc. oral history project records, Archives of Manitoba.

Bell, Joe, and Agnes Bell. Oral History Interview with Joe and Agnes Bell of St. Lazare, Manitoba. April 30, 1993. Accession No. 1997—44, Location Code C2422. Métis Women of Manitoba Inc. oral history project records, Archives of Manitoba.

Breland, Therese. Oral History interview with Therese Breland of Winnipeg, Manitoba. June 5, 1993. Accession No. 1997—44, Location Code C2455. Métis Women of Manitoba Inc. oral history project records, Archives of Manitoba.

Carpick, Eve, and Kathryn McLeod. Oral History interview with Eve Carpick and Kathryn McLeod of The Pas, Manitoba. May 12, 1993. Accession No. 1997—44, Location Code C2425. Métis Women of Manitoba Inc. oral history project records, Archives of Manitoba.

Chartrand, Jules. Oral History interview with Jules Chartrand of Winnipeg, Manitoba. June 1, 1993. Accession No. 1997—44, Location Code C2451. Métis Women of Manitoba Inc. oral history project records, Archives of Manitoba.

DeLaronde, Kathleen. Oral History interview with Kathleen DeLaronde of the Pas, Manitoba. May 12, 1993. Accession No. 1997—44, Location Code C2424. Métis Women of Manitoba Inc. oral history project records, Archives of Manitoba.

Dysart, Hilda. Oral History interview with Hilda Dysart of South Indian Lake, Manitoba. May 18, 1993. Accession No. 1997—44, Location Code

C2439. Métis Women of Manitoba Inc. oral history project records, Archives of Manitoba.

Garrick, Henry. Oral History interview with Henry Garrick of Wabowden, Manitoba. May 13, 1993. Accession No. 1997—44, Location Code C2430. Métis Women of Manitoba Inc. oral history project records, Archives of Manitoba.

LaFreniere, Rose. Oral History interview with Rose LaFreniere of St. Francois Xavier, Manitoba. June 3, 1993. Accession No. 1997—44, Location Code C2543. Métis Women of Manitoba Inc. oral history project records, Archives of Manitoba.

McIvor, Rebecca. Oral History interview with Rebecca McIvor of the Pas, Manitoba. May 13, 1993. Accession No. 1997—44, Location Code C2427. Métis Women of Manitoba Inc. oral history project records, Archives of Manitoba.

McLeod, Kenneth. Oral history interview with Kenneth McLeod of Norway House, Manitoba. May 20, 1993. Accession no. 1997—44, Location Code C2444. Metis Women of Manitoba Inc. oral history project records, Archives of Manitoba.

Mohr, Ernest. Oral history interview with Ernest Mohr of Crane River, Manitoba. April 28, 1993. Accession No. 1997—44, Location Code C2412. Métis Women of Manitoba Inc. oral history project records, Archives of Manitoba.

Morriseau, Bella. Oral history interview with Bella Morriseau of Crane River, Manitoba. April 28, 1993. Accession No. 1997—44, Location Code C2414. Métis Women of Manitoba Inc. oral history project records, Archives of Manitoba.

Potoski, Bernice. Oral history interview with Bernice Potoski of Riverton, Manitoba. April 14, 1993. Accession No. 1997—44, Location Code C2402. Métis Women of Manitoba Inc. oral history project records, Archives of Manitoba.

Pottinger, Mary. Oral history interview with Mary Pottinger of Eriksdale, Manitoba. April 22, 1993. Accession No. 1997—44, Location Code C2407. Métis Women of Manitoba Inc. oral history project records, Archives of Manitoba.

Walter, Frank. Oral history interview with Frank Walker of Selkirk, Manitoba. April 13, 1993. Accession No. 1997—44, Location Code C2397. Métis Women of Manitoba Inc. oral history project records, Archives of Manitoba.

Case Law

R. v. Van der Peet (1996) 2 S.C.R. 507, 1996 Supreme Court of Canada. https://scc-csc.lexum.com/scc-csc/scc-csc/en/item/1407/index.do.

Secondary Literature

Andersen, Chris. "Residual Tensions of Empire: Contemporary Métis Communities and Canadian Judicial Imagination." In *Canada: State of the Federation (2003): Reconfiguring Aboriginal State Relations*. Edited by Michael Murphy. Montreal and Kingston: McGill Queen's University Press for the Institute, 2005: 295—328.

Andersen, Chris. "From Difference to Density." *Cultural Studies Review* 15, no. 2 (2009): 80—100.

Andersen, Chris. *Métis: Race, Recognition and Indigenous Peoplehood*. Vancouver: University of British Columbia Press, 2014.

The Bannock Factory. "Bannock-in-a-box." Accessed November 17, 2020. http://www.thebannockfactory.com/Products.htm.

Borrows, John. *Freedom and Indigenous Constitutionalism*. Toronto: University of Toronto Press, 2016.

Colpitts, George. *Pemmican Empire: Food, Trade, and the Last Bison Hunts in the North American Plains, 1780–1882*. Cambridge: Cambridge University Press, 2016.

Coulthard, Glen. *Red Skin, White Mask*: *Rejecting the Colonial Politics of Recognition*. Minneapolis: University of Minnesota Press, 2014.

Deloria, Philip Joseph. *Indians in Unexpected Places*. Lawrence: University Press of Kansas, 2004.

Ens, Gerhard J., and Joe Sawchuk. *From New Peoples to New Nations: Aspects of Metis History and Identity from the Eighteenth to the Twenty-First Centuries*. Toronto: University of Toronto Press, 2016.

Hogue, Michel. "Still Hiding in Plain Sight? Historiography and Métis Archival Memory." *History Compass* 18, no. 7 (2020): 1–11.

Jenson, Jane, Francesca Polletta, and Paige Raibmon. "The Difficulties of Combating Inequality in Time." *Daedalus* 148, no. 3 (2019): 136–63.

Lawrence, Bonita. *"Real" Indians and Others: Mixed-Blood Urban Native Peoples and Indigenous Nationhood*. Vancouver: UBC Press, 2004.

Legault, Gabrielle. "Making Métis Places in British Columbia: The Edge of the Métis Nation Homeland." *BC Studies* no. 209 (Spring 2021): 19–36.

Lewis, Courtney. "Frybread wars: biopolitics and the consequences of selective United States healthcare practices for American Indians." *Food, Culture & Society* 24, no. 4 (2018): 427–48.

Lyons, Scott Richard. *X-Marks: Native Signatures of Assent*. Minneapolis: University of Minnesota Press, 2010.

Macdougall, Brenda. *One of the Family: Metis Culture in Nineteenth Century Northwestern Saskatchewan*. Vancouver: University of British Columbia Press, 2010.

Macdougall, Brenda, and Nicole St-Onge. "Scuttling Along a Spider's Web: Mobility and Kinship in Metis Ethnogenesis." In *Contours of a People: Metis Family, Mobility and History*, edited by Brenda Macdougall, Nicole St-Onge, and Carolyn Podruchny, 59–92. Norman: University of Oklahoma Press, 2012.

Mamawi Project. "Samantha Nock Poem." *Instagram*, April 2, 2020. https://www.instagram.com/p/B-fAL45DofG/

Manitoba Historical Society, *Manitoba Heritage Cookery: Selections from Personal Collections*. Winnipeg, Manitoba Historical Society, 1992.

McCullough, Alan B. "The Confrontations at Rivière aux Îlets-de-Bois." *Manitoba History* 67 (2012): 2–13.

Mihesuah, Devon. "Indigenous Health Initiatives, Frybread and the Marketing of Nontraditional 'Traditional' American Indian Foods." *NAIS: Journal of the Native American and Indigenous Studies Association* 3, no. 2 (2016): 45–69.

Payment, Diane. "'La Vie en Rose'? Métis Women at Batoche 1870–1920." In *Women of the First Nations: Power, Wisdom, and Strength*, edited by

Christine Miller and Patricia Churchryk, 19–36. Winnipeg: University of Manitoba Press.

Pigeon, Émilie, and Carolyn Podruchny. "The Mobile Village: Metis Women, Bison Brigades, and Social Order on the Nineteenth-Century Plains." In *Violence, Order, and Unrest: A History of British North America, 1749–1876*, edited by Elizabeth Mancke, Jerry Bannister, Denis McKim, and Scott See. Toronto: University of Toronto Press, 2019: 236–63.

Raibmon, Paige. *Authentic Indians: Episodes of Encounter from the Late-Nineteenth Century Northwest Coast*. Durham, NC: Duke University Press, 2005.

Rhulmann, Sandrine. "Are Buuz and Bans Traditional Mongolian Foods? Strategy of Appropriation and Identity Adjustment in Contemporary Mongolia." In *Eating Traditional Food: Politics, Identity and Practices*, edited by Brigitte Sebastia, 86–103. London: Routledge, 2016.

Rifkin, Mark. *Settler Common Sense: Queerness and Everyday Colonialism in the American Renaissance*. Minneapolis: University of Minnesota Press, 2014.

Roth, Christopher F. "Without Treaty, without Conquest: Indigenous Sovereignty in Post-Delgamuukw British Columbia." *Wicazo Sa Review* 17, no. 2 (2002): 143–65.

Sawchuk, Joe. *The Metis of Manitoba: Reformulation of an Ethnic Identity*. Toronto: P. Martin Associates, 1978.

Sebastia, Brigitte. "Eating Traditional Food: Politics, Identity and Pracitices." In *Eating Traditional Food: Politics, Identity and Practices*, edited by Brigitte Sebastia, 1–19. New York: Routledge, 2017.

Stevenson, Allyson, and Cheryl Troupe. "From Kitchen Tables to Formal Organization: Indigenous Women's Social and Political Acitivism in Saskatchewan to 1980." In *Compelled to Act: Histories of Women's Activism in Western Canada*, edited by Sarah Carter and Nanci Langford, 218–52. Winnipeg: University of Manitoba Press, 2020.

St-Onge, Nicole. *Saint-Laurent, Manitoba: Evolving Métis Identities, 1850–1914*. Regina: Canadian Plains Research Centre, 2004.

Teillet, Jean. *The North-West Is Our Mother: The Story of Louis Reil's People, the Métis Nation*. Toronto: HarperCollins, 2019.

Thistle, Jesse A., and Jerry Thistle. "When Canada Opened Fire on My Kokum Marianne with a Gatling Gun." *Graphic History Collective*. July 3, 2017. http:// graphichistorycollective.com/project/poster-8-batoche-1885-canada-opened -fire-kokum-marianne-gatling-gun.

Thrush, Coll. "Vancouver the Cannibal: Cuisine, Encounter, and the Dilemma of Difference on the Northwest Coast, 1774–1808." *Ethnohistory* 58, no. 1 (Winter 2011): 1–35.

Van Rosendall, Julie. "Shane Chartrand's Bannock." *Globe and Mail*, February 17, 2018.

Vizenor, Gerald. *Native Liberty: Natural Reason and Cultural Survivance*. Lincoln: University of Nebraska Press, 2019.

Voth, Daniel. "'Descendants of the Original Lords of the Soil'": Indignation, Disobedience, and Women Who Jig on Sundays." *NAIS: Journal of the Native American and Indigenous Studies Association* 7, no. 2 (2020): 87–113.

Voth, Daniel, and Jesse Loyer. "Why Calgary Isn't Métis Territory: Jigging towards an Ethic of Reciprocal Visiting." In *Visions of the Heart: Issues Involving Indigenous Peoples in Canada,* edited by Gina Starblanket and David Long with Olive Patricia Dickason, 106–25. Oxford: Oxford University Press, 2020.

Media

"Back to Batoche '78." *New Breed Magazine*, August 1978, 6–9.
Welsh, Christine. *Women in the Shadows*, NFB Online, directed by Norma Bailey. Toronto: National Film Board of Canada, 1991.

Notes

1. Often seen as interchangeable with frybread, bannock has a unique historical trajectory. Mihesuah, "Indigenous Health Initiatives," 49–50.

2. "Bannock-in-a-box," *The Bannock Factory* (accessed November 17, 2020), http://www.thebannockfactory.com/Products.htm.

3. Lewis, "Frybread Wars," 427–48.

4. Hogue, "Still Hiding in Plain Sight," 1–11.

5. "Survivance" is a useful term in contemporary Indigenous politics that speaks to an ongoing presence. In *Native Liberty*, Gerald Vizenor describes survivance as "an active sense of presence over historical absence." In this sense, to write of Métis survivance forces historians to understand the spaces and places that were critical to continued Métis presence. In this article I focus on bannock and the kitchen table as one of these spaces where Métis continued to be Métis throughout the twentieth century. Vizenor, *Native Liberty*, 1.

6. First, while I am apprehensive about reenforcing a gendered binary, I am constrained by the archival material I engaged for this project, which actively employed this framework. Second, an early review of this article noted the history of men baking bannock while traveling either on buffalo hunts or on the canoe routes and asked about the connections between bannock and Métis masculinities. I have decided against investigating the topic of Métis masculinities in this project primarily because of my reliance on the Oral History Project archive.

7. Often called Canada's "forgotten people," Métis peoples, in the century between the Northwest Resistance of 1885 and the *Constitution Act* of 1982, were purposefully marginalized my Canada. The passiveness of "forgetting" obscures the active targeting of Métis peoples by state policies. It is more accurate to frame this "forgetting" as intentional neglect.

8. I elaborate the histories of both unilateral policies later. For a larger discussion of the impacts of Bill C-31 see Lawrence, *"Real" Indians and Others*.

9. Lawrence, *"Real" Indians and Others*; also see Borrows, *Freedom and Indigenous Constitutionalism*.

10. "Metis Women of Manitoba Inc. Oral History Project Records," Archives of Manitoba (accessed July 24, 2019), http://pam.minisisinc.com/SCRIPTS

/MWIMAIN.DLL/122896985/1/1/1267?RECORD&DATABASE=DESCRIPTION
_WEB_INT.

11. Coulthard defines recognition politics as a liberal variant of coercion. The ultimate goal is the continued dispossession of Indigenous lands through the enforced reliance of Indigenous Peoples on the settler state. Appeals to the state for recognition only serve to center the state as the ultimate authority on Indigenous existence and identity. See Coulthard, *Red Skin, White Mask*.

12. Métis sociologist Chris Andersen argues that misconceptions of Métis "hybridity" undergird the adjudication of Métis rights. See Andersen, *Métis*.

13. Rifkin, *Settler Common Sense*, 12.

14. While the Supreme Court has extended rights to Métis in cases such as *R v. Powley* and *Daniels*, it has done so in a way that has allowed misconceptions of Métis identity to proliferate. Inappropriate claims to Métis-ness serve only to center colonial assumptions about our Peoplehood, and often distort the claimants' own Indigeneity. See Andersen, *Métis*.

15. McIvor, interview.

16. Potoski, interview.

17. Morriseau, interview.

18. Chartrand, interview.

19. Andersen, "Residual Tensions of Empire," 298.

20. LaFreniere, interview.

21. LaFreneire, "Oral History Interview."

22. Macdougall and St-Onge, "Scuttling Along a Spider's Web," 59—92.

23. LaFreniere, interview.

24. Work by scholars such as Brenda Macdougall and Jean Teillet centers the critical role of women in sustaining Métis kinship practices through the nineteenth century as well. See also Teillet, The *North-West Is Our Mother*.

25. Stevenson and Troupe, "From Kitchen Tables to Formal Organization," 218—19.

26. Stevenson and Troupe, "Kitchen Tables," 245.

27. Mihesuah, "Indigenous Health Initiatives," 49.

28. Van Rosendall, "Shane Chartrand's Bannock."

29. Rifkin, *Settler Common Sense*, xvi.

30. Ibid.

31. See: Raibmon, *Authentic Indians*. And Deloria, *Indians in Unexpected Places*.

32. Andersen, "From Difference to Density," 92.

33. Lyons, *X-Marks*, 107. I am generally inclined to follow Lyons's assertion that we should "resist any stabilizing or coherent description of culture as a noun [but instead should] comprehend culture as a conversation marked by diversity and contest, yet ultimately seeking to protect women or minority groups from subordination and marginalization." This formulation demands that we ask what work culture does in the world rather than simply seek to define an inherent essence.

34. I made this choice because so many of the interviews seemed to take place at the kitchen table. Ultimately, this is my own speculation; but the

auditory experience—mugs on wood, a kettle boiling—located these conversations in space. In doing so, I also consciously follow Lyons's conceptualization of the kitchen table. See Lyons, *X-Marks*, 20–21. The kitchen table is not a stable, overromanticized object but a historically contingent and dynamic site that reveals and contests the power dynamics of the interview. The kitchen table is socially constructed and politically engaged.

35. Rhulmann, "Are Buuz and Bans Traditional Mongolian Foods?," 86–87.

36. The pizza test refers to the legal criteria that link Aboriginal rights with traditional activity. In Delgamuukw, "the Crown's lawyers continually prob[ed] Gitksan and Wet'suwet'en witnesses on whether they ever ate pizza, where they earned their money, and how much time they actually spent on the land." All in an effort to discount their claims through modern cultural adaptations. See Roth, "Without Treaty, without Conquest," 143–65.

37. Jenson, Polletta, and Raibmon, "The Difficulties of Combating Inequality in Time," 155.

38. Andersen, *Métis*, 105.

39. For a discussion of Métis collective political Peoplehood see Andersen, *Métis*.

40. See Douglas Sprague's arguments quoted in McCullough, "The Confrontations at Rivière aux Îlets-de-Bois," 2.

41. In retrospect, Métis organizations regard Section 35 recognition as a political victory. At the time, the Métis Association of Alberta was the only Indigenous group to approve of the constitution.

42. Borrows, *Freedom and Indigenous Constitutionalism*, 120–25.

43. Jenson, Polletta, and Raibmon, "The Difficulties of Combating Inequality in Time," 154.

44. Andersen, *Métis*, 164.

45. Andersen argues that the Supreme Court decided to protect only those cultural practices that "Non-Aboriginals would not themselves engage in." See Andersen, "Residual Tensions," 296.

46. Ibid, 298.

47. Borrows, *Freedom and Indigenous Constitutionalism*, chap. 4.

48. Andersen, Métis, 66.

49. Thrush, "Vancouver the Cannibal," 9.

50. Ibid., 16.

51. Ens and Sawchuk, *New Peoples*, 503.

52. Andersen, "Residual Tensions of Empire," 298.

53. McLeod, interview.

54. Chartrand, interview.

55. Ibid.

56. *R. v. Van der Peet* (1996) 2 S.C.R. 507, 1996 Supreme Court of Canada.

57. Jenson, Polletta, and Raibmon, "The Difficulties of Combating Inequality in Time," 155.

58. Mohr, interview.

59. DeLaronde, interview.

60. Bell, interview.

61. Ibid.

62. Ibid.

63. Chartrand, interview; Bell, interview.

64. Potoski, interview; Bell, interview.

65. Carpick and McLeod, interview.

66. Ibid.

67. Chartrand, interview.

68. Mohr, interview.

69. Breland, interview.

70. Chartrand, interview.

71. George Colpitts provides the most direct study of pemmican in a historical context: Colpitts, *Pemmican Empire*.

72. For the gendered dynamics of Métis bison hunts see: Pigeon and Podruchny, "The Mobile Village," 236–63.

73. Mohr, interview.

74. Much like frybread, see Lewis, "Frybread Wars," 427–48.

75. Anderson, interview.

76. Bell, interview.

77. Ibid.

78. Allard, interview.

79. Bell, interview.

80. St-Onge, *Saint-Laurent*, 68.

81. Christine Welsh, *Women in the Shadows*, NFB Online, directed by Norma Bailey (Toronto: National Film Board of Canada, 1991).

82. Sawchuk, *The Metis of Manitoba*, 40.

83. Hogue, "Still Hiding in Plain Sight?," 8.

84. LaFreniere, interview.

85. Pottinger, interview.

86. Breland, interview.

87. Author's family anecdote.

88. Anderson, interview.

89. McLeod, interview.

90. Allard, interview.

91. LaFreniere, interview.

92. Ibid.

93. Ibid.

94. Sebastia, "Eating Traditional Food," 2.

95. LaFreniere, interview.

96. Mohr, interview.

97. LaFreniere, interview.

98. Allard, interview.

99. Métis scholars have written differently. Jesse Thistle's collaborative piece with the graphic history collective is a great example of how to write histories that center Métis women at the heart of political moments traditionally seen as male dominated; see Thistle and Thistle, "When Canada Opened Fire on My Kokum Marianne with a Gatling Gun," *Graphic*

History Collective July 3, 2017, https://graphichistorycollective.com/project/poster-8-batoche-1885-canada-opened-fire-kokum-marianne-gatling-gun.

100. Few historians have written of women's experience during these events with a notable exception of Payment, "'La Vie en Rose'?," 19–36.

101. See Lawrence, *"Real" Indians and Others*, 56.

102. Dysart, interview.

103. In the 1990s most provincial organizations dropped nonstatus members from their rolls and added nationalist rhetoric to their names and constitutions, for example the Association of Métis and Non-Status Indians of Saskatchewan became the Métis Nation, Saskatchewan. Ens and Sawchuk, *From New Peoples*, 369.

104. Baker, interview.

105. Delaronde, interview.

106. McIvor, interview.

107. Delaronde, interview.

108. Ibid.

109. Baker, interview.

110. Ibid.

111. Dysart, interview.

112. Baker, interview.

113. Ibid.

114. Carpick, interview.

115. Dysart, interview.

116. "Back to Batoche '78," *New Breed Magazine*, August 1978, 6–9.

117. Ibid.

118. Voth, "Descendants of the Original Lords of the Soil," 87–113.

119. Macdougall, *One of the Family*, 54. See also Macdougall, "Space and Place within Aboriginal Epistemological Traditions," 64–82.

120. Legault, "Making Métis Places in British Columbia," 2.

121. Voth and Loyer, "Why Calgary Isn't Métis Territory," 120.

122. Garrick, interview.

123. Chartrand, interview.

124. Bell, interview.

125. Anderson, interview.

126. Frank Walter, interview.

127. Breland, interview.

128. Ibid.

129. Voth, "Descendants of the Original Lords of the Soil," 106.

130. LaFreniere, interview.

131. Mihesuah, "Indigenous Health Initiatives."

ALEJANDRA DUBCOVSKY *and* GEORGE AARON BROADWELL

"Anohebasisiro Nimanibota / We Want to Talk to the Honored One": Timucua Language and its Uses, Silences, and Protests

Abstract

In 1688, five Timucua Native chiefs wrote a brief letter welcoming the new Spanish governor to La Florida, or so the accompanying Spanish translation of the letter suggests. The original Timucua words tell another story. Combining two methodologies, linguistic anthropology and history, we seek to offer more than a new translation of a neglected seventeenth-century Native-language text. First, we examine the ways in which the Timucua letter-writers used their language. We show the select grammatical and rhetorical strategies Timucua writers used to make arguments, communicate displeasure, and express themselves by comparing the 1688 epistle with the only other surviving Timucua letter, written in 1651. Second, we ground the letter in its historical context. Placing the 1688 Timucua epistle alongside other letters and dispatches from the time, we explore the different ways Timucua people made sense of the violence and disruptions affecting their homelands. Centering Timucua words and experiences shows the limits of colonial control and, more importantly, the powerful possibilities afforded by working with Native language texts.

THIS IS A STORY OF A TRANSLATION. Or rather, this is a story of multiple translations. The first translation occurred in 1688, when five Timucua Native leaders came together and wrote a letter to the Spanish Crown. Gathered in their own town—far from San Agustín, the main Spanish settlement in Florida—and writing in Timucua, not Spanish, these chiefs were careful about how they communicated their message. They had to find ways of expressing Timucua concerns that would prove legible to Spanish officials. This first translation of Timucua voices into a colonial medium intended for an imperial audience was quickly followed by a second translation. The Spanish friars supervising the whole ordeal produced a Spanish translation of the Timucua epistle that would accompany the 1688 Timucua letter all the way to Spain. Much like the Timucua translation, the Spanish version also had an agenda. The Spanish translation added, omitted, and changed critical information from the chiefs' Timucua epistle, producing a text that the Franciscans thought better communicated the situation in Florida. For 335 years this incomplete and edited Spanish translation has been the one that scholars have consulted.

We offer a new and more accurate translation of the Timucua letter. This new translation requires reckoning with both the political and social context of the 1688 Timucua letter as well as reading and analyzing the Timucua language. By carefully exploring the Timucua grammar, syntax, and word choice of this seemingly simple and relatively short epistle, we work through multiple layers of meaning and mistranslations in this deeply colonial document. The 1688 Timucua letter does not offer unfiltered access into Timucua mindsets or preoccupations; however, as Daniel Heath Justice argues in *Why Indigenous Literatures Matter,* this document exists because of Native writers "who are writing and speaking into and against an oppressive colonial context that displaces, erases, or disfigures the broader narrative about Indigeneity in order to justify the occupation and exploitation of [their] lands, communities, and relations."[1] Our translation of the 1688 Timucua letter underscores not only the absolutely vital importance of working with Native-language sources and texts but also the methods necessary to properly read, document, and engage with materials written "into and against an oppressive colonial context." While many would agree that Timucua language sources matter, very few have ever tried to work with them, and therein lies the problem. We argue that the Timucua language is not just valuable in the abstract; in its uses, silences, and protests it offers new insights into Native efforts to defend "lands, communities, and relations" in the early South.

A New Translation

Our aim seemed simple enough: create a new translation of the 1688 Timucua letter.[2] The Timucua chiefs who wrote this epistle made their home across a vast territory of over twenty-thousand square miles, encompassing what is now northern Florida and southern Georgia. At least thirty-five separate Timucua chiefdoms shared many societal, political, economic, and cultural links: their language tied them together. The Timucua language has robust early textual documentation from the seventeenth century, especially when compared to other Indigenous languages spoken north of Mexico. In what is now the United States, Timucua documents are the oldest published Native-language sources. Despite the large number of materials in

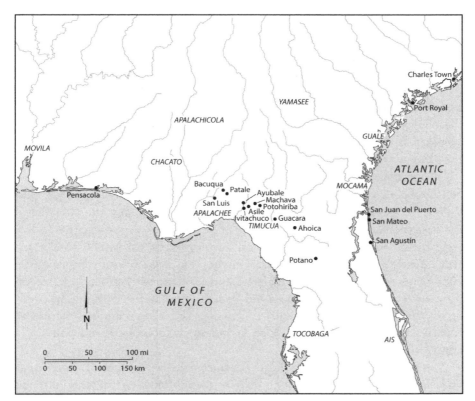

FIGURE 1. Map of main Timucua and Apalachee Mission towns, circa 1688. Map made by Bill Nelson.

the Timucua language, we still do not know how Timucua fits into the larger picture of Native languages in the Southeast. Timucua is not a Muskogean language, like Choctaw, Creek, or Chickasaw, nor is it clearly connected to any other language family of North America or the Caribbean. Linguists characterize it as a linguistic isolate (like Basque). It is hard to know how many people spoke the language, but it seems that tens of thousands of people spoke primarily Timucua by the time Spanish conquistadors reached the area in the early sixteenth century.[3]

We embarked on a translation of the 1688 Timucua letter knowing full well the difficulties that lay ahead. No complete grammar or dictionary of the Timucua language is available from the colonial period; the language has not been spoken in nearly 250 years; and it is mostly recorded in complicated, dense, and deeply religious Spanish materials from the seventeenth century. Still, we had reason to be optimistic. Since 2013 we have actively collaborated, studied, analyzed, and published on the Timucua language. George Aaron Broadwell is an anthropological and historical linguist by training and has carefully built a corpus of the extant Timucua texts, along with their parallel Spanish translations. A dictionary based on the corpus of all the known Timucua textual material is publicly available at https://www.webonary.org/timucua/. The current corpus is about 148,000 orthographic words of Timucua and includes a wide range of styles and authors.[4] Alejandra Dubcovsky is a historian of early America who studies Timucua people and the sources that document them. With a team of Native and non-Native scholars, Dubcovsky curates a website that offers lessons and resources on the Timucua language, https://hebuano.com/.[5]

As we began our translation of the 1688 letter, two interconnected questions began to trouble us. The first had to do with language. This epistle felt terse, even curt. The 1688 epistle seems tightlipped compared with the courteous and honorific language of other texts, especially the earlier 1651 "Jesus Maria Letter," the only other surviving Timucua letter.[6] Contextualizing the 1688 letter within earlier Timucua literary expressions allowed us to compare Timucua texts and think about Timucua literacy in its own terms, not simply vis-à-vis Spanish translations or understandings. What linguistic choices did Timucua speakers have available to them? How could Timucua people use their language in socially and politically appropriate ways?

The line of questioning that centers Native writers and their preoccupations did not come solely from comparing two colonial documents with one another but sprang directly from our involvement with other community-centered Native language projects—primarily from our work with Choctaw and Zapotec communities and language speakers.[7] Time and time again in our conversations, community members wanted to know how to speak their languages and how to do so in socially meaningful ways. No Timucua communities exist today, yet our work with descendants and historically connected groups, including, but not limited to, the Seminole Tribe in Florida, Seminole Nation of Oklahoma, Apalachee Nation, and Choctaw Nation of Oklahoma, have emphasized that discrepancy even further. We were now ready to address the questions that we have been repeatedly asked in other contexts: How did Timucua people use their language? How did the language reflect Timucua society?

As we began framing our new translation centering Timucua writings and literary strategies, a second question emerged, which had less to do with language and more to do with context. The 1688 Timucua letter was part of a series of documents made and requested by the then newly appointed governor of Florida, Diego de Quiroga y Losada, to detail the situation in the colony. These assorted documents included a report of Quiroga y Losada's *visita* (survey) of the region, juxtaposing the efforts and attitudes of his predecessor, Governor Marquez de Cabrera, with his own; letters detailing English activities in San Jorge (Charles Town); accounts of the rising violence in Apalachicola and the urgent need for military infrastructure in the region; and communications about a new partnership with Don Carlos, an important Indian leader from South Florida, who suddenly seemed interested in an alliance after having turned away Spanish officials and efforts for decades. Quiroga y Losada was particularly pleased by Don Carlos' friendly overtures, making a point to mention them in almost all his correspondence. In fact, many of the reports written by Spanish government and military officials gathered alongside the 1688 Timucua letter provide the same information over and over again, as if their repetition would help focus the myriad concerns and tensions in Florida and forge them into a single narrative about the growing violence Spanish officials faced as they supported their dwindling numbers of Native allies. How did the Timucua letter fit into that Spanish narrative?

The 1688 Timucua epistle seems almost like an afterthought, included at the very end of this packet of materials sent to the Crown and hardly connected to the key developments Quiroga y Losada touted. The 1688 Timucua letter and its Spanish translation were preceded by a letter in the Apalachee language written by Apalachee chiefs. The history of relations among Timucua and Apalachee people is complicated, marked as much by tension and difference as by peaceful coexistence. Though our focus remains on the 1688 Timucua letter, the 1688 Apalachee epistle provides important context for the rising violence, English incursions, and population loss that plagued the region—concerns that the Timucua letter vaguely alluded to but never explicitly mentioned.[8] Read alongside these longer and far more detailed documents, the Timucua letter recounts how Timucua people chose to describe the violent changes affecting their lands. A close reading of the original allows us to see the letter's rhetorical devices as purposeful, powerful tools employed by the Native writers to address both local and colonial seats of power.

Reading Timucua Again

Both the 1651 and 1688 handwritten Timucua letters can be found in the Archivo General de Indias in Seville, Spain, the main Spanish colonial archive containing materials from the Americas. An excellent copy of the 1688 letter can also be found in the John Carter Brown Library. Here we transcribe the original 1688 Timucua letter and offer a more literal translation of the Timucua than has been available up to now.[9]

erei heca Anoconica	To the King, our lord
Nanemi Anoquelamitonoma ni eiabobila hacu heqeno cumenatimococo Anoquelamitonoma ni eiabotela queniqe Anohebasisiro nimanibotaqe	We have always lived as your servants, but now we very full-heartedly are your servants, and we want to talk to you.
AnonaioHolata puqua himesobonibilahacu dontiecu naquimosi nienebobitila.	Many chiefs of the white people were sent but we did not see one like Don Diego.
Anonaio Holata yoqua caremate eiatamalahacu naquimosini enebobitila	There were other chiefs of the white people, but we didn't see them like this.
naquenema betaleq diosiquimi leqeysaco niquosoboni habe namo tani cale	We say we will give thanks to God for this
Holata ynemimate Anoquelacaremate Amunapuqua ninabarasobota niquosoboniqeysaco manta eiatanicala	We are thankful that all our chiefs and servants are covered in much clothing.
Acu anonaio Holata ponobi ioqucaremala cXnisobonemaqu mosinisobo mobilenincono	If the other chiefs of the white people who came had acted toward us in the way he [hon] acted toward us,
Cristiano nipuquacocolebohela Cristianoleno lenolehabema	We would be more numerous as Christians and like Christians should be.
tacubani hebasibonela minete pataquilononebeleca ynta Cristiano Anoutima niparifosibonelahacu	He [hon] has spoken justice for us; he [hon] has gone around for us in the Christian land where there is great misery, but
pataquilomoquayquimileqe misamano haninibiti la.	He [hon] did not fail to go to mass, [despite] the great misery
Santole nelene la mano nimanibotela	We think that he [hon] is a saint.

ytecare nabosonoletahabe caremate nihebasibota mosoniqeysaco manta eiatanicale	We are thankful that the fathers who should be praised did speak to us and
misaocotonoletahabecaremate nihebanecasibota homotaminiqeysaco manta eiatanicale	We are thankful that they went and thoroughly taught us to be the ones who must listen to the mass.
naquenemabetaleqe caqi anonaio Holata hibantema diosiquimileqe anilapusimitanicale diosibalunu ohonta haue tomanco caquani hibasinota hero nimanibotaqe anihebasimita nicale.	He taught us that we should hear mass, and we ended up living giving thanks. For this reason, we say that we want this man to remain with us after God gave [him/us?] life; we request for God's sake that this chief of the white people [hon] remain.
san mateo enero ela otumayuchoqe piqinahu eromano 88 don fransisco naystale Acu fransisca martine don P s P Holata don diego Machaba Holata bentura asile Holata gregorio S. ju[an guacara]	San Mateo January twenty-eight Year 88, Don Francisca says, This Francisco Martinez Don Pedro San Juan Holata, Don Diego Machaba Holata. Bentura, Asile Holata Gregorio San Juan Holata

Why Write This Letter?

In late January of 1688, five chiefs gathered in the San Matheo de Tolapatafi mission, in the western part of Timucua lands. It does not seem that the men had gathered for the sole purpose of writing a letter to the Spanish king; it seems instead that the letter grew out of pressures and conversations with Fray Francisco Rojas and other *doctrineros* (Franciscans in charge of mission sites), who were most eager to shape relations with the recently arrived Governor Quiroga y Losada. The Franciscans living in Timucua towns and missions were keen on setting the right tone with the new governor because tensions between Quiroga y Losada's predecessor, Governor Cabrera, and the Franciscans in Florida had deteriorated beyond repair. In fact, both sides had become openly hostile.[10]

Cabrera's entire tenure in Florida had been marked by tensions with the Catholic friars. He had reached Florida in the early 1680s, and, disembarking in Apalachee (near present-day Tallahassee) instead of San Agustín, he spent his first months in office surveying the activities of the Franciscans. He was immediately appalled by the conditions in the mission and the

excessive power Franciscans had over the daily lives of Apalachee men and women. He openly attacked the Franciscans and made it clear that, as governor, he was the main authority in Florida.[11]

The Franciscans insisted that Cabrera was solely acting in self-interest and that he had no desire to protect Native people or defend them from any abuse; his actions were a power grab and an attempt to interfere with and undermine Franciscan efforts. The well-documented fight between Cabrera and the Franciscans turned ugly in the mid-1680s, as the Franciscans refused to grant communion to or hear confession from Cabrera, and the governor opened even more inquiries into Franciscan activities in Apalachee and Timucua—some of these underexplored documents reveal the extreme level of brutality deployed by Franciscan friars in La Florida.[12]

In 1687, a new governor, Diego de Quiroga y Losada, reached the colony. The Franciscans hoped Quiroga y Losada would not interfere in their missionization practices and would defer to their authority. In the early months, relations seemed quite promising, Quiroga y Losada took the time to survey the region, and for a brief moment it seemed that the secular and religious orders in Florida would unite. This truce proved short lived, as Quiroga y Losada followed in his predecessor's footsteps, openly criticizing the state of Florida missions and the violent and irresponsible behavior of the Franciscans: eventually he carried a case all the way to the highest court of the Indies.[13] All that would come later, however. In early 1688, the future of Franciscan-government relations was still to be decided.

The Timucua backdrop of the 1688 letter is equally as complex as the Spanish context. The writers of the letter signed their names as Don Francisco Holata of San Matheo [de Tolapatafi], Don Pedro Holata of San Juan de Guacara, Don Diego Holata of Machaba, Bentura Holata of [San Miguel de] Asile, and Gregorio Holata of San Juan [de Arapaha?]. These men identified both by their Timucua title of *holata* (chief) and by the Spanish honorific marking "Don," meaning "sir" or denoting someone of status.[14]

The men were all from towns now located in Yustaga, the westernmost region of Timucua that bordered powerful Apalachee towns.[15] In other words, these men had more and more regular dealings with Apalachee leadership than they did with the small number of Timucua chiefs who still lived near San Agustín or along the Atlantic coast. The Franciscan missionaries had received their first invitation into Timucua almost eight decades earlier. Though Spanish sources often laud their own success in Timucua, Timucua chiefs had tremendous influence over where and when Franciscans made inroads. To put it bluntly, Franciscans depended on Timucua welcome and permission. In his overview of the mission activities in Florida, Fray

Francisco Alonso de Jesus flaunted Franciscan success in the region: "There are more than 20 thousand souls baptized and more than 50,000 catechized among the catechumens."[16] He praised Franciscans for bringing *más policía* (order) and *ejercicio* (employment) to the region. Timucua holatas agreed, but they viewed this order and employment in a much more negative light. They complained about the rising demands placed on their labor, manpower, and lands. Though there were many small moments of unrest, the so-called Timucua rebellion of 1656 perhaps most readily showcased Timucua frustration with Spanish colonial officials.[17] Gathered at San Pedro, Timucuas from the towns of Santa Cruz de Tarihica, San Francisco de Chuaquín, San Francisco de Potano, Santa Fé de Toloco, San Pedro de Potohiriba, and Santa Elena de Machaba, agreed to fight against Spanish encroachments.

The violence in 1656 proved short-lived but with long-lasting repercussions. Most of the people who had joined the fight were from western towns, like the writers of the 1688 Timucua letter. Up until that point, Spanish officials had very limited control over these towns and realized they needed to consolidate their power in the region. First, they demanded the relocation of most Timucua towns; by the time Don Francisco Holata, Don Pedro Holata, Don Diego Holata, Bentura Holata, and Gregorio Holata gathered to write their epistle, most western Timucua towns had been forcefully moved along the *Camino Real* (a path that connected San Agustín to San Luis, or what is now Tallahassee). Second, most Timucua leadership had changed; only chiefs loyal to Spanish authority had remained in power, and families with ties to those who had resisted Spanish rule had been removed from political office. The five holatas who wrote the 1688 letter had spent their entire lives under this new Timucua leadership, which had to be more responsive to the demands of San Agustín. Third, and perhaps unsurprisingly, Timucua people began to leave their towns in large numbers. Depopulation became a critical issue for Timucua holatas, who after the 1660s not only had to deal with more intrusive and less reciprocal Spanish policies but also faced intensifying violence in the region. Slaving raids, sponsored and supported by the new English colony in South Carolina, began targeting Timucua towns with alarming frequency after 1670.[18]

The 1688 letter allowed Timucuas to describe the mounting pressures in their towns. Not many Native letters or petitions from La Florida survive, unlike in many other parts of Spanish America. The 1688 Timucua letter nonetheless shows that Timucuas had a long history of literacy and writing; they clearly understood the form and format of their epistle and used careful language to present themselves in this colonial format.[19] Before looking at the content of the letter it is thus important to consider its language.

The Letter's Language

We know little about the everyday experiences of Timucua people in Spanish missions, but we know Timucua people quickly understood the power of the written word.[20] Franciscans wrote with cautious excitement that their new converts were quick to learn to read and write. They believed that the ease with which Timucua people took to the Roman script and the written word would surely facilitate conversion, but Franciscans were also worried about the implications of literacy and complained that Timucua men and women wrote letters to one another that Spanish officials were not privy to.[21] Francisco Pareja, a leading Franciscan among Timucua missions, noted: "Many Indian men and women have learned to read in less than six months . . . [and] they write letters to one another in their own language."[22] Fray Francisco Alonso de Jesús in his 1630 *Memorial* mentioned the prevalence of Timucua literacy: "many who know how to read and write, to which they are all inclined, men as well as women."[23] Finding specific mentions of Timucua authors is harder, but we know of Don Manuel, an Indian chief from the Timucua town of Asile, who wrote the earliest preserved Timucua letter in 1651; Lucas Menéndez, a prominent Timucua chief who orchestrated an attack that Spanish officials would refer to as the start of the Timucua rebellion in 1656, both wrote and intercepted many letters; and a few years later, Benito, from the small town of Santa Elena de Machaba, also wrote many letters to the governor seeking to assert his rightful place as chief.[24]

Timucua writers also assisted in the creation of all published Timucua texts. The first bilingual Spanish-Timucua book appeared in print in 1612, and it was soon followed by other religious materials including confessionals, *doctrinas,* and longer catechisms intended to assist Franciscan friars with their evangelization project in La Florida. The last known Spanish-Timucua book was published in 1635—though a recent rediscovery of a 1628 catechism suggests that perhaps more Timucua-Spanish materials remain to be found. These published books contain thousands of pages in the Timucua language; some are monolingual Timucua materials with no Spanish equivalent while others are translations of the accompanying Spanish text, but these translations rarely match the Spanish text word for word. The Timucua sections add information, delete critical details, and even include dialect variations of Timucua. Franciscans never explicitly acknowledged their contributions, but Timucua people were "ghost authors" of these texts. The presence of these unnamed and unrecognized Timucua writers can be seen in almost every one of these two thousand published pages.

In other words, the 1688 letter is not sui generis. The authors who penned this letter were likely second or even third generation writers.[25] They began their epistle with a show of loyalty to the Spanish Crown:

> Nanemi Anoquelamitonoma ni eiabobila hacu heqeno cumenatimococo. Anoquelamitonoma ni eiabotela queniqe Anohebasisiro nimanibotaqe /We have always been servants of His Majesty but now with even more reason and full-heartedly, we are and so we wish to speak.[26]

This opening statement was very similar to the one used by Don Manuel in the 1651 letter.

> Anano conica Reynachigeleta Holataleta Holataleta. Nimelabobotanio ocotosibonihaue naqueneniqe Ananoconica benito Ruis Rey nachiqeleta pononema nihebasinemano Utima ni hete cosoni habe nimasinibila/Our Lord representing the King, living as Chief, we are speaking to you. May we be heard, and may we receive mercy. Our Lord Benito Ruiz, representing the King, has come, and said to me, "May I be loaned this land," he told me.[27]

After these niceties, the 1688 letter offers a rather vague description about the "big misery" afflicting Timucua; the 1651 letter, on the other hand, spares no detail. In his 1651 epistle, Don Manuel records the long history of Spanish abuses in the area and bemoans the many unfulfilled promises from San Agustín. Spanish officials had promised axes and hoes, which never arrived. Spanish officials had then vowed to provide clothes and other goods, which also failed to materialize. Don Manuel used his letter to assert his power, reminding Spanish officials that Timucua men and women supplied the labor that fed the people of San Agustín. Don Manuel argued that while Timucua people had kept the Spanish colony afloat, the Spanish governor had failed to live up to his words: "Hebanomichu ninapicha sosi ne le/He failed to comply with his word."[28]

Though the 1688 Timucua letter lacks the explicit critiques and verbal punches of the 1651 letter, it is no less angry. Perhaps thirty additional years of dealing with Spanish colonization had disabused Timucua chiefs of what they could achieve with a letter. The 1688 Timucua authors made a different kind of argument through their language, and it is important to dwell on their words, syntax, and literary choices. To understand our claim that the language of 1688 is curt—and perhaps even contemptuous—we must return to our earlier question: What linguistic choices did Timucua speakers have available to them? We focus on the ways that Timucua writers chose to convey respect or lack of respect for the persons mentioned in a text.

Timucua has an elaborate system of honorific marking by which a speaker or writer signals the social status of those mentioned.[29] This honorific system has at least three notable components: an honorific particle *ano ~ ani* that appears before the verb when one of its arguments is honored; an honorific possessive suffix *-mitono*, which appears when a possessor is honored; and a special honorific use of the passive *-ni* when the subject is honored.[30] The opening line of the 1651 letter has two uses of the honorific *ano ~ ani:*

Anano conica Reynachigeleta· Holataleta hiuantema anihebasinitanicala·

Here is our analysis, in more linguistic detail, of this opening line:

1 **ANANO CONICA**   **REYNACHIGELETA**   **HOLATALETA**

an	**anoco**	**-nica**	**Rey**	**-na**	**chige**	**-leta**	**holata**	**-leta**
hon	lord	1:pl:poss	king	ins	represent	indef	be:chief	indef

HIUANTEMA   **ANIHEBASINITANICALA**

hiua	**-nte**	**-ma**	**ani**	**heba**	**-si**	**-ni**	**-ta**	**-nica**	**-la**
live	dur	def	hon	speak	ben	hon:pass	part	1:pl:erg	dec

Our (honored) Lord representing the king, living as chief, we are speaking to you (honored).

Here we use a common linguistic method of analysis known as "interlinear glossing" to examine the structure of Timucua sentences. The first line shows the original orthography and word breaks, while the second line separates each word into its morphemes (constituent meaningful parts). The third line gives an English gloss that corresponds to each Timucua morpheme.[31] The final line of the example gives an English translation of the entire line.

In this example, the first word of the line, *ananoconica* "our (honored) Lord" contains a shortened form of the honorific particle *ano~ ani*. The last word *anihebasinitanicala* has two honorific elements. The first is, again, the honorific *ani,* while the second is the passive suffix *-ni*.

We see similar elements in example (2), where the honorific possessor stuff *-mitono* occurs on the phrase *qiemitonoma* (his honored son), and the honorific passive appears on the verbs *pono* (come) and *heba* (speak).

2 **NAQUENIQE**   **ANONAYOHOLATA**   **QIEMITONOMA**

naqueni	**-qe**	**ano**	**nayo**	**holata**	**qie**	**-mitono**	**-ma**
do:this	if	person	white	chief	son:(of:a:man)	3:poss:hon	def

PONONEMANIHEBASINEMA

pono	**-ne**	**-ma**	**ni-**	**heba**	**-si**	**-ne**	**-ma**
come	hon:pass	def	1:abs	speak	ben	hon:pass	def

CANIMASINELA

ca=	ni-	ma	-si	-ne	-la
thus=	1:abs	say	ben	hon:pass	dec

So, when the son of the chief of the white people came, I spoke thus to him.

The honorific passive needs some special explanation. In Timucua, a standard use of the passive is like the English passive. The honorific passive, however, does not have a good analog and is difficult to translate. It appears when the subject or object of the verb is honored. We have rendered it as, "We are speaking to you (honored)." But this uses an active form of the English verb *speaking*, and the pronoun *you* is absent from the Timucua. A less readable translation but one that perhaps conveys a bit of the flavor of the Timucua text might be: "It is spoken by us to the honorable one." In our analysis, use of the honorific passive shows the highest level of respect, while the *ano~ ani* particle and the *-mitono* suffix are respectful, but not at the highest level.

The 1651 letter shows a consistent pattern: nearly every verb that refers to the actions of the Spanish governor and his representatives is in the honorific passive. By contrast, verbs that refer to actions of the Natives are in plain, nonpassive forms. Consider example (3) where the verbs *naqueni* (do this) and *mo* (say) are in the plain forms since they concern speech and actions by Timucua people.

3 **ANOPALUCUNUMABETA**   **LEQE**   **HEBANOYNEMI**   **NAQUE NI**

ano	palucu	-nu	-ma	beta	-leqe	hebano	ynemi	naqueni
person	fear	nmlz	def	obl	foc	word	all	do:this

HALANI   **MOBILA**   **HACU**   **HONIANQUA**   **NI**   **MOBILA**

-ha	-la	ni-	mo	-bi	-la	=hacu	honihe	yanqu	ni-	mo	-bi	-la
irr	dec	1:abs	say	pst	dec	=but	1:sg	only	1:abs	say	pst	dec

from fear I said all these words, I will do it, but only I said it

We hasten to add that what we see here is linguistic deference, probably skillfully deployed to flatter and persuade the Spanish authorities. As is true in the contemporary world, polite or deferential language is often at variance with nonlinguistic behavior. Still, the writers of the 1651 letter thought that a skillful verbal argument, using the Timucua honorific system adroitly, might sway the authorities toward justice in the ongoing disputes about the lands Spanish officials called the "Asile hacienda" and Timucuas called home.

The 1688 letter is much more selective in its use of honorific passives. When the Timucua writers discuss the actions of the new governor, Don Diego, we see consistent honorific language. In example (4) the verbs *heba* (speak) and *parifo* (go around) are both in the honorific passive.

4 **TACUBANI**　　　　　**HEBASIBONELA**　　　　　　　　　　　　　**MINETE**

tacuba	ni-	heba	-si	-bo	-ne	-la	mine	-te
justice	1:abs	speak	ben	pl:abs	hon:pass	dec	resp	CFoc

　　PATAQUILONONEBELECA　　　　　**YNTA**　　**CRISTIANO**　**ANOUTIMA**

pataquilo	-no	nebeleca	yn	-ta	Cristiano	Ano	uti	-ma
miserable	nmlz	big	be	part	Christian	person	earth	def

　　NIPARIFOSIBONELAHACU

ni-	parifo	-si	-bo	-ne	-la	=hacu
1:abs	go:around	ben	pl:abs	hon:pass	dec	=but

He (honored) has spoken justice for us; he (honored) has gone around for us in the Christian land where there is great misery, but

By contrast, when the actions of other Spanish civil and religious authorities are discussed, there is little or no honorific language. Consider example (5), which contrasts the actions of Governor Quiroga y Losada with those of other Spanish officials who previously held this office. When the subject of the verbs *pono* (come) and *iso* (do) is the other Spanish officials ("the chiefs of the white people"), then the verbs appear in the plain (nonpassive) form. When the subject is the new governor, Don Diego, then the honorific passive form *isone* is used. As we have previously noted, this is difficult to convey in the English translation. We have added the designation (hon) before the verb "acted," which describes the actions of Governor Quiroga y Losada, and provided no special designation before the verb describing the actions of "other chiefs of the white people:"

5 **ACU**　**ANONAIO**　　　　**HOLATA**　**PONOBI**　　**IOQUCAREMALA**

Acu	ano	naio	holata	pono	-bi	ioqua	-care	-ma	-la
All	person	white	be:chief	come	pst	other	plural	def	dec

　　CXNISOBONEMAQU MOSINISOBO

ca=	n-	iso	-ne	-ma	quimo	n-	iso	-bo
thus=	do	pl:abs	hpas	def	in:the:same:way	1:abs	do	pl:abs

MOBILENINCONO

-mo	**-bile**	**-ninco**	**-no**
3:pl:subj	past:2:(remote)	counterfactual	nmlz

If the other chiefs of the white people who came had acted toward us in the way he [hon] acted toward us

The Timucua writers use both honorific and nonhonorific verbs in the same sentence, praising the current governor while delivering a putdown to previous Spanish administrations. These differences would have been quite clear to the Timucuas composing the letter. Linguistic analysis allows us to see the strategic shifts in the language and more clearly reveals how Timucua authors deployed their language in ways that were sensitive to the social and historical environment.

Beyond the Words on the Page

The 1688 Timucua letter was intended to showcase support for the new governor and affirm Timucua allegiance to the Spanish Crown, but it did so in the most succinct way possible. The leaders wrote this letter with the encouragement of local Franciscans, who, much like the Timucua chiefs, had welcomed the change in leadership in San Agustín. Opening with the statement, "Nanemi Anoquelamitonoma ni eiabobila/ We have always lived as your servants," the Timucua writers do not seem to be embellishing or using hyperbole; they were reminding Governor Quiroga y Losada of their long-standing amity with San Agustín. Don Francisco Holata of San Matheo, Don Pedro Holata of San Juan, Don Diego Holata of Machaba, Bentura Holata of Asile, and Gregorio Holata of San Juan had outlasted Quiroga y Losada's predecessor, and they could also survive him.

Timucua praise for the new governor was muted. It mostly came in the form of a comparison: the Timucua holatas hoped that unlike the previous neglectful and abusive governors, Quiroga y Losada would be more attentive to Timucua needs. The Timucua holatas argued that the bar Quiroga y Losada needed to clear was quite low, and they hoped he would succeed. The biggest compliment they offered the new governor had little to do with his policies or plans; the Timucua writers insisted that the most impressive quality of Quiroga y Losada was that he never failed to attend mass, *misamano haninibiti la*. Hinting at, but never explicitly mentioning the ongoing struggles between secular and religious authorities in the colony, the epistle argued that the most impressive accomplishment of Quiroga y Losada's short tenure was his willingness to listen to the Franciscans on a regular basis. It is easy to find such Franciscan talking points in the 1688 Timucua letter. Like in most surviving Timucua writings, the religious framing is more overtone than undertone. But the Timucua holatas and leaders wrote this letter in their own language; although disentangling their words from Franciscan arguments is messy and not always possible, Timucuas were very careful in how they framed their letter.

The Timucua writers made no demands. They tersely thanked the governor for the clothing he had recently provided, and made no additional request of tools, goods, or military protection. In its content and style, the 1688 Timucua letter is different from both the earlier 1651 Timucua letter and from the other letters, reports, and documents that accompanied it, including the letter by Apalachee chiefs.[32] By 1688, it seems that the Timucuas gathered at the town of San Matheo knew what to expect and what not to hold out hope for. Though writing demure, supplicant letters to the Crown was a literary strategy that Timucua people had used in the past, the Timucua writers of the 1688 letter opted for a different approach.[33] Their careful and succinct grammatical and syntactic decisions reflect both their deep understanding of Spanish practices and their equally deep frustrations with their shortcomings.

Silent Slavery

The Timucua letter speaks vaguely of *pataquilononebeleca ynta Cristiano Anoutima,* or "a great misery in the lands of the Christians." The word *pataquilo* is repeated twice in the letter. It is an interesting word that has negative connotations, meaning despicable, exhausted, and even defeated. The Timucua letter thus details a tired and disparaged people; the accompanying 1688 Apalachee letter talks with a little more precision of the many "injured," "afflicted," and "orphaned" who remain in Apalachee towns. Both letters remain relatively silent as to the cause. Why were Timucua people exhausted and defeated? Why were Apalachee people injured and left orphaned? The long answer was the one-hundred-plus years of Spanish colonialism in the region and the dramatic population decline due to abusive labor, disease, violence, and outmigration. There was also another, more immediate reason why "entire towns were [now] fleeing to the *montes.*"

Indian slavery had become a growing problem in Timucua.[34] English raids against Spanish mission towns had steadily increased since the founding of Charles Town in 1670, and though most of those early attacks focused on the Guale missions on what is now the Georgia coast, the ripples of that violence spread throughout the region.[35] Since much of the scholarship is rooted in English archives and sources, we know more about the slave raiders than those they targeted. Timucua people suffered some of the worst parts of the rising violence in the region, which incentivized Native people to raid and enslave their neighbors in exchange for firearms and other goods. Spanish officials consistently refused to provide weapons to their Native allies, and thus Timucuas, Guales, Apalachees, and other Native groups in the region found themselves a target of Indian raiders, supplied and armed by the English.

The 1688 Timucua letter alludes to this violence. Its details specify that "pataquilono nebeleca/the great misery" was happening in Cristiano Ano utima, literally in "the land of Christian people." Did this misery *only* affect *Cristiano* uti (land)? What about non-*Cristiano* uti? What about Timucua uti? Or what about the *montes* where people fled to? Both the 1688 Timucua and Apalachee letters connect the mounting violence in the region to the unprotected mission towns. Arguing that "good," "loyal," and "Christian" people were suffering at the hands of "heathen" and English attacks, these epistles try to convince Spanish officials to protect their own colonial enterprise.[36] The 1685 slaving raid on the Timucua town of Santa Catalina de Ahoica led to the capture of many and left a wake of death and destruction that deeply unsettled the neighboring Timucua towns.[37]

Given the level of violence consuming the region, it might be surprising that these mentions of Indian slavery are subtle and folded into other discussions. But the Timucua writers were trying to describe something that only in hindsight seems obvious. At the time, the scale and impact of Indian slavery were not yet clear; what was clear was a disorienting violence that seemed only to be growing. The 1688 Timucua letter is trying to describe a level of destruction and loss that, even now, is hard to fathom.

Not Everything Shatters

The Timucua letter thanks Quiroga y Losada for traveling among towns and helping all those who are suffering. Once again, the letter is vague and offers no specifics. The Spanish translation of the Timucua letter goes into a bit more detail about Quiroga y Losada's new policies and particularly praises the governor for traveling to "Vasisa" (also spelled "Basisa"). The mention of this town is fascinating both for its specific inclusion in the Spanish translation of the Timucua letter and for its omission in the Timucua version. Perhaps the Timucua writers thought adding this specific detail was unimportant, or maybe they knew little about the town since it was beyond their sphere of influence. According to the accompanying 1688 Apalachee letter, this town was "en los montes/in the hills" beyond Spanish and Catholic control. Quiroga y Losada had visited other, long-neglected Timucua and

Apalachee towns, so why had he stopped at this town? And why had the visit proven important enough to receive mention in both letters? What was so special about Vasisa?

Vasisa was new. Vasisa was a town that had been established and grown as both a result of and response to Spanish colonization and growing English incursions. Although these towns and spaces are perhaps more pervasive than we have assumed in the colonial South, the narrative of the time from both Spanish as well as English sources depicts a shrinking Native world buckling under the violence of slaving, disease, and invasion.[38] Robbie Ethridge has described how these destabilizing and tumultuous processes created "shatter zones," or "large regions of instability from which shock waves radiate out for sometimes hundreds and hundreds of miles."[39] While the description of what was likely one of several Native towns beyond any European sphere of influence does not fully reverse well-known stories of shattering and declension from this period, Vasisa interrupts this entrenched narrative with other possibilities.

Vasisa was likely home to Apalachees, Timucuas, and perhaps Chacatos who had moved away from the Camino Real. When Don Francisco Holata of San Matheo, Don Pedro Holata of San Juan, Don Diego Holata of Machaba, Bentura Holata of Asile, and Gregorio Holata of San Juan spoke of Timucua people leaving and relocating elsewhere, they could have meant resettlement into towns like this one. And with this mention, both direct in translation and indirect in the original, a letter addressed to the Spanish Crown revealed a bigger and still-growing Native world.

What the Spanish Heard

Governor Quiroga y Losada had little information about the people and land he was supposed to govern. One of his first actions as governor was to conduct a careful survey of the region. In his letter to the Crown that included both the 1688 Timucua and Apalachee letters, the new governor explained that it had been more than "thirty years"—from the violent aftermath of the so-called Timucua rebellion—since any Spanish official had formally visited the main towns in Timucua and Apalachee. He noted that a great number of Native people had chosen to leave the region under Spanish control since they were "abused and insulted during the time of my predecessor, many of them, including entire towns, have fled to the *montes* [hills]."[40]

There are no "montes" in Florida; *fleeing to the montes* was a common Spanish idiom meaning that the people in question had moved beyond Spanish control. Timucuas knew that well; in their 1651 letter they use this metaphor to explain the out-migration of people from Timucua towns.[41]

Timucuas chose to embrace an idiom also selectively deployed by similarly positioned Indigenous writers across colonial Latin America. In doing so, Timucuas invoked a strategy of resistance: fleeing to "sites of refuge" or places beyond Spanish control, such as the new town of Vasisa.[42] Quiroga y Losada began his survey by noting a sharp decline in the Native population of Florida; he contextualized this decline in the actions and agency of Native people.

The governor wanted Timucuas to return from the *montes*. He wanted Timucuas and all Native allies to come back into Spanish missions and boasted relative success after "treating and consoling the Natives." He depicts himself as a charitable and kind governor, who through gifts and attention was able to get some Timucua and Apalachee people to return into the Spanish fold. Governor Quiroga y Losada viewed the 1688 Timucua letter as evidence of his efforts to build stronger relations in Indian country.[43]

Overall, the governor says very little about the Timucua letter and people in his writings; instead he devotes most of his attention to describing the burgeoning relations with "the Great Cacique of the Keys Carlos." The governor uses his introduction to the 1688 Timucua epistle to talk about another visit, a somewhat unexpected and fortuitous one that had also taken place in 1688 from the Cacique Carlos, who wanted to forge an alliance between South Florida Native groups and San Agustín.[44] Spanish officials had desperately sought a partnership with these groups since the earliest days of Spanish colonization in the region. Calusa, Tequesta, Ais, and Tocobaga communities had been, at best, lukewarm toward Spanish advances, expelling any and all Spanish settlements in their towns.[45] Cacique Carlos's sudden interest in opening paths to San Agustín spoke of a possible reversal. It is not at all surprising that Governor Quiroga y Losada would dedicate most of his letter to this new, lucrative, and long-sought partnership rather than to the ones already established. The emerging relation between Spanish Florida and South Florida Natives was all potential; the reality in Timucua was far more muddied.

Where is Diosi?

God, or at least the outward practice of Catholicism, was of vital importance to the Timucua writers. In their letter they repeatedly emphasized the new governor's religious piety and the importance of attending mass and listening to the Franciscans' teachings. At a quick glance, the 1688 Timucua letter seemed to take a pro-Franciscan stand and argue that what made Quiroga y Losada a good governor, especially compared to his predecessor, was his subservience to the Catholic church. It is hard to know how much this emphasis on Catholic practices came from the Franciscans supervising the writing of this letter and how much came from the Timucua writers themselves.

In their letter, the Timucua writers thanked God for granting them this new governor, *naquenemabetaleqe caqi anonaio Holata hibantema diosiquimileqe.* The Spanish translation of this sentence reads: "Y por esta causa damos a **VM** las gracias/and for this reason we thank **His Majesty**." It is unlikely that Francisco Rojas, the Franciscan translator, misunderstood the word "Dios." Instead, it seems that he made a purposeful decision to invoke the Crown, not God, in his translation. Rojas's word choice perhaps alludes to the bitter fight between the Franciscan order and government officials in Florida. The Franciscan fray made it clear that Quiroga y Losada's appointment and authority as governor of Florida came solely from the Crown. The Timucua writers expressed a different understanding of the existing hierarchy. God, not the Crown, deserved thanks. Perhaps the Timucua writers had misunderstood what the Franciscans in their towns wanted them to say; perhaps the holatas had referred to God because the Franciscans were the most tangible source of Spanish power in their towns; or perhaps they had purposefully bypassed the Crown altogether and addressed instead a higher power. Recognizing this fascinating mistranslation requires working through the Timucua words.

Conclusion

The 1688 Timucua letter is the last known surviving piece of Timucua writing. While it is in many ways subdued compared to the 1651 letter or earlier writings, it is addressed directly to the king and offers a biting critique of Spanish leadership in Florida. In a handful of short sentences, the 1688 letter blames the abusive Spanish leadership in Florida for causing misery in Timucua and pushing people away from their lands and against Christianity. The writers then describe a different future: "Had other chiefs of the white peoples . . . acted Christian in the same way they acted; we would be more numerous." Or, had Spanish officials behaved according to the Christian values they touted, Timucua would be in a different place.[46]

The brief 1688 letter speaks not only of destruction—describing Indian slavery, depopulation, and violence—but also of Timucua agency—detailing the creation of new towns and spaces, the evolution of Native leadership, and the persistence of Timucua people. Timucua writers did more than document their changing homelands. They demanded change. They focused on Native priorities and pressures. They created narratives that treated colonialism as contingent, not inevitable. Read in Timucua, the 1688 letter shows the persuasive power and potential found in Native language texts.

ALEJANDRA DUBCOVSKY is associate professor of history at the University of California, Riverside.

GEORGE AARON BROADWELL is Elling Eide Professor of Anthropology and Chair of the Department of Linguistics at the University of Florida, Gainesville.

Appendix

Here is a transcription of the Spanish translation of the Timucua letter (with original spelling); we have provided an English translation after each line.

Al Rey ñro Señor =siempre emos sido vasallos a V.M.
To the King, Our Lord, we have always been your vassals,
Pero aora con mejor razon y de ttodo Coraçon lo somos Y asi queremos de hablar
But now with better judgment and full heart we wish to speak
= V.M. a Ymbiado muchos Governadores
Your Majesty has sent many Governors
Pero Como Don Diego no emos vistto ninguno,
But as for Don Diego, we have never seen another like him
otros que an sido Gobernadores estan aqui
Other Governors have been here
pero Como heste no emos vistto ninguno,
But we have never seen anyone like him
Y por estta Cavssa damos a V.M. las gracias; nos ha socorrido
For this reason, we give thanks to your Majesty; we give thanks because he has assisted us,
A los Casiques y pobres Vasallos de V. MG.
the caciques and poor vassals of His Majesty,
Con rropa Por Cuya Causa esttamos muy agradecidos,
with clothes for which we are very grateful
Dios se lo pague a V.M; Y si los señores
God reward your Majesty, and if the lord
Gobernadores que an venido fueran Como el
Governors who have come were like him [Don Diego]
que oy esta fueramos mejores xptianos y
Today we would be better Christians
Su md a travajado mucho en ñro vien con tan malos
Your Majesty has worked hard for our good, with such bad
tiempos y por si mimos a visitado ttodos los
Times and has himself visited all
lugares de xptianos y de ynfieles Como fue
Places of the Christians and the Heathens, like he went to
Vasisa y nos a dado mucho Consuelo y con todos
Vasisa, and has given much counsel and with all

esttos travajos nunca a dejado de oir misa Y asi
These works have never failed to listen to Mass and thus
decimos que hes vn hombre santto ha nos
We say he is a saintly man
enCargado mucho que honrremos que rreberenziemos
Much obliged that we honor and revere
A los Sacerdotes que nos asisten Como su merced
The priests who have helped us, like your grace
lo hacia delante de nosotros, Suplicamos a V.M.
And he did so before us, we beg Your Majesty
se sirva de Continuarnos muchos años Al sr
That he remains in this service for many years, and to the Lord
Governador que es porque procura nro vien
Governor who is ensuring for our wellbeing
AConsejandonos Como buen xptiano que
Advising us like a good Christian
hoygamos misa y atendamos mucho A lo que
To listen to mass and heed the many things that the
Los Relijiosos nos enseñan, Bolvemos a suplicar
friars teach us, and again we beg
a V. Mg. nos Continue el sr Don Diego Nuestro
Your Majesty keep, Sir Don Diego, Our
Governador para nro Consuelo nro señor
Governor, for our council, our lord
de en todo a V.M. ttodo Gozo y salud, Como
In everything, your Majesty, much happiness and health, like
esttos Pobres Vasallos le desean escrita en Sn
These poor vassals wish to write you in San
Matheo en el mes de henero Veinte y ocho de
Matheo in the month of January, twenty-eight of
mil seis cienttos y ochenta y ocho años escripta
Six thousand one hundred and eighty-eight years written
y firmada de los Caciques y que nos allamos
And signed by the caciques who find ourselves
presentes Don Francisco cacique de San Matheo
Present Don Francisco cacique of San Matheo
Don Pedro Casique de San Pedro =
Don Pedro Casique of San Pedro =
Don Bentura Cacique de Asile = Don Diego Cacique
Don Bentura Cacique of Asile = Don Diego Cacique
De Machaua = Gregorio Cacique de S Ju de
Of Machaua = Gregorio Cacique of S[an] Ju[an] of
GuaCara fransco Martinez residente en San Matheo
GuaCara fransco Martinez dweller of San Matheo

References

Anderson, David G., and Kenneth Sassaman. *Recent Developments South-eastern Archaeology: From Colonization to Complexity.* Washington D.C.: SAA, 2012.

Anderson, J. O., Frances F. Berdan, and James Lockhart, editors. "Petitions, Correspondence, and Other Formal Statements." In *Beyond the Codices: Nahua View of Colonial Mexico,* University of California Press, 1979.

Archivo General de Indias (AGI), Sevilla, Spain.

———. "Horruque, Ays, Oribia, Abia, and Caparaca," May 13, 1605, Santo Domingo (SD) 224 folio 74–748.

———. "Governor Juan Marquez de Cabrera to the King," December 8, 1680. SD 226.

———. "Governor Juan Marquez de Cabrera to the King," March 20, 1686, AGI SD 227.

———. "Diego Qurioga y Losada to the King," April 18, 1692, AGI SD 227B.

———. "Cacique of Machaba," circa 1674, SD 234.

———. "Francisco de Pareja to the king," March 8, 1599, AGI SD 235.

———. "Autos y Cartas de los Caciques," folio 731–39. SD 839.

———. "Quiroga y Losada to the King," April 1, 1688. SD 839 folio 731.

———. "Jesus María Letter," December 9, 1651. Escribanía de Cámara (EC) 155B, folios 381–82.

———. "Crimes by Governor Marquez Cabrera," by Alonso Solana, September 4, 1688, AGI EC 156A.

———. "Domingo Leturiondo," 1677–1678, AGI EC 156B.

———. "Visitation to San Pedro," February 13, 1657, EC 15. No 188 and 1467.

———. "Testimony of Cacique Clemente Bernal of San Juan del Puerto," May 3, 1660. AGI Contaduría, 963.

———. "Testimony of Don Joseph de Prado, Royal Treasurer," April 1660. AGI Contaduría, 963.

———. "Testimony of Adjutant Pedro de la Puerta," April 1660. AGI Contaduría, 963.

———. "Testimony of Captain Augustín Pérez de Villa Real," April 1660. AGI Contaduría, 963.

Beltrán, Aguirre. *Regiones de refugio: el desarrolla de la comunidad y el proceso dominical en mestizo América.* Mexico City: Institution Indigenista Interamericano, 1967.

Blanton, Justin B. "The Role of Cattle Ranching in the 1656 Timucuan Rebellion: A Struggle for Land, Labor, and Chiefly Power." *Florida Historical Quarterly* 92, no. 4 (2014): 667–84.

Broadwell, George Aaron. "Honorific Usage in Timucua Exempla." In *Preaching and New Worlds: Sermons as Mirrors of Realms Near and Far,* edited by Timothy J. Johnson, Katherine Wrisley Shelby, and John D. Young, 280-94. London: Taylor & Francis, 2018.

———. "Shadow Authors: The Texts of the Earliest Indigenous Florida Writers." In *Franciscans and American Indians in Pan-Borderlands Perspective,* edited by Jeffrey Burns and Timothy Johnson, 139–52. Oceanside, CA: Academy of American Franciscan History, 2018.

Broadwell, George Aaron, and Alejandra Dubcovsky. "Chief Manuel's 1651 Timucua letter: The Oldest Letter in a Native Language of the United States." *Proceedings of the American Philosophical Society* 164, no. 4 (2020): 1–43.

Broadwell George Aaron, and Christina Snyder. "The Criminalization of Whooping in the Nineteenth-Century Choctaw Nation: A Case Study in Language and History Organizers," featuring Frankie Hiloha Bauer, Edward Green, Jamie Henton, Seth M. Katenkamp, Julie L. Reed, Michael C. Stoop, and Matthew Tyler. Presentation at American Society for Ethnohistory, Chapel Hill, North Carolina, November 10–13, 2021.

Blackhawk, Ned. *Violence over the Land: Indians and Empires in the Early American West.* Cambridge, MA: Harvard University Press, 2006.

Bushnell, Amy Turner. "Debitage of the Shatter Zone: Indoctrination, Asylum, and the Law of Towns in the Provinces of Florida." In *Petitioning in the Atlantic World: Empires, Revolutions and Social Movements,*" edited by Miguel Dantas da Cruz, 137–56. New York: Palgrave Macmillan, 2022.

Carpenter, Daniel. *Democracy by Petitioning: Popular Politics in Transformation, 1790–1870.* Cambridge, MA: Harvard University Press, 2021.

Crawford, James M. "Timucua and Yuchi: Two Language Isolates of the Southeast." In *The Languages of Native America: Historical and Comparative Assessment,* edited by Lyle Campbell and Marianne Mithun, 327–54. Austin: University of Texas Press, 1979.

Cobb, Charles R. *The Archaeology of the Southeastern Native American Landscapes of the Colonial Era.* Gainesville: University Press of Florida, 2019.

de Luna, Kathryn M. "Sounding the African Atlantic." *William and Mary Quarterly* 78, no. 4 (2021): 581–616.

Dubcovsky, Alejandra, and George Aaron Broadwell. "Writing Timucua: Recovering and Interrogating Indigenous Authorship." *Early American Studies: An Interdisciplinary Journal* 15, no. 3 (2017): 409–41.

Dubcovsky, Alejandra. *Informed Power: Communication in the Early South.* Cambridge, MA: Harvard University Press, 2016.

———. "Defying Indian Slavery: Apalachee Voices and Spanish Sources in the Eighteenth-Century Southeast." *William and Mary Quarterly* 75, no. 2 (2018): 295–322.

———. "Asymmetries of Power: Timucua-Apalachee Relations in the Early 18th Century." In *Facing Florida: Essays in Culture and Religion in Early Modern Southeastern America,* edited by Timothy J. Johnson and Jeffrey M. Burns, 91–102. San Diego: Academy of American Franciscan History, 2021.

Ellis, Elizabeth N. *The Great Power of Small Nations: Indigenous Diplomacy in the Gulf South.* Philadelphia: University of Pennsylvania Press, 2022.

Ethridge, Robbie. "Creating the Shatter Zone: Indian Slave Traders and Collapse of Southeastern Chiefdoms." In *Light on the Path: The Anthropology of the Southeastern Indians,* edited by Robbie Ethridge and Thomas J. Puckhahn, 207–16. Tuscaloosa: University of Alabama Press, 2006.

——————. *From Chicaza to Chickasaw: The European Invasion and the Transformation of the Mississippian World, 1540—1715.* Chapel Hill: University of North Carolina Press, 2010.

Florescano, Enrique. "El Abasto y La Legislación de Granos En El Siglo XVI." *Historia Mexicana* 14, no. 4 (1965): 567—630.

Gallay, Alan. *The Indian Slave Trade, the Rise of the English Empire in the American South 1670—1717.* New Haven, CT: Yale University Press, 2002.

Gatschet, Albert S. "The Timucua Language." *Proceedings of the American Philosophical Society* 16, no. 99 (1877): 626—42. Sequential lectures published in Ibid., 17, no. 101, 490—504, and 18, no. 105, 465—502.

Goddard, Ives. "The Description of the Native Languages of North America Before Boas." In Vol. 17 of *The Handbook of North American Indians*, 17—42. Washington D.C.: Smithsonian Institution, 1996.

Goetz, Rebecca Anne. "Indian Slavery: An Atlantic and Hemispheric Problem." *History Compass* 14, no. 2 (2016): 59—70.

Hall, Joseph M. *Zamumo's Gifts: Indian-European Exchange in the Colonial Southeast.* Philadelphia: University of Pennsylvania Press, 2009.

Hann, John H. "Summary Guide to Spanish Florida Missions and Visitas: With Churches in the Sixteenth and Seventeenth Centuries." *The Americas* 66, no. 4 (1990): 417—513.

——————. *Missions to the Calusa.* Gainesville: University of Florida Press: Florida Museum of Natural History, 1991.

——————. "Political Leadership among the Natives of Spanish Florida." *Florida Historical Quarterly* 71, no. 2 (1992): 188—208.

——————. "1630 Memorial of Fray Francisco Alonso de Jesús on Spanish Florida's Missions and Natives." *The Americas* 50, no. 1 (1993): 85—105.

——————. "Visitations and Revolts in Florida, 1656—1695." *Florida Archaeology* 7 (1993).

Hoffman, Paul E. *Florida's Frontiers.* Bloomington: Indiana University Press, 2002.

Jennings, Matthew. *New Worlds of Violence: Cultures and Conquests in the Early American Southeast.* Knoxville: University of Tennessee Press, 2011.

Justice, Daniel Heath. *Why Indigenous Literatures Matter.* Waterloo: Wilfrid Laurier University Press, 2020.

Kelton, Paul. *Epidemics and Enslavement: Biological Catastrophe in the Native Southeast, 1492—1715.* Lincoln: University of Nebraska Press, 2007.

Kimball, Geoffrey. "A Grammatical Sketch of Apalachee." *International Journal of American Linguistics* 53, no. 2 (1987): 136—74.

——————"An Apalachee Vocabulary." *International Journal of American Linguistics* 54, no. 4 (1988): 387—98.

Kirkness, Verna J., and Ray Barnhardt. "First Nations and Higher Education: The Four R's—Respect, Relevance, Reciprocity, Responsibility." *Journal of American Indian Education* 30, no. 3 (1991): 1—15.

Lillehaugen, Brooke Danielle, and Xóchitl Flores-Marcial, "Extending Pedagogy through Social Media: Zapotec Language in and beyond Classrooms," *Native American and Indigenous Studies* 9, no. 1 (2022): 62—101.

Linklater, Tanya Lukin. "Desirous Kings of Indigenous Futurity: On the Possibilities of Memorialization." In *Desire Change: Contemporary Feminist Art in Canada,* edited by Heather Davis, 149–62. Montreal: McGill-Queen's University Press, 2017.

Leonard, Wesley Y. "Producing Language Reclamation by Decolonising 'Language'." In Vol. 14 of *Language Documentation and Description*, edited by Wesley Y. Leonard and Haley De Korne, 15–36. London: EL Publishing, 2007.

Masters, Adrian, and Bradley Dixon. "Indigenous Petitioning in the Early Modern British and Spanish New World." In *Petitioning in the Atlantic World: Empires, Revolutions and Social Movements,* edited by Miguel Dantas da Cruz, 105–136. New York: Palgrave Macmillan, 2022.

Masters, Adrian. "A Thousand Invisible Architects: Vassals, the Petition and Response System, and the Creation of Imperial Caste Legislation." *Hispanic American Historical Review* 98, no. 3 (2018): 377–406.

McDonough, Kelly. "Indigenous Remembering and Forgetting: Sixteenth-Century Nahua Letters and Petitions to the Spanish Crown." *Native American and Indigenous Studies* 5, no. 1 (2018): 69–99.

McEnroe, Sean F. "Sites of Diplomacy, Violence, and Refuge: Topography and Negotiation in the Mountains of New Spain." *The Americas* 69, no. 2 (2012): 179–202.

Mexía, Álvaro. "The Derrotero of Álvaro Mexía, 1605." In *A Survey of Indian River Archaeology, Florida,* translated. by Charles D. Higgs, 265–74. New Haven, CT: Yale University Press, 1951.

Milanich, Jerald T. *Laboring in the Fields of the Lord: Spanish Missions and Southeastern Indians.* Washington, D.C.: Smithsonian Institution Press, 1999.

———. *The Timucua.* Malden, MA: Blackwell, 1999.

Newell, Margaret Ellen. *Brethren by Nature: New England Indians, Colonists, and the Origins of American Slavery.* Ithaca, NY: Cornell University Press, 2015.

Owensby, Brian. *Empire of Law and Indian Justice in Colonial Mexico.* Stanford, CA: Stanford University Press, 2008.

Pareja, Francisco. *Arte y Pronunciación de la Lengua Timucua y Castellana.* Mexico City: Imprenta de Ioan Ruiz, 1614.

Peres, Tanya M., and Rochelle A. Marrinan, eds. *Unearthing the Missions of Spanish Florida.* Gainesville: University of Florida Press, 2021.

Puente, Jose Carlos de la. *Andean Cosmopolitans: Seeking Justice and Reward at the Spanish Royal Court.* Austin: University of Texas Press, 2018.

Radding, Cynthia. *Landscapes of Power and Identity: Comparative Histories in the Sonoran Desert and the Forests of Amazonia from Colony to Republic.* Durham, NC: Duke University Press, 2006.

Reséndez, Andrés. *The Other Slavery: The Uncovered Story of Indian Enslavement in America.* Boston: Houghton Mifflin Harcourt, 2016.

Romero, Sergio. "Grammar, Dialectal Variation, and Honorific Registers in Nahuatl in Seventeenth-Century Guatemala." *Anthropological Linguistics* (2014): 54–77.

Rushforth, Brett. *Bonds of Alliance: Indigenous and Atlantic Slaveries in New France.* Chapel Hill: University of North Carolina Press, 2012.

Schneider, Tsim D. "Placing Refuge and the Archaeology of Indigenous Hinterlands in Colonial California." *American Antiquity* 80, no. 4 (2015): 695–713.

Shefveland, Kristalyn Marie. *Anglo-Native Virginia Trade, Conversion, and Indian Slavery in the Old Dominion, 1646–1722.* Athens: University of Georgia Press, 2016.

Smith, Buckingham. *Documents in the Spanish and Two of the Early Tongues of Florida (Apalachian and Timuquan).* In the collections of the John Carter Brown Library. Washington, D.C., 1860.

Snyder, Christina. *Slavery in Indian Country: The Changing Face of Captivity.* Cambridge, MA: Harvard University Press, 2010.

Stojanowski, Christopher M. "Spanish Colonial Effects on Native American Mating Structure and Genetic Variability in Northern and Central Florida: Evidence from Apalachee and Western Timucua." *American Journal of Physical Anthropology* 128 (2005): 273–86.

Tavárez, David. "'We Will Wait to Be True People, Christians': An Idolatry Confession in Zapotec." *Ethnohistory* 69, no. 3 (2022): 325–50.

Tuck, Eve, and K. Wayne Yang. "Decolonization Is Not a Metaphor." *Decolonization: Indigeneity, Education and Society* 1, no. 1 (2012): 1–40.

Tuck, Eve, and C. Ree. "A Glossary of Haunting." In *Handbook of Autoethnography,* edited by Stacy Holman Jones, Tony E. Adams, and Carolyn Ellis, 639–58. New York: Routledge, 2013.

Worth, John E. *The Timucuan Chiefdoms of Spanish Florida: Vol. 1, Assimilation.* Gainesville: University Press of Florida, 1998.

————. *The Timucuan Chiefdoms of Spanish Florida: Vol. 2, Resistance and Destruction.* Gainesville: University Press of Florida, 1998.

————. "Razing Florida: The Indian Slave Trade and the Devastation of Spanish Florida, 1659–1715." In *Mapping the Mississippian Shatter Zone: The Colonial Indian Slave Trade and the Regional Transformation in the American South,* edited by Robbie Ethridge and Sheri M. Shuck-Hall, 295–311. Lincoln: University of Nebraska Press, 2009.

Wyss, Hilary E. *English Letters and Indian Literacies: Reading, Writing, and New England Missionary Schools, 1750–1830.* Philadelphia: University of Pennsylvania Press, 2012.

Yannakakis, Yanna. "Making Law Intelligible: Networks of Translation in Midcolonial Oaxaca." In *Indigenous Intellectuals: Knowledge, Power, and Colonial Culture in Mexico and the Andes,* edited by Gabriela Ramos and Yanna Yannakakis, 79–103. Durham, NC: Duke University Press, 2014.

Notes

An earlier version of this paper was presented at the Indigenous Studies Seminar series hosted by the Library & Museum at the American Philosophical Society. We want to thank everyone in the audience for their thoughtful suggestions. We are also very grateful to the journal's four anonymous reviewers, whose excellent suggestions greatly improved the essay.

1. Justice, *Why Indigenous Literatures Matter,* 78.

2. "Autos y Cartas de los Caciques."

3. Although pre-Columbian population estimates are hard to come by, John Worth collects data for about thirty-thousand Timucuas during the earliest moments of Spanish settlement but argues that earlier estimates are "essentially wild guesses." Jerald Milanich estimates that there were about two hundred thousand. See Worth, *The Timucuan Chiefdoms of Spanish Florida,* 2: 2—5; and Milanich, *The Timucua,* 60—61. For discussion of general patterns, see Anderson and Sassaman, *Recent Developments Southeastern Archaeology,* 152—90; Cobb, *The Archaeology of the Southeastern Native American Landscapes of the Colonial Era,* 64—101. For Timucua dialects, Pareja, *Arte y Pronunciación,* folio 8—9; Milanich, *The Timucua,* 41—44.

4. Dubcovsky and Broadwell. "Writing Timucua," 409—41; Gatschet, "The Timucua Language," 626—42; Crawford, "Timucua and Yuchi," 327—54; Goddard, "The Description of the Native Languages of North America," 17—42; Broadwell, "Honorific usage in Timucua exempla," 280—94; Ibid, "Shadow Authors," 139—52.

5. The guiding principles of respect, relevance, reciprocity, and responsibility, or the four "r's," guide this collaborative and ongoing language work. Respect for tribal members as well as for their knowledge, concerns, and time was at our foundation; we consulted both early and consistently with interested communities to develop a research agenda that was relevant to them, not simply to us, and we endeavored to create more reciprocal relations. Finally, we have a responsibility to the historical and current voices represented in this language work. Kirkness and Barnhardt, "First Nations and Higher Education: The Four R's," 1—15; Leonard, "Producing Language Reclamation," 15—36.

6. "Jesus María Letter"; Broadwell and Dubcovsky, "Chief Manuel's 1651 Timucua Letter," 1—43. For the importance of "words" and "sounds" in historic documents, see de Luna, "Sounding the African Atlantic," 581—616.

7. For more on the Choctaw language project see the forthcoming and collaborative work, Broadwell and Snyder, "The Criminalization of Whooping in the Nineteenth-Century Choctaw Nation." For more on the Zapotec language project see: https://ticha.haverford.edu/en/ and Lillehaugen and Flores-Marcial, "Extending Pedagogy," 62—101.

8. For the Apalachee letter, see "Autos y Cartas de los Caciques"; Kimball, "A Grammatical Sketch of Apalachee," 136—74; Kimball, "An Apalachee Vocabulary," 387—98. For thinking about the relations between Apalachee and Timucua people, see Dubcovsky, "Asymmetries of Power," 91—102; Stojanowski, "Spanish Colonial Effects on Native American," 273—86; Hann, "Political Leadership among the Natives of Spanish Florida," 188—208.

9. See the Appendix.

10. "Governor Juan Marquez de Cabrera to the King," December 8, 1680. "Governor Juan Marquez de Cabrera to the King," March 20, 1686.

11. Hoffman, *Florida's Frontiers,* 166—67.

12. For complaints about Governor Cabrera, see "Crimes by Governor Marquez Cabrera," September 4, 1688. For Cabrera's description of Franciscan

abuses, see Governor Juan Marques Cabrera to the King, March 20, 1686. AGI SD 227B.

13. "Diego Qurioga y Losada to the King," April 18, 1692.

14. Worth has extensively chronicled the leadership structure and titles in Timucua, but by the late 1680s much of Timucua's complex leadership structure had been reduced. Titles as holata aco ("chief of many" or "big chief") and parucusi (paramount chief) were far less common. Titles like holata and cacique were often used interchangeably by Timucua officials seeking to make their leadership structure legible. Although these five men were clearly part of Timucua leadership, their precise roles and relations to one another are hard to decipher. See Worth, *The Timucuan Chiefdoms* 1:86—92. For the ongoing efforts to redefine Timucua leadership, see Hann, *Visitations and Revolts in Florida*, 196—216.

15. The only other surviving Timucua letter also comes from a town in this region.

16. Hann, "1630 Memorial of Fray Francisco Alonso de Jesús," 85—105, quote 100. San Juan de Guacara was originally located on the Suwannee River at Charles Springs but moved to the region after the 1656 rebellion from the east. See Worth, *The Timucuan Chiefdoms of Spanish Florida*, 2:103—104.

17. For the so-called Timucua Rebellion see Worth, *The Timucuan Chiefdoms of Spanish Florida* 2:38—65; Blanton, "The Role of Cattle Ranching," 667—84; and Dubcovsky, *Informed Power*, 68—96.

18. For a good overview of Indian slaving in the region, see Gallay, *The Indian Slave Trade*, 19—248; Snyder, *Slavery in Indian Country*, 46—79 Ethridge, "Creating the Shatter Zone," 207—218; Ibid, *From Chicaza to Chickasaw*, 194—231; Hall, *Zamumo's Gifts*, 95—116; Shefveland, *Anglo-Native Virginia Trade*, 44—60. For good overviews on Indian slavery in other regions see, Rushforth, *Bonds of Alliance*, 15—72; Newell, *Brethren by* Nature, 17—42; Reséndez, *The Other Slavery*,1—12; Goetz, "Indian Slavery," 59—70.

19. The 1688 Apalachee letter that was sent to the Crown along with the Timucua letter also evinces a similar understanding. For thinking about the language, style, and content of Native petitions in Spanish America, see: Owensby, *Empire of Law and Indian Justice*, 49—89; and McDonough, "Indigenous Remembering and Forgetting," 69—99, especially 85—68.

20. For the newest work on Native people in the Florida missions, see Peres and Marrinan, *Unearthing the Missions of Spanish Florida*, 1—34.

21. For overviews of Spanish efforts in Timucua territory see Worth, *The Timucuan Chiefdoms of Spanish Florida*, 1:57—68. Milanich, *Laboring in the Fields of the Lord*, 82—104; Kelton, *Epidemics and Enslavement*, 82—83.

22. "Francisco de Pareja to the king," March 8, 1599.

23. Hann, "1630 Memorial of Fray Francisco Alonso de Jesús," 85—105, quote 100.

24. "Testimony of Don Joseph de Prado, Royal Treasurer," "Testimony of Adjutant Pedro de la Puerta," "Testimony of Captain Augustín Pérez de Villa Real," April 1660. Dubcovsky and Broadwell, "Writing Timucua," 409—41. "Cacique of Machaba," circa 1674.

25. Dubcovsky and Broadwell, "Writing Timucua," 409—41; Wyss, *English Letters and Indian Literacies,* 33—74.

26. "Autos y Cartas de los Caciques."

27. "Jesus María Letter," December 9, 1651.

28. Ibid.

29. Broadwell, "Honorific usage in Timucua exampla," 280—294. The honorific system of Timucua resembles that described for Classical Nahuatl, as discussed in Romero, "Grammar, dialectal variation, and honorific registers," 54—77.

30. Broadwell, "Honorific Usage in Timucua Exempla," 280—294.

31. The explanations for the abbreviations in the interlinear gloss may be found at https://hebuano.wordpress.com/linguistic-terms/.

32. For a recent and comparative overview of Native petitions in Latin America see Masters and Dixon, "Indigenous Petitioning," 104—36. In the same volume Amy Bushnell chronicles the fragmented petition practice in Florida, "Debitage of the Shatter Zone," 137—56.

33. For more about the petition form, see McDonough, "Indigenous Remembering and Forgetting," 69—99. Carpenter, *Democracy by Petitioning,* 3—22; Masters, "A Thousand Invisible Architects," 377—406; Puente, *Andean Cosmopolitans,* 1—20. For a similar example in Nahuatl, see Anderson, Berdan, and Lockhart, *Beyond the Codices,* 166—220; and for Zapotec see Yannakakis, "Making Law Intelligible," 79—103.

34. "Visitation to San Pedro," February 13, 1657. "Testimony of Cacique Clemente Bernal of San Juan del Puerto." Dubcovsky, "Defying Indian Slavery," 295—322. Worth, "Razing Florida," 295—311.

35. Gallay, *The Indian Slave Trade,* 40—100. Jennings, *New Worlds of Violence,* 119—36. For an overview on the impact of slaving and violence, see Ethridge, *From Chicaza to Chickasaw,* 194—231; and Blackhawk, *Violence over the Land,* 226—74.

36. "Autos y Cartas de los Caciques."

37. "Domingo Leturiondo." Hann, "Summary Guide to Spanish Florida Missions and Visitas," 471—73.

38. For the complex ways Native nations made and remade their geopolitical power, see Ellis, *The Great Power of Small Nations,* 1—44.

39. Ethridge, "Creating the Shatter Zone," 208.

40. "Quiroga y Losada to the King," April 1, 1688.

41. Broadwell and Dubcovsky, "Chief Manuel's 1651 Timucua Letter," 1—43.

42. For a similar use in a Zapotec testimony, see Tavárez, "'We will wait to be true people, Christians,'" 325—350. For a Nauhatl example, see Florescano, "El Abasto y La Legislación de Granos En El Siglo XVI," 567—630. For "sites of refuge" see Beltrán, *Regiones de* refugio; Radding, *Landscapes of Power and Identity,* 162—95. McEnroe, "Sites of Diplomacy, Violence, and Refuge," 179—202. Schneider, "Placing Refuge and the Archaeology of Indigenous Hinterlands in Colonial California," 695—713.

43. "Quiroga y Losada to the King," April 1, 1688.

44. Ibid.

45. For earlier Spanish efforts in South Florida, "Horruque, Ays, Oribia, Abia, and Caparaca." Mexía, "The Derrotero of Álvaro Mexía," 265–274. Hann, *Missions to the Calusa.*

46. Ibid. For discussions of Indigenous futures, Tuck and Yang, "Decolonization Is Not a Metaphor," 1–40; Linklater, "Desirous Kings of Indigenous Futurity," 149–68, quotation, 150; Tuck and Ree, "A Glossary of Haunting," 639–58.

RUSSEL LAWRENCE BARSH

*Beyond Rights: The Nisga'a Final Agreement and the Challenges
of Modern Treaty Relationships*
by Carole Blackburn
University of British Columbia Press, 2021

THE EXTENSIVE REVISION and "patriation" of the Canadian constitution forty years ago was an opportunity for Indigenous Peoples to flex their political muscles at home and abroad. From marches in Ottawa to an outspoken "embassy" in London, Indigenous Peoples demanded the recognition of inherent aboriginal rights and full implementation of treaties in accordance with their original spirit and intent as founding documents of the legitimacy of the Crown in Canada. As a result, both aboriginal and treaty rights were broadly entrenched in the *Constitution Act, 1982*. The new constitution also recognized the possibility of new treaties settling territorial disputes with First Nations.

In the United States, Congress not only extinguished the president's authority to make treaties with Indian tribes 150 years ago, but also asserted power to break treaties already made. In Canada, additional treaties with Indigenous Peoples are not only possible, but once made, they are constitutionalized.

There was great public interest (and concern) in this opportunity a generation ago. Few modern treaties have actually been negotiated and approved in Canada, however, making Carole Blackburn's narrative of the Nisga'a Final Agreement (2000) especially important. The author had opportunities to observe the negotiations and the process of implementation and enjoyed access to many of the participants on the Nisga'a side of the table.

I approached this book from the perspective of an advocate for Indigenous Peoples seeking lessons that can be learned from the Nisga'a. In the 1980s to 1990s, I participated in diplomacy on behalf of the Mi'kmaq Grand Council and helped organize tripartite "treaty clarification" discussions as a senior advisor to the Treaty Commissioner in Saskatchewan. I wrote analyses on land-claims negotiations in the Americas for United Nations agencies and a volume of case studies, published by the International Labour Office, with my Pikani (Blackfoot) colleague Krisma Bastien.

It is no secret that the promise of using modern treaties to resolve land claims in Canada has foundered, with few final agreements, and much of the caseload trapped somewhere in the pipeline. What can other Canadian First Nations learn from the Nisga'a experience about "getting to *Yes*," to borrow a cliché from the business world.

Blackburn appropriately underscores that modern treaties (indeed all Indigenous political reconciliations with the state) are two-way streets that require confidence building and pragmatic baby steps and must be part of ongoing and unending relationships. Agreements are necessarily imperfect; but they may do a great deal of good if they result in some degree of formal recognition of Indigenous identity and genuine power-sharing with other state actors. Good agreements will lead eventually, in principle, to the good-will to replace them with even better agreements.

But acknowledging this reality, we are compelled to conclude that the entire Canadian project of modern treatymaking is doomed to fail. Since there is no detailed definition of "aboriginal and treaty rights" in the *Constitution Act, 1982*, negotiations with each First Nation begin effectively at zero, and leave the balance of negotiating power with the federal and provincial authorities. If one First Nation succeeds in achieving a deal, it raises or lowers the bar for others; while those with earlier agreements may feel cheated if any subsequent agreements are more generous. At the same time, state negotiators who regard agreements as an irrevocable erosion of state power have little incentive to make progress, leading to endless delay. Federal and provincial technocrats have no doubt also realized that scores of different jurisdictional and power-sharing agreements across the country is unmanageable and must be avoided, except perhaps in relatively unpopulated, Indigenous-majority regions of Canada where only a fraction of First Nations live.

First Nations may have gained some modest leverage from S.C. 2021, c. 14, adopting the United Nations Declaration on the Rights of Indigenous Peoples (UNDRIP) as a source of law. Henceforth, the Supreme Court of Canada may use UNDRIP to determine what, exactly, comprise "aboriginal rights," and thereby establish a fresh starting-point for negotiating new treaties with Indigenous Canadians. It is unlikely that federal or provincial authorities in Canada will change their negotiating position without court decisions, however.

Systemic failure and remedies that "even the odds" for Indigenous negotiators reach far beyond the scope of Blackburn's book, which, in its overall approach, seems aimed at persuading nonaboriginal Canadians that the "new treaty" project under the *Constitution Act, 1982,* is really a good thing—albeit imperfect. That this is still an open question more than twenty years after the Nisga'a settlement is perhaps a sign that the political mood in Canada has shifted to the right, eroding much of the goodwill that Nisga'a people won during and after the negotiations Blackburn describes.

Canada and its Indigenous nations have changed since 2000, of course, and if anything, the relevance of land-claims treaties has paled as issues such as the murder of women and residential school students are holding the attention of Indigenous and non-Indigenous Canadians. An argument could be made that the Nisga'a Final Agreement, in 2022, is something of an historical relic outside of northern British Columbia. Recognizing the changes that have taken place in the country, and the pursuit of "reconciliation," would have provided much-needed context for ascertaining what the Nisga'a experience has to offer to First Nations today.

RUSSEL LAWRENCE BARSH is director of the nonprofit conservation biology laboratory KWIAHT, Lopez Island, Washington.

PHILLIP ROUND

Postindian Aesthetics: Affirming Indigenous Literary Sovereignty
edited by Debra K. S. Barker and Connie A. Jacobs
University of Arizona Press, 2022

POSTINDIAN AESTHETICS GATHERS nineteen essays from a wide variety of Indigenous writers and scholars who explore the many ways contemporary Native literature is pushing the boundaries of readers' aesthetic expectations for art produced by Indigenous Peoples in the twenty-first century. Gerald Vizenor's memorable and useful description of late twentieth-century Native experience as "postIndian" is brought together with more recent theorizations of Indigenous aesthetics and literary sovereignty to demonstrate how truly varied and genre-bending Native literature has become. In his forward to the volume, Osage scholar Robert Warrior celebrates the collection's energetic reaffirmation of the pleasures of reading Indigenous texts and especially the way the authors of the individual essays find interesting ways to harmonize two sometimes very divergent approaches to the appreciation of Indigenous literatures. As Warrior notes, Native literary criticism has, over the past decade, featured two main methodologies—those that emphasize close readings and those that underline social and cultural contexts. In *Postindian Aesthetics*, by contrast, craft and context appear as mutually constitutive aspects of Indigenous literary practice. The editors of this collection define the "postindian aesthetics" of its title as "a philosophy of art and beauty grounded in Native expressive cultures informed by Indigenous philosophy" (6). In so doing, they have opened up a much wider canon with a far more varied set of aesthetic approaches to writing than previous critics have allowed.

By bringing less-discussed authors into the ongoing scholarly debates over the place of ethnography and cultural criticism in Native literary studies, the essayists in this collection marshal new methodologies to match the true diversity of aesthetic practices and geographic and linguistic range that animate the arts in Indian country today. *Postindian Aesthetics* reintroduces its readers to underrepresented writers from the twentieth-century North American Indigenous literary canon (Lucy Tapahanso, Jeanette C. Armstrong, and Ray Young Bear) and to newer authors like Esther Belin, Sherwin Bitsui, and Orlando White, who began their careers in the twenty-first century—all with an eye to matching their critical methodologies with the aesthetic challenges these authors present.

Among the new theorizations featured in this volume, several shared realizations / revisions are underscored here, all of which flow from those often unspoken and under-theorized assumptions that have been at the foundation of the interpretation of Indigenous literatures in the recent past. First among these is the tendency of critics to seek something "recognizably Indian" in works by Native authors. The collection's editors and contributors here seek to unpack what Robert Warrior has called the "provocative aesthetics" (3) of these works, arguing that while many of these practices are indeed "edgy," such "provocations" are actually often drawn from the most quotidian aspects of Native life in North America today. Like settler writers, some Native authors come from working-class backgrounds, and many are urban, with their families having been relocated from ancestral homelands during the 1950s as part of federal Indian policy.

The essays in *Postindian Aesthetics* continually and usefully remind us that these authors' "expressive cultures," rooted as they are in the incredibly wide variety of Indigenous homelands present in North America today, demand an appreciation of the real differences that exist between those who hail from the Columbia Plateau and the Great Basin, the removed communities in Oklahoma, and the urban centers of Chicago, Minneapolis, and Los Angeles. In her essay on Jeanette Armstrong, for example, Jane Halladay explains how the Okanagan writer grounds her English-language literary offerings in first-language knowledge of her community's language (Nsyilxcən) and her own community activism, which has included work as a translator for Okanagan elders in her homelands. For Halladay, Armstrong "both describes and enacts" Okanagan (Syilx) epistemologies and representational practices to "craft a distinctive Syilx literary aesthetic" (22). In Esther Belin's poetry, by contrast, writing itself has become the homeland, and essayist Jeff Berglund describes Belin's own relocation history as central to her repositioning of Diné philosophy and aesthetics within a stimulating array of concrete poetry, extralinguistic marks, and formatting techniques so as to "build a home— the world—" like the one in which "we live" (196). For the Haida artist Michael Nicoll Yahgulanaas, manga provides a medium for provocatively combining a Haida worldview with Japanese artistic practices in a way that, as Jeremy Carnes explains, blurs the lines between high art and comics and settler and Indigenous craft, allowing the Haida artist to participate in a global and cosmopolitan aesthetic sphere.

Postindian Aesthetics offers its readers the kind of reading pleasures Robert Warrior cites as often lacking in contemporary literary criticism. Through these essays, we experience Esther Belin's own engagement with

Sherwin Bitsui's verse, as we experience Orlando White's poetry through Bitsui's essay appreciating his fellow Diné author's work. Each essay is supported by a rich works-cited section that will allow readers to pursue these new interpretive strategies in their own readings of contemporary Indigenous literature. Both scholars and students will be rewarded with refreshing new takes on literary craft as practiced by Native artists today.

PHILLIP ROUND is John C. Gerber Professor of English at the University of Iowa.

BRYAN KAMAOLI KUWADA

Hawai'i is My Haven: Race and Indigeneity in the Black Pacific
by Nitasha Tamar Sharma
Duke University Press, 2022

EVERY HAWAIIAN SCHOLAR I mentioned the first part of the book's title to rolled their eyes. Not from foreknowledge of the book itself, but because of how accustomed Hawaiians are to outsiders and tourists considering our 'āina a special refuge and how we are mostly just background to people's vacations and fantasies. But my friends became intrigued once my they found out that the book considered the possibilities that Hawai'i offered for pono (righteousness/balance/justice), particularly with regard to Black people here.

Nitasha Tamar Sharma spent a decade interviewing and working with nonmilitary Black folx in Hawai'i, from Black Hawaiians and Black locals to new college students and old-timers who have lived here for decades. Along with the painful, funny, heart-wrenching, inspiring, loving life stories that Sharma presents to us as the piko (umbilicus/center) of this book, her main intervention is the insistence that race is a vital yet underused lens through which to examine life in Hawai'i, a place not structured along the Black/white binary that has informed so much of continental thinking about race. Sharma convincingly argues that examining Hawai'i through a racial lens would make for important shifts in Native and Indigenous studies, mixed-race studies, African American studies (particularly Afropessimism), American studies, ethnic studies, and in popular understandings of Hawai'i itself. Sharma troubles foundational categories that often go uninterrogated in discussions of race, identity, belonging, settler colonialism, and Black and Native relations as she calls us to move beyond the limitations of Black/white and settler/Indigenous binaries and received conceptions of ethnicity and descent.

Sharma's first chapter brings back into focus the two-centuries-long history of the African diaspora in Hawai'i. Her second chapter deals with her ethnographic work with Black Hawaiians, Black locals, and "expansive Blackness" (the power of a "Black And ____" identity) with the third chapter focusing on Black transplants. The fourth chapter focuses on anti-Black racism in contemporary Hawai'i and the Native Hawaiian community, which has changed from the nineteenth-century Hawaiian kingdom, where

Black women and men were welcomed and found many different places for themselves. The fifth chapter focuses on cross-sectional kuleana (rights/responsibilities/privileges) as a way to navigate Black and Native futures in Hawai'i. Sharma ends with a conclusion that ties together identity, politics, and knowledge.

While Sharma's book is undeniably important, powerfully articulated, and well worth reading, there is one disappointing aspect worth pointing out. The subtitle is "Race and Indigeneity in the Black Pacific," and Sharma lays out a somewhat thoughtful framing for her usage of the term "Black Pacific" in the introduction as she connects it to the Black Atlantic and mentions different ways Blackness is understood in the Pacific, particularly with Indigenous Australians and Melanesians; the rest of the book does not earn this use of the term "Black Pacific." The Pacific and Oceania are used almost interchangeably with Hawai'i, not accounting for the vastly different experiences of African Americans in Hawai'i and Black peoples in the greater Pacific. While this does not undermine any of the major points that Sharma is making, if you are looking for a book that really engages the Black Pacific with an understanding of the broader Pacific, this is not it.

There is also a certain lack of understanding of Hawaiian culture/history/concerns that is unfortunately evident in this otherwise well-argued book. For just a quick example, we are long past the time where it is acceptable for academics to talk about nineteenth-century Hawai'i without Hawaiian-language sources, so their absence in her first chapter was noticeable, particularly since tracking the usage of "lāhui," a word that went from meaning something akin to "nation" in the early nineteenth century to something more akin to "race" in the early twentieth, would have provided strong evidence for her assertion that Hawaiians began to take onboard American understandings of race during that time.

Yet I do not necessarily see her lack of 'ike (knowledge/understanding) in these areas (there are others besides the example given above) as shortcomings. They actually reiterate her assertions about the necessity of Black and Hawaiian communities working together toward pono in Hawai'i and helping each other fill in gaps where they can. Sharma asserts that "expansive belonging" and cross-sectional kuleana are necessary for us to live ethically together and create futures that are more humane and freer from violence. Thus, this is an interesting and important work for scholars in the fields mentioned above. But for Hawaiian scholars and/or activists invested in a more pono future for Hawai'i, this book is required reading.

BRYAN KAMAOLI KUWADA is assistant professor in the Kamakakūokalani Center for Hawaiian Studies, University of Hawai'i-Mānoa.

PABLO MILLALEN LEPIN (*English*)

Red Scare: The State's Indigenous Terrorist
by Joanne Barker
University of California Press, 2021

RED SCARE: THE STATE'S INDIGENOUS TERRORIST by Joanne Barker (Lenape, a citizen of the Delaware Tribe of Indians) opens with a prologue that highlights two scenarios linked to the struggles of Indigenous Peoples in Canada and the United States: on the one hand, Indigenous opposition to the violations of the rights of the treaties and to the oppression of Indigenous women, and on the other hand, Indigenous resistance to oil extraction in Standing Rock (North Dakota) and the demand for a legal instrument that addresses violence against Indigenous women in the United States. In both cases, sexual violence generated and perpetuated the traumas and subordination of Indigenous women. These processes illustrate the tensions between Indigenous Peoples and what the author characterizes as "imperialist States," states characterized by the use of "invasion, occupation, land theft, extraction, exploitation and sexual violence for centuries" (ix).

Barker argues that Indigenous Peoples and their members are identified as "terrorists" (5). In other words, "Indigenous peoples who maintain governance and territorial-based lifeways are perceived as threats to the state's security and social stability" (21). Given the colonial stigma of "terrorists," states have granted themselves the authority to act with impunity, attack human dignity, and even kill.

Barker's book is developed over four chapters. The first focuses on the threat that some ideologies (such as communism, socialism, anarchism, atheism, and the combination thereof) constitute to the security and social stability of the states. The second and third chapters focus on two ways in which Indigenous People have been framed as terrorists by Canada and the United States of America to protect their imperialist agendas. First, *The Murderable Indian,* a terrorist figure against whom the state uses all available tools: repression, discipline, and imprisonment. This figure is particularly relevant with regard to the opposition of industrial projects (e.g., oil and gas) resulting from collusion between states and corporate governments. The second, *The Kinless Indian,* is a figure "without any linear or community-based relationship to Indigenous People" (25). *The Kinless*

Indian encourages Indigenous identity fraud, which is prevalent in the Cherokee and Métis contexts and absolves the state of their responsibilities for the violence, impacting Indigenous governance and self-determination. In the fourth chapter, Barker reflects on reciprocity, a value embodied in Indigenous governance, as viable alternative to state imperialism.

Barker illustrates her argument with an interdisciplinary and activist approach, drawing on reflections and contributions from activists and researchers in the fields of critical Indigenous and race studies, Indigenous feminism, and anti-imperialist studies. Through these intersections, Barker demonstrates that in the eyes of the state, racialized Indigenous bodies are indistinguishable from terrorists.

The author makes a significant contribution to the field of critical Indigenous studies. Her analysis of colonial state discourse includes Indigenous methodology, drawing on stories that interpret the world from Indigenous Peoples' point of view. For example, Sky woman, a Lenape story about earth formation, adds a feminist methodology with an Indigenous and anti-imperialist approach, by proposing the concepts of "rematriation" and "rootedness." Rematriation is "the return of the land to Indigenous governance" (116). Rootedness is characterized by interdependence and reciprocity, where Indigenous Peoples "do not compete for space" (123), as the state and corporate governments do but instead share, respect, and promote reciprocity.

Red Scare resonates in Abiayala (Latin America). For example, in Wallmapu, the ancestral lands of the Mapuche people, the Mapuche movement opposed the large-scale forestry companies and settlers. As a consequence, the outgoing government of Sebastián Piñera in Chile subjected the Mapuche to a militarization plan that installed Chilean soldiers in "conflict zones." The government narrative continually invoked the figure of the "terrorist" to justify the "state of exception" over Mapuche territory.

Given the significance of the topic it would have been helpful to include some images for added impact on the academic audience, activists, and those outside of Turtle Island's geographies. *Red Scare* shows the colonial and imperialist responses that states deploy to Indigenous claims. The book is an invitation to participate in a broader debate among those who are represented as "terrorists" by imperialist states and corporate governments and all those who stand in solidarity with the struggles of Indigenous Peoples constantly exposed to colonial stigmatization.

PABLO MILLALEN LEPIN (Mapuche) is a member of the Centro de Estudios e Investigación, Comunidad de Historia Mapuche. He is a Ph.D. candidate at the Institute for Latin American Studies (LLILAS) at the University of Texas at Austin.

PABLO MILLALEN LEPIN (*Español*)

Red Scare: The State's Indigenous Terrorist
por Joanne Barker
University of California Press, 2021

EL LIBRO *RED SCARE: THE STATE'S INDIGENOUS TERRORIST* de Joanne Barker (Lenape, una ciudadana de la tribu Delaware) comienza con un prólogo que pone de relieve dos escenarios ligados a las luchas de los Pueblos Indígenas en Canadá y Estados Unidos: por un lado, la oposición Indígena a las violaciones de los derechos de los Tratados y a la opresión de las mujeres Indígenas; por el otro, la resistencia Indígena a la extracción de petróleo en Standing Rock (Dakota del Norte) y la demanda de un instrumento legal que aborde la violencia contra las mujeres Indígenas en Estados Unidos. En ambos casos, la violencia sexual generó y perpetuó los traumas y la subordinación de las mujeres Indígenas. Estos procesos ilustran las tensiones entre los Pueblos Indígenas y lo que la autora conceptualiza como "Estados imperialistas", Estados caracterizados por el uso de la "invasión, ocupación, robo de tierras, extracción, explotación y violencia sexual durante siglos" (ix).

Barker argumenta que los Pueblos Indígenas y sus miembros son identificados como "terroristas" (5). Según Barker, "Los Pueblos Indígenas que mantienen una gobernabilidad y modos de vida basados en el territorio son percibidos como amenazas a la seguridad del Estado y la estabilidad social." (21) Con este estigma colonial de "terroristas", los Estados se han autoconcedido la autoridad para actuar con impunidad, atentar contra la dignidad humana e incluso asesinar.

El libro de Barker se desarrolla en cuatro capítulos. El primero tiene su foco en la amenaza que constituyen algunas ideologías (como el comunismo, el socialismo, el anarquismo, el ateísmo, y la combinación de los mismos) para la seguridad y estabilidad social de los Estados. Luego, los capítulos segundo y tercero, se enfocan en dos formas en las que los Pueblos Indígenas han sido enmarcados como terroristas por Canadá y Estados Unidos para proteger sus agendas imperialistas. Primero, bajo la figura del "Indígena Asesinable" (*The Murderable Indian*), aquel que es etiquetado como terrorista y contra quién el Estado utiliza todas las herramientas disponibles: represión, disciplina y encarcelamiento. Esta figura es particularmente relevante con respecto a la oposición a proyectos industriales (por ejemplo, de petróleo y gas) que resultan de la colusión entre Estados y gobiernos corporativos. Segundo, el "Indígena sin Parentesco" (*The Kinless Indian*), que corresponde a personas "sin relación lineal o comunitaria con los Pueblos Indígenas" (25). Esta figura motiva el fraude a la identidad Indígena que prevalece en los contextos Cherokee y Metis y absuelve a los Estados de sus responsabilidades por la violencia, lo que afecta la gobernabilidad y autodeterminación Indígena. Por último, en el cuarto capítulo, Barker reflexiona sobre la reciprocidad, un valor encarnado en la gobernanza Indígena, como alternativa viable al imperialismo estatal.

Para ilustrar su argumento, Barker adopta un enfoque interdisciplinario y activista, basándose en reflexiones y contribuciones de activistas e investigadores de los campos de los estudios críticos Indígenas y de raza (*Indigenous critical race studies)*, feminismo Indígena (*Indigenous feminism)* y enfoques anti-imperialistas (*anti-imperialism approaches)*. A través de estas intersecciones, Barker demuestra que los cuerpos Indígenas racializados, a los ojos de los Estados, son indistinguibles del terrorismo.

La autora hace una contribución significativa al campo de los estudios críticos Indígenas. Su análisis de los discursos estatales coloniales incluye metodología Indígena que se nutre de historias que dan forma a la interpretación del mundo desde los Pueblos Indígenas. Por ejemplo, *Sky Woman* (Mujer Cielo), una historia Lenape sobre la formación de la tierra, añade una metodología feminista con un enfoque Indígena y anti-imperialista al proponer los conceptos de "rematriación" y "*Rootedness*", que podríamos traducir como raigambre o enraizamiento. La rematriación es "la devolución de la tierra a la gobernanza indígena" (116). *Rootedness* se caracteriza por la interdependencia y la reciprocidad, donde los Pueblos Indígenas "no compiten por el espacio" (123), como lo hacen el Estado y los gobiernos corporativos, sino que se comparte, respeta y se promueve la reciprocidad.

Red Scare es un libro que resuena en Abiayala (América Latina). Por ejemplo, en Wallmapu, el territorio histórico del Pueblo Mapuche, el Movimiento Mapuche se opuso a las grandes empresas forestales y a los colonos. Como consecuencia, el gobierno saliente de Sebastián Piñera en Chile sometió a los Mapuche a un plan de militarización en las llamadas "zonas de conflicto". La narrativa gubernamental invocó continuamente a la figura del "terrorista" para justificar este "Estado de excepción" sobre el territorio Mapuche.

Dada la importancia de este tema, hubiese sido de gran ayuda incluir algunas imágenes en el libro para obtener un mayor efecto en la audiencia académica, activista y la que se ubica fuera de las geografías de la Isla Tortuga. *Red Scare* muestra las respuestas coloniales e imperialistas que los Estados despliegan ante las reivindicaciones Indígenas. El libro es una invitación a participar en un debate más amplio entre quienes son representados como "terroristas" por los Estados imperialistas y sus gobiernos corporativos y todos aquellos que solidarizan con las luchas de los pueblos Indígenas constantemente expuestos a la estigmatización colonial.

PABLO MILLALEN LEPIN (Mapuche) es integrante del Centro de Estudios e Investigación, Comunidad de Historia Mapuche. Es candidato a doctor en el Instituto de Estudios Latinoamericanos (LLILAS) de la Universidad de Texas en Austin.

JAIME M. N. LAVALLEE

Prophets and Ghosts: The Story of Salvage Anthropology
by Samuel J. Redman
Harvard University Press, 2021

PROPHETS AND GHOSTS is a well-organized history of "salvage anthropology" defined as "the collecting and preservation of human culture deemed to be threatened . . . . not just collecting songs and stories but trying to document *everything* about a society and its heritage" (6). Redman acknowledges the challenges of an undertaking this large and that it is not a complete history—the breadth and depth would be more than this approximately three-hundred-page book could accommodate. Instead, he tackles the major players—institutions, government, and collectors—that shaped the course of salvage anthropology for the betterment (and for the not-so-betterment) of the field and the people that it studied. As a professor, I applaud the organization of the book and the chapters. Redman lays out the reasoning for each chapter, asking the reader to ponder questions within it. The inclusion of the impact of art by both Indigenous and non-Indigenous artists is a welcome connection to the ideologies of salvage anthropology, as well as the ways in which Indigenous Peoples connected to their own heritage and interactions with collectors (chapter 4). Chapter 5, "Cultural Salvage in California," achieves Redman's goal of showcasing a case study of salvage anthropology and its effects.

The book unfolds history with a who's who of anthropology: individuals and their influences, as well as institutions. Often providing insight into personal motivations and sometimes cautiously speculating about what they might have been for the collector or institution—the juicy tidbits at times motivated me to read just a few more pages. The interwoven stories are illuminating as they bring the reader along for the ride throughout history, and they are also grounded in academically rigorous research. *Prophets and Ghosts* would be a suitable introduction for many, and any of the individual chapters would provide a good background of where salvage anthropology came from (chapters 1—5) and where it could go (chapter 6).

Redman acknowledges that salvage anthropology is deeply embedded in colonialism. Settler colonialism created and perpetuated the "myth of the vanishing Indian." Salvage anthropologists sought out the "true" and "authentic Indian" bypassing adaptations (115—16) while simultaneously reflecting modern Western society's views of "true and authentic" (123, 146–47) and valuable (157). These ideas continue to the present day; for example, within Canadian Aboriginal law, Indigenous Peoples must prove their Aboriginal rights only through connections to precontact practices and traditions; the original practice must not have a whiff of European influence or it is deemed non-Aboriginal and denied any present-day relevance. Thus, Indigenous Peoples are confined to precontact notions of hunting, fishing, and gathering; they are not seen as past and current economic actors who have always been capable of making a living from the resources around them.

Redman does not tiptoe around the difficulties inherent in a field that was mostly exploitive, romanticized, and colonial. Collecting Indigenous Peoples' material culture was intended to "preserve" the sacred but not to allow its practice (82). The denial of Indigenous Peoples' basic human and civil rights is set within the historical context of nationalism, expansionism, and assimilationism. Without the government, museums, universities, and collectors removing Indigenous material culture (and thus the means of intergenerational transmission of knowledge), the goals of settler colonialism would not have been possible.

Social evolution, which arose from Darwinism (24–25), aided in the creation and motivation behind salvage anthropology, and, ultimately, its professionalization into anthropology. Social evolution meant there was an inevitability and justification of the more civilized society (white) to dominate, eradicate, and assimilate the lesser civilized society (Indigenous). This played a major role in the race to collect, and thereby influenced what to keep and what was ascribed value as important knowledge and then later as art (31).

Redman points out moments when salvage anthropologists and Indigenous Peoples collaborated. He has shown, where possible, the agency of Indigenous Peoples' cooperation to preserve their culture, such as the Omaha (67–70), as well as revitalization efforts that have arisen in recent times (chapter 6). Ironically, without the materials collected by salvage anthropology, cultural revitalization would not be possible for some or not nearly as robust (156).

Redman concludes by acknowledging the challenges of dealing with the past and present-day effects of salvage anthropology and its intertwining with settler colonialism. But he also holds out hope that the humanism and cross-cultural education that became a later goal of anthropology will promote healing, revitalization, and new connections with new questions, new answers, and new solutions.

JAIME M. N. LAVALLEE (Muskeg Lake Cree from Treaty 6 in Saskatchewan) is assistant professor at the University of Saskatchewan College of Law.

MICHAEL DAVID KAULANA ING

Remembering Our Intimacies: Mo'olelo, Aloha 'Āina, and Ea
by Jamaica Heolimeleikalani Osorio
University of Minnesota Press, 2021

THIS IS A BEAUTIFUL BOOK. Jamaica Heolimeleikalani Osorio is a leader in the newest generation of Indigenous scholars articulating what it means to be Indigenous (in her case, Kanaka—Hawaiian) in the contemporary world. The pages of her book (re)member the past to show how relationality for Kanaka was unraveled by colonial projects and, more importantly, how relations might be rewoven into an 'upena (net) that binds together human beings as well as the places and other beings that inhabit the world. Osorio accomplishes these goals in just over two hundred pages that are equal parts literary analysis, theoretical engagement, personal narrative, and poetry. The result sets the stage for future Kanaka scholarship.

Osorio centers the mo'olelo (story, account, history) of Pele and her family as they move to the islands that become known as Hawai'i and settle on the island of Hawai'i. Pele is the akua (deity) associated with volcanic activity. Pele's kāne (male lover) resides on the island of Kaua'i, so she sends her favorite (and youngest) sister, Hi'iakaikapoliopele (Hi'iaka in the bosom of Pele) to bring him to her. The mo'olelo reccounts Hi'iaka's journey from the island of Hawai'i to Kaua'i and back, accompanied by friends (and lovers) and their encounters with others that challenge them in various ways. The story is one of intimacy—with other people and with the lands they are from and travel through. Osorio engages in an "intimate and intense practice of reading, analysis, and interpretation" to discover a series of ha'awina (lessons) (16). Part of her goal is to encourage Kanaka to "take up the study of our mo'olelo as vigorously as we study our kingdom and legal history," which Osorio accomplishes (138). As someone who studies the ethical dimensions of literature, I deeply appreciated Osorio's readings.

The mo'olelo of Hi'iaka, in its several versions, show us what it means to care for each other in ways that are often very different than those of the Christian hetero-patriarchal structures that have become dominant in Hawai'i. Osorio engages with related conversations in Indigenous, queer, and feminist studies to show several interventions made by nā mea Hawai'i (Hawaiian material). One important intervention highlights the notion of aloha ʻāina, which Osorio describes as "the central orienting framework for any attempt to understand what it means to be Kanaka Maoli" (9). Both words are rich in meaning, with aloha often connected with love and ʻāina associated with land; but aloha ʻāina is more than simply the love of land. Building on nineteenth-century Kanaka writers such as Joseph Nāwahī, Osorio explains that "Aloha ʻāina is that pull to place, that internal compass orienting Kānaka Maoli toward intimacy and self-governance" (13). Rooted in her reading of the Hiʻiaka moʻolelo, Osorio develops an "aloha ʻāina literary consciousness" to show the many facets of this central tenet (91). On one level, aloha ʻāina is a knowledge of the lands we inhabit—knowing winds, rains, history, and more. This knowledge is a precondition for moving from a malihini (foreigner) with the land to a kamaʻāina (literally, a child of the land; a person with a deep relationship to the land).

On another level, aloha ʻāina becomes "the standard by which we understand our pilina [relations] with each other. Our relationship to our ʻāina is our kumu [source], and every pilina we practice thereafter echoes the pilina learned from our beautiful home" (119). In other words, ʻāina is not simply the setting for an event, nor is it only a metaphor for how we ought to relate with each other. Rather, ʻāina are "active participants in [our] narrative" (91). ʻĀina is "an actor who moves, changes form, and (re)members events" (92). What we see in the Hiʻiaka moʻolelo are figures that quite literally embody their ʻāina; hence, their intimacies are descriptions of their ʻāina. Like them, "our aloha for ʻāina [should be] so intimate that we aspire to be ʻāina" (97). One of the major takeaways of the book is that "the most intimate thing we can do with another person is to share our ʻāina with them" (107). This could entail a sexual intimacy but also has far-reaching implications for what it means to be human beings situated with each other in shared spaces—some spaces we are born to and others we move to and bear kuleana (responsibility) to know.

MICHAEL DAVID KAULANA ING (Kanaka) is associate professor of religious studies at Indiana University, Bloomington.

DANIELLE D. LUCERO

Pueblo Sovereignty: Indian Land and Water in New Mexico and Texas
by Malcolm Ebright and Rick Hendricks
University of Oklahoma Press, 2019

MALCOLM EBRIGHT AND RICK HENDRICKS return to the Southwest in *Pueblo Sovereignty: Indian Land and Water in New Mexico and Texas.* Their extensive archival study examines the legal history of Pueblo peoples' shifting relationships with their sovereign land and water rights during more than four hundred years of occupation by Spanish, Mexican, and U.S. colonists. *Pueblo Sovereignty* builds on the authors' 2014 book *Four Square Leagues,* arguing that the protections afforded the Pueblos by Spanish/Mexican law subsequently served as a key legal anchor that ensured the New Mexico Pueblos retained portions of their original land base under U.S. occupation.

The authors' five case studies, Pojoaque, Nambé, Tesuque, and Isleta (all in New Mexico) and Ysleta del Sur (Texas), demonstrate the challenges to and successes of Pueblo sovereignty in the Southwest. Threats of land loss and actual dispossession are detailed for each Pueblo, with the archival narrative showing how communities utilized every tool at their disposal to protect their land and water. As the authors note: "Sovereignty, in the sense of exercising the right to control one's land—what can and should happen on it—is the lens through which Pueblo Indians see the world" (x–xi).

The introduction delineates the separate legal structures employed by the Spanish, Mexican, and American governments and how these impacted the Pueblos' control over their land, water, and other nonhuman relatives. The case studies highlight the critical role that tribal attorneys and Indian agents played in the Pueblos' ability to (un)successfully defend their sovereignty. Where a Pueblo lacked suitable allies, their efforts for land and water protection often failed. However, when Pueblos combined self-advocacy with effective bureaucratic and legal counsel, they were successful in defending and asserting their sovereignty.

The first chapters focus on three neighboring Tewa Pueblos in the Española Valley. Chapter 1 describes how Pojoaque Pueblo continuously maintained their right to land even when its people were forced to reside with other nearby Native communities. Chapter 2's detailed account of land encroachment at Nambé Pueblo highlights the need for legal representation in the courts and the essential role played by government advocates. Chapter 3 recounts how Tesuque Pueblo's history of rebellion, from the 1680 Pueblo Revolt to the 1922 Tesuque Fence War, impacted the Pueblo's ability to protect its resources.

Chapter 4 is a case study of Ysleta del Sur, a Pueblo near El Paso, Texas. The authors situate the origins of Ysleta del Sur in the aftermath of the Pueblo Revolt and demonstrate how the Ysleta people weathered land encroachment *and* physical changes to the Rio Grande Valley while simultaneously asserting their status as a sovereign nation to state and federal authorities. The final case study, chapter 5, shows how the Pueblo of Isleta in New Mexico successfully protected their land and asserted their status as a sovereign nation during the nineteenth and twentieth centuries. At Isleta, strong tribal leadership (exemplified by Pablo Abeita), masterful political and legal negotiations, calculated land purchases, relentless defense against encroachment, and the skillful use of bureaucratic allies and legal counsel ensured the protection of Isleta's land, water, and culture. *Pueblo Sovereignty* concludes that the Pueblos' past assertions of legal, political, and territorial sovereignty continue to set the standard for contemporary Pueblo communities.

While *Pueblo Sovereignty* is an excellent historical analysis, as a Pueblo scholar, I found the concept of Pueblo sovereignty to be underdeveloped. The lack of comparison between the Pueblos is a weakness, especially considering how integrated Pueblo communities were in the past and continue to be today. Greater engagement with Native American and Indigenous studies literature would have helped reframe and analyze the concept of sovereignty from a uniquely Pueblo perspective. Additionally, for a book that explores complicated and overlapping spatial histories, there are only three maps! More maps would help readers better visualize and track the authors' compelling narrative of encroachment, dispossession, and Pueblo reacquisition.

Despite these critiques, Ebright and Hendricks make several important contributions. The archival research is excellent, and any researcher interested in understanding the complexity of Pueblo experiences under successive Euro-American occupations only has to explore the footnotes to find rich sources. Perhaps most importantly, the inclusion of the oft-overlooked Ysleta del Sur, whose history is intertwined with the Pueblo Revolt and Spanish reconquest, enhances and complicates our understanding of Pueblo identity on its own terms without bending to the imposed boundaries of the state of New Mexico. Overall, *Pueblo Sovereignty* provides a good introduction to the complicated history of Pueblo rights and sovereignty under Spanish, Mexican, and American rule.

DANIELLE D. LUCERO (Isleta Pueblo) is a doctoral candidate in justice and social inquiry at Arizona State University.

ROSE STREMLAU

Choctaw Confederates: The American Civil War in Indian Country
by Fay A. Yarbrough
University of North Carolina Press, 2021

THE TITLE OF THIS BOOK is misleading. This monograph, Fay A. Yarbrough's second (after her 2008 *Race and the Cherokee Nation: Sovereignty in the Nineteenth Century*) is broader in scope and makes contributions beyond an analysis of 1861–65. Yarbrough reaches back into the seventeenth century to provide context and extends the last chapter through Reconstruction to the beginnings of the allotment era of the late nineteenth century. *Choctaw Confederates* begins with a wonderful vignette contrasting a speech in which principal chief Peter Pitchlynn, who led his nation between 1864 and 1866, characterized Choctaws as "more committed to the Confederate cause than white southerners were" with the near total absence of Choctaws from present-day scholarship and public programming about the Civil War (1). The book explains the reasons for the former and corrects the latter.

Overall, Yarbrough argues that Choctaws supported the Confederate cause for three reasons: first, they hoped that advocates of states' rights would respect their sovereign right to self-government and collective ownership of their land; second, they were invested politically and economically in the institution of chattel slavery; and third, they were southern not only in the location of their homeland but in their social and economic relationships with white and Black Americans.

Yarbrough organizes the narrative into six chapters. The first is a useful summary of Choctaw social and political history through the removal era of the 1830s. The author deftly threads the continuity of Choctaw self-government through the challenges posed by settler colonialism. In the second chapter, Yarbrough emphasizes that "as the Choctaw adopted the practice of racialized slavery, they did so in a manner that preserved Choctaw identity" on the farms and plantations that lined the Red River in Indian Territory (48). Yarbrough explains that although Choctaws produced cotton for sale, their focus on corn production and stock raising demonstrated the persistence of ancestral economic practices. Like other scholars who have addressed this topic in the last decade, Yarbrough concurs that the trope of the benevolent Indian enslaver is not an accurate descriptor, and in an outstanding discussion of Choctaw practices of enslavement, she weaves together insights on Choctaw legal history, gender roles, and the development of Choctaw anti-Blackness. In the third chapter, which focuses on Choctaw diplomacy at the beginning of the war, Yarbrough provides an in-depth analysis of their political strategy in the face of Republican designs on land, concerns over the loss of federal annuities and investments, relations with Arkansas and Texas, threats posed by intruders and squatters, and concerns over the future of slavery. She concludes that Choctaws did not side with the Confederacy: "Rather than the Choctaw Nation moving toward the southern position, it was white southerners who moved toward the Native position," particularly on sovereignty and land rights (91).

Yarbrough demonstrates how to use the expansive Compiled Service Records of Confederate Choctaw veterans in her fourth chapter. Drawing insight from the review of approximately eighteen-hundred personnel records, she tracks enlistment patterns and common experiences. Choctaw men joined early in the war in response to threats to their homeland and to attain status, and the failure of the Confederate government to provision them and protect Indian Territory undermined confidence in the broader war effort. Developing ideas about gender introduced in earlier chapters, Yarbrough explains the evolution of traditional notions of masculinity and warfare as shaped by demilitarization and settler colonialism; light horse-men served as the bridge connecting these earlier ideals about manhood and power to the Civil War generation. In the last chapter, Yarbrough makes clear that the differences between Choctaw national and Confederate state responses to Reconstruction and race relations provide insight both into social relations in the Choctaw nation and U.S. national debates about race and tribal sovereignty that emerged in the postwar decades.

Yarbrough's important monograph is one of only a small number of published books on Indian Territory during the Civil War. Despite a recent turn in the field of Civil War history to recognize the importance of Native peoples in the South and West to larger military, political, and economic changes, this region remains understudied. Yarbrough's excellent monograph brings to the fore several critical and important debates in the larger scholarship of the Native South, particularly the development of racialized thinking and emergent anti-Blackness. Scholars of gender in Native North America will want to read this book for the author's innovative analysis of Choctaw masculinity. In sum, this book is a must-read for those interested in the history of the Civil War, Choctaws, the Native South, ideologies of race in Indian Country, gender roles, and tribal sovereignty.

ROSE STREMLAU is associate professor of history at Davidson College.

KERRY F. THOMPSON

Archaeologies of Indigenous Presence
edited by Tsim D. Schneider and Lee M. Panich
University Press of Florida, 2022

IN THE U.S. SETTLER-COLONIAL NARRATIVE, Native Americans exist simultaneously as romantic phantoms of a glorified past and inconvenient reminders of the ongoing brutality of colonialism. American archaeology is a narration of Native American pasts built on the material remains of those pasts by people with the social, economic, and political capital to exert scientific authority. Recent decades have seen the growth of inclusivity in American archaeology, and today a growing body of archaeologists practice Indigenous archaeologies. Significant work, however, remains to be done. The editors of and contributors to this volume "identify and counter archaeological practices that . . . continue to support narratives of cultural loss among North America's Native groups" (1). Rather than simply laying down a challenge, the volume's contributors also provide examples of the "different ways that archaeologists can center long-term Indigenous presence in the practices of fieldwork, laboratory analysis, scholarly communication, and public interpretation" (1). The book is eminently suitable for upper-level undergraduates, graduate students, and professionals and is a rich resource for courses in archaeology, archaeological theory, Indigenous perspectives in anthropology, and Indigenous archaeology.

The editors are prominent scholars in the field of Indigenous archaeologies who have worked primarily in California. Both have written extensively on myriad challenges presented by the discipline of archaeology in the development of Indigenous archaeologies. Tsim D. Schneider is a citizen of the Federated Indians of Graton Rancheria and an assistant professor of anthropology at the University of California, Santa Cruz. Lee M. Panich is an associate professor of anthropology and department chair at Santa Clara University in Santa Clara, California. The volume is situated within an established context of previous work by both Schneider and Panich and contributes to both theory building and development of practical applications in Indigenous archaeologies. The selected authors represent a wide range of geographies, but all take the colonialist nature of archaeology as the starting point for expanding conversations about what we think we know, and how we "know" Indigenous pasts.

Twelve chapters are grouped into two thematic parts. In Part I contributors untangle Western constructions of Native American authenticity, disappearance, and invisibility. Throughout Part I, authors encourage the reader to question the frames within which we perform archaeological work (Kretzler), reflect on the impact of our teaching and what we recognize as legitimate (Dickson and Steinmetz), foreground Indigenous lived experience (Laluk and Scheidecker et al.), attend to the erasure of Indigenous presence as a consequence of renaming places and archaeological sites (Trabert), and interrogate our conceptual shortcuts (Beaudoin). Part I provides the questions and concepts with which the study of Indigenous pasts can be reframed to be more inclusive of Indigenous paradigms, voices, and experiences.

Contributors to Part II offer examples of how the inclusion of various dimensions of the study of colonialism and its consequences for Indigenous people into archaeological field methods and interpretations can expand our understanding of Indigenous pasts. Authors examine the ingrained assumption that European goods denote the absence of Native presence (Hull), the information potential of nontraditional materials repurposed in traditional or adaptive ways (Russell), biographies of place (Scheiber), European goods as indicators of Indigenous trade networks (Walder), and examination of smaller and often overlooked sites to understand changing regional settlement patterns (Jordan). In the last chapter of Part II, authors Cowie and Teeman demonstrate how archaeological work on sites resulting from colonialist practices can be entangled with ongoing intergenerational trauma in Native American communities.

The volume concludes with a rich and nuanced discussion of "presence" and the ways in which the work of the different contributors to this volume expresses overlooked dimensions of Indigenous presence. The authors of the volume's final chapter illuminate the ways in which the Coast Miwok and Southern Pomo people continue to navigate forces that would erase their presence. Using ongoing and adaptive cultural resource management practices, collaborative and community based participatory research, and teaching as vehicles, the authors illustrate that we can know how our ancestors adapted to the changes wrought by colonialism if we foreground Indigenous presence.

KERRY F. THOMPSON is a citizen of the Navajo Nation, an archaeologist, and Professor of Anthropology and Associate Vice Provost for Curriculum and Assessment at Northern Arizona University.

FARINA KING

A History of Navajo Nation Education: Disentangling Our Sovereign Body
by Wendy Shelly Greyeyes
University of Arizona Press, 2022

GREYEYES PERSUASIVELY ARGUES how and why the Navajo Nation must disentangle itself from the colonizing influences of the United States, especially in its education systems. She foregrounds her book with the detailed and often obscured history of Diné education, referring to the organization and administration of schools and training on the reservation. She compiles previous histories and studies of Diné educational organizations and adds to the historical narrative by considering the issues of Diné education into the twenty-first century. Greyeyes offers a history of the Navajo Nation Department of Diné Education (DODE) that only appeared in fragments before this book.

The foreword of former assistant secretary of the interior for Indian affairs Kevin K. Washburn endorses the legitimacy of her analysis. Greyeyes shows how the sovereignty of the Navajo Nation has formed through education since the Navajo Treaty of 1868, and how colonial entanglements with the United States affect Diné sovereignty into the present. Her work differentiates between decolonization and disentanglement, while relating these movements by recognizing how Diné nationhood stemmed from a colonial context and mimicked the United States for survival.

Many Indigenous Peoples confronted similar limited choices when the U.S. encroached on their lands under the banners of the Doctrine of Discovery and imposed legal relationships, seeking to control Indigenous Peoples as "domestic dependent nations" (43). Indigenous ways of being and Euro-American governance have interwoven over the years, enabling Indigenous Peoples to survive and to resist and navigate their perpetual Peoplehood for generations.

In the case of Diné education, Greyeyes contends that sovereign entanglement must continue to unravel for Diné to reclaim their lands, knowledge, epistemology, and future as a people—which are all interconnected. However, the knots of this entanglement impede Diné self-determination and sovereignty. While Bureau of Indian Affairs (B.I.A.) and Bureau of Indian Education (B.I.E.) schools have followed assimilationist agendas, especially in the family separation policies of the Indian boarding schools, state public education presents serious challenges to the Navajo Nation and its pursuit of disentangled sovereignty.

Greyeyes delineates several state impediments to Diné education, emphasizing how states follow "the priorities of state legislatures and not the visions of the Navajo people" (133). States have vied for control over Navajo land and affairs, specifically through schools that the U.S. federal government funded in provisions such as the Johnson O'Malley Act of 1934 (JOM). Greyeyes considers how DODE seeks equality and the status of state educational agencies (SEAs) due to confrontations with different entities, especially states, since the twentieth century.

Public schools on tribal lands are part of a matrix of educational systems. State control over Diné education from the state capital and a top-down approach from beyond Diné Bikéyah (Navajo land) restrain Diné sovereign education. Greyeyes also highlights internal tensions between Diné tribal leaders, local school boards, and communities and families. Greyeyes moves toward reconciliation by seeking to understand the Diné people and the debates on Diné education both inside and outside the Navajo Nation.

The book offers a timeline of Navajo Nation education, including an appendix, but the narrative is sometimes disrupted by missing transitions between significant milestones in Diné educational history. Greyeyes provides bolded headings as signposts between the various sections, which summarize the parts; however, the pieces of the book could be interwoven more to connect dynamics such as Diné migrations to urban centers and the growth of public-school systems on the reservation. These transitions could help readers to trace the web of Diné education that Greyeyes assesses, including the federal, state public, tribally contracted and community, and denominational and private schools both in and beyond Diné Bikéyah (for example, in cities and border towns). The graphs and images from DODE data serve to illustrate such dynamics (see p. 100 for an example).

Since the American colonization of Navajo country in the nineteenth century, schools have operated as auxiliaries of the colonizing project to suppress Diné Peoplehood, either aiming to eradicate, whitewash, or control Diné. But Diné have persevered through these onslaughts on their existence and families, including their children and youth, by fighting for their self-determined and sovereign education to this day. Greyeyes paves a way for Diné to face these present and future challenges by unpacking the complexities of Diné education and school systems along with her recommendations based on thorough research, including conversations and lessons from many of the pathbreakers who preceded her.

FARINA KING, Diné historian, is the Horizon Chair of Native American Ecology and Culture and associate professor of Native American studies at the University of Oklahoma.

MEREDITH L. McCOY

Without Destroying Ourselves: A Century of Native Intellectual Activism for Higher Education
by John A. Goodwin
University of Nebraska Press, 2022

WHILE HISTORICAL SCHOLARSHIP on federal and public schools for Native students has rapidly expanded in the past thirty years, scholarship on the perspectives of Indigenous people relative to higher education has been somewhat under-explored. Stepping into this gap, John A. Goodwin's *Without Destroying Ourselves: A Century of Native Intellectual Activism for Higher Education* offers a useful overview of some of the key players in Native histories of higher education from the 1870s through the 1970s. Henry Roe Cloud, Elizabeth Bender Cloud, D'Arcy McNickle, Jack Forbes, Robert K. Thomas, Robert V. Dumont, Dillon Platero, Sam Ahkeah, and Ned Hatathli feature most prominently in this telling. Of these, Henry Roe Cloud takes center stage, with early chapters establishing him as the measuring stick against which later experiments in higher education are evaluated.

Goodwin articulates a vision of Native leaders' strategies for advancing Indigenous priorities through the mechanism of higher education, emphasizing how Native people have "search[ed] for cracks in governmental bureaucracies in which they could plant the seeds of their own Indigenous agendas" (2). In doing so, he nuances some familiar stories and demonstrates continuities in Indigenous thinking about possibilities for higher education. Goodwin's analysis points to persistent challenges, including funding and conflicting visions for the "how" of implementing Indigenous forms of higher education. His descriptions of how Native leaders in the past have navigated these challenges may allow the reader to consider the benefits and challenges of specific interventions with ramifications for the present. To support this reflection, the book concludes with a brief set of considerations for policy, funding, and practice moving into the future.

As an intellectual history, *Without Destroying Ourselves* focuses primarily on the perspectives and visions of prominent Native leaders. Goodwin's narrative focuses on "moments of ambiguity and struggle" as he centers their "creativity to employ institutional frameworks compatible with and recognizable to the world of settler colonialism" while "protecting and advancing

Native-driven goals" (5). He argues that Native leaders in higher education have demonstrated a particular adaptability in strategy and messaging to accomplish these efforts. To support this argument, Goodwin draws upon their own materials, including diaries, speeches, letters, and oral histories, among others. Of the secondary literature he engages, Renya Ramirez's interpretation of the efforts of Henry and Elizabeth Cloud notably informs Goodwin's analysis.

Goodwin notes the potential drawbacks of centering "a particular chorus of leading voices," as the emphasis on individuals can at times obscure collective efforts (186). Even so, scholars seeking information on the American Indian Institute and Haskell (particularly relative to Henry Roe Cloud and, to a lesser extent, Elizabeth Bender Cloud) will find the first part of the book to be of aid. The book's exploration of community-wide initiatives is stronger in the second half of the book, particularly in Goodwin's discussions of Navajo Community College and Deganawidah-Quetzalcoatl University. The final chapter on tribal colleges focuses particularly on the origins of Turtle Mountain Community College, Sinte Gleska University, Sitting Bull College, and Oglala Lakota College. Of these experiments, Goodwin is perhaps most critical of Jack Forbes and the work of D-Q University, wondering whether Forbes was "so emotionally invested in his own effort" that he cast himself as "particularly innovative" at the cost of acknowledging the legacies of previous activism.

While many of the cast of the book are familiar, other familiar stories are surprisingly absent. Bacone College, for example, founded in 1880, does not appear in the book, nor does the University of North Carolina at Pembroke, founded as Croatan Normal School in 1887. Both of these stories would have usefully expanded Goodwin's discussion of early issues facing Indigenous leaders in higher education. Additionally, some engagement with the 1994 Tribal Land-Grant Colleges and Universities Program would have pointed us toward Goodwin's understanding of more recent developments for tribal colleges.

Despite these omissions, the book provides a helpful overview of the history of Native leaders' "enthusiastic, tenacious, and truly inventive" activism for higher education in the face of colonial control (15). This book will likely be most useful to those scholars interested in the core thinkers highlighted in the book, as well as to those looking to understand rhetorical and philosophical trends in activism for Native higher education over time.

MEREDITH L. McCOY (Turtle Mountain Band of Chippewa descent) is assistant professor of American studies and history at Carleton College.

MARINA TYQUIENGCO

Placental Politics: CHamoru Women, White Womanhood,
  and Indigeneity under U.S. Colonialism in Guam
by Christine Taitano DeLisle
University of North Carolina Press, 2022

CHAMORU HISTORIAN CHRISTINE TAITANO DELISLE'S *Placental Politics: CHamoru Women, White Womanhood, and Indigeneity under U.S. Colonialism in Guam* is a timely and expertly researched examination of the roles and relationships of *famalao'an* CHamoru (CHamoru women) and white American women in the history of Guåhan (Guam) in the period of American colonization from 1898 to today. DeLisle provides a novel Indigenous CHamoru feminist approach to the period on Guåhan, which has resonances more broadly in Micronesia and the U.S. colonized Pacific.

DeLisle defines placental politics as "women enacting and employing knowledge and sacred practices, like the burying of the ga'chong i påtgon—I am specifically marking the idea of distinctly Native and gendered forms of being modern" (6). The *ga'chong i påtgon* (friend of the child) is the CHamoru word for the placenta; burying it near the home is a CHamoru practice to ensure a healthy and rooted child. This practice serves as a basis for placental politics, a theoretical framework that centers famalao'an CHamoru and their practices of care for community, family, and environment. Drawing on and acknowledging the work of previous generations of CHamoru and BIPOC scholars, such as Laura Marie Torres Souder and Teresia Teaiwa, DeLisle weaves together wide-ranging sources seamlessly.

The first chapter focuses on "i CHe'cho i pattera," or the work of *pattera* (midwives) in homes and hospitals, using historical accounts and several interviews with patteras, using the term "Tan" to indicate *respetu* (or respect) for her female elders. She emphasizes the role that CHamoru women played in U.S. colonial efforts. Training nurses, beginning in 1907 with the establishment of the first nursing school on Guåhan, was meant in part to displace the established patteras and thus diminish the influence of older CHamoru women. The interviews demonstrate how the pattera role was a financial opportunity for women, which required negotiations between helping other women and their own domestic caregiving opportunities. Significantly, pattera often incorporated medical training they received with kostumbren CHamoru, referring to CHamoru customs, and inafa'maolek, an organizing principle of society meaning to do good for the community, thus integrating new knowledge into existing cultural understandings.

The next two chapters highlight white American women significant to the history of Guåhan. DeLisle infuses these chapters with nuance, acknowledging Susan Dyer's and Helen Paul's American paternalism and, at times, earnest desire to help and support the CHamoru people. DeLisle examines Susan Dyer, the wife of American Naval Governor George Dyer, mainly in the context of new womanhood, an early twentieth-century conception of more independent and capable women. Dyer's efforts to found the Susan Dyer Women's Hospital and organize leisure activities for navy officers exemplify her new woman status. DeLisle emphasizes the whiteness and imperialism inherent in Dyer's pursuits, while also showing the affection that some CHamoru women felt for her, such as the hospital's lay matron Tan Rosa Perez, who kept the hospital running after Dyer left the island. The chapter on Helen Paul, the well-educated, artistic wife of Lieutenant Commander Carroll Paul, draws on critical readings of ethnographic photography to discuss Helen Paul's photography of CHamoru people and land. It starts with a reference to Paul's student and later CHamoru political leader, Agueda Iglesias Johnston, who credits Paul with the design of the Guåhan flag. It reveals a major twist in the flag's history in its final pages, revealing that a then young CHamoru man Francisco Feja, or Tun Kiko Feja, designed the Guåhan seal that makes up most of the flag.

Johnston's role in acknowledging Paul gestures to Johnston's own complexity as a historical figure. DeLisle argues, "American education in the first half of the twentieth century offered nonelite CHamorus and women opportunities for social mobility" (167). Delisle succeeds in her aim to complicate understandings of Agueda Iglesias Johnston, who began as a star student, then teacher and principal—eventually becoming an important CHamoru political leader. DeLisle examines Johnston's public speeches and unpublished writings to contend that Johnston's deep American patriotism and CHamoru values were not as at odds as the contemporary reader might expect. She demonstrates Johnston's expression of placental politics with her discussion on Johnston's founding of an organization for *manåmko'*, (or Elders), an effort rooted in the CHamoru value of respetu for manåmko'.

Placental Politics is a timely book for a multitude of audiences that will inspire more CHamorus and other Indigenous scholars to critically engage with famalao'an-centered histories.

MARINA TYQUIENGCO (CHamoru) is associate curator of Native American Art, Museum of Fine Arts, Boston.

JULIANNE NEWMARK

*Assembled for Use: Indigenous Compilation and the Archives
of Early American Literatures*
by Kelly Wisecup
Yale University Press, 2021

AT THE CENTER of Kelly Wisecup's *Assembled for Use* lie crucial questions concerning "users" and "readers" of Indigenous compositions from (primarily) the eighteenth and nineteenth centuries, compositions or works that we might, in fact, call Indigenous multimodal communications. Wisecup asks us, in her introduction, to consider "what we might learn by *reading* texts long assumed to both lack readers and elicit *use* rather than reading" (emphasis added, 9). I have italicized the terms "reading" and "use" in this crucial sentence because doing so foregrounds central themes that resonate throughout Wisecup's excellent volume. When we, as Indigenous literary and cultural studies scholars, engage with archival materials, are we perceptive to structural and rhetorical encodings within these materials? Wisecup asks that we take a critical stance both toward archives themselves and toward long-held assumptions concerning the genres of material composition and how "use-value" was/is assigned to certain kinds of creations, whereas what we might call "readerly value" was/is assigned to other kinds of creations.

Over her book's 210 pages, Wisecup asks her readers to work toward destabilizing—following the lead of Indigenous archives and materials themselves—our conceptions of "texts" and to engage, instead, with rich Indigenous assemblages, such as compositions that defy the formal conventions of, for example, an accounting ledger, or that exist as scrapbooks comprising clippings, or that vibrate across the words used in the recording on paper of a recipe or traditional healing practice. Across five chapters and four shorter "Interludes," Wisecup examines how Indigenous composers (we might call them "compilers," "authors," or "resistance" rhetoricians) repurpose colonial forms to give them new meaning within and beyond Indigenous communities.

Wisecup's five long-form chapters proceed in a recognizable, or perhaps "traditional," academic mode; the chapters exist as primarily textual arguments supported by appropriately cited images, figures, and short and long primary text citations. We would expect this form from a monograph published by a major university press. On a metatextual level, however, Wisecup asks us to think *beyond* the formal parameters of her document (and to follow her by working *beyond*) through her interweaving of stories—of the authors whose works she discusses as well as stories of her own; of her experience as a teacher, grant collaborator, non-Native community-engaged scholar; and archival researcher.

In her longer chapters Wisecup focuses on writers such as Samson Occom and Simon Pokagon; in her shorter, interchapter "Interludes," samples of her foci include William Apess, E. Pauline Johnson, and Carlos Montezuma. Wisecup is insistent upon a community lens, destabilizing authorial centrality by revealing how these writers represented cultural and familial geographies and tribal and pan-tribal networks. Embracing this commitment to multivocality, Wisecup asks us to be attentive to much more than words on pages. The material texts she studies are not flat, locked into a particular historical time (she writes consistently of the afterlives of Indigenous compilations) and were often not accessible only at their time of creation to the visual, "readerly" senses; many of the works she studies are, in fact, richly dimensional vis-à-vis the sensorium (210). Examples of this are the tactile nature of paste in a scrapbook (such as Montezuma's) or of needles and stitching as used in bookmaking (such as in Charlotte Johnston's poetry albums).

Wisecup writes in her epilogue, "The making, uses for, and circulations of Indigenous compilations expand our understandings of the hands that made early Native literatures, allowing us to recognize the relations among people already familiar in literary histories and those absent from such narratives but significant as requestors of healing, senders and readers of letters, singers of hymns, sewers of makaks, speakers of dialogues in an Indigenous language, and tellers of histories" (206). Wisecup's *Assembled for Use* is a text that one can read and use again and again, perhaps with chapters selected for a graduate seminar, phrases and passages cited in scholarly works of others, methodologies adopted and expanded by authors engaged in archival projects in Indigenous studies. Above all, Wisecup is explicit about one of her book's central messages: that "Indigenous compilations' afterlives call for research methodologies that acknowledge, build on, and sit in relation to compilations' capacious archives, textual forms and circulations, their seemingly quotidian uses, and the critical perspectives they foster" (210). Wisecup effectively asks us all to *do more* as Indigenous studies scholars and archival researchers to destabilize colonial genre conventions and instead foreground networked anticolonial compilations—just as the authors she discusses did for so long.

JULIANNE NEWMARK is director of the Technical and Professional Communication Program in English at the University of New Mexico.

BONNIE ETHERINGTON

Navigating CHamoru Poetry: Indigeneity, Aesthetics, and Decolonization
by Craig Santos Perez
The University of Arizona Press, 2021

CRAIG SANTOS PEREZ PROVIDES the first full-length examination of contemporary CHamoru poetry in this monograph: a necessary endeavor, as imperialism has long constrained the visibility of Micronesian literatures. CHamoru refers to the Indigenous Peoples of Guåhan (Guam) and the Northern Mariana Islands. Perez's poetic works introduced me to the expansiveness of CHamoru literatures, via his *from unincorporated territory* series (2008–2023) and *Habitat Threshold* (2020). These works embody and articulate an intertextual navigation of Guåhan (Guam), CHamoru diaspora, and Guåhan's Oceanic and global relations. Navigation forms the dominant structure of Perez's scholarly book, which deftly delineates the critical presence of CHamoru literature in Oceania as well as further afield and argues that the work of CHamoru poetry is bound up in the work of decolonization.

Perez offers his book as an act of "chenchule'," a CHamoru "complex and intimate system of social reciprocity, mutual aid, and relational gift-giving" (xvii). In other words, this book acts as a gift to Perez's readers as it establishes how CHamoru literature is dynamic and agential, that contemporary CHamoru literature is an ongoing expression of CHamoru literary and artistic Indigenous articulations, and that such literature is a vital part of decolonial activism in the face of Spanish, Japanese, and U.S. colonialism.

Two crucial points underpin Perez's navigation of CHamoru poetry, which in his interpretation "encompass[es] written texts, orature, and contemporary 'spoken word'" (26). First, he rejects what he calls "*fatal impact literary theory*" (28, original emphasis). He asserts that CHamoru literature is still alive and well, shaped by contextual and cultural pressures and transformations and also an integral and ongoing part of CHamoru past, present, and future. Secondly, Perez articulates a "Pacific literary methodology" of "wayreading" (31). Taking cues from scholars including Vicente Diaz, who describes how navigation offers "a critical framework through which to envision and interpret the mobile complexities of Native Pacific cultures and identities," Perez approaches CHamoru literary texts through the lens of Indigenous Pacific and Native American literary contexts and epistemologies, expressing that "Native cultures *move* the way islands move," and therefore modes of interpretating Indigenous texts must also acknowledge those texts' dynamic mobility and persistence (31—32, original emphasis).

While Perez's book focuses specifically on poetic works published since 1990, the range of his text is vast, reinforcing the impact and reach of CHamoru literatures and their authors historically as well as more recently, including CHamoru authors who live in CHamoru spaces as well as those who live in diaspora. His chapters' organization echoes practices of navigation: starting with landfall, and acknowledging the entanglement of land and sea, then attending to connections between CHamoru architectural and storytelling forms. Then Perez moves beyond the reef, drawing on the image of the outrigger canoe as he voyages through issues of diaspora and Indigeneity, arguing that poetry can act as a locative source, a "map" (130). Returning (literarily speaking) to Guåhan, Perez foregrounds CHamoru oral literature through the kåntan chamorrita chanting form, and its contemporary manifestations in spoken word and intertextually driven written poems: these poems "weave a community of voices" that embody and express diverse collaborations as well as claim a literary heritage that reinvigorates traditions displaced by colonialism (132). Perez concludes his monograph by extending this concept of a community of CHamoru voices, reiterating that literature offers coordinates for resurgent decolonial futures.

The many strengths of this book lie in Perez's precise descriptions and definitions of its literary methodology and its rich scope, which means that the book doubles as a critical historical text as well as an effective and accessible literary resource. This resource offers insight to scholars well beyond those who are solely interested in CHamoru literatures. The book has implications for those invested in world literature studies, transoceanic and Pacific studies more broadly, Indigenous studies, and anyone grappling with studies in aesthetics and expressions of colonialism, decolonization, self-determination, and sovereignty. The book's illustrations help locate readers in place and the specifics of place. Characteristic of both Perez's poetics and his rigorous academic essays, the monograph is linguistically dexterous and also lucid. It is a chenchule' that offers itself as a critical document for CHamoru readers, while being valuable to non-CHamoru readers with diverse areas of interest.

This monograph is a gift indeed, a model of writing a scholarly work in a reciprocal, relational manner, a gift that emphatically elucidates how CHamoru literature has always mattered and continues to matter.

BONNIE ETHERINGTON is a lecturer in literary and creative communication at Te Herenga Waka—Victoria University of Wellington.

VALERIE LAMBERT

Power Balance, Increasing Leverage in Negotiations with
*   Federal and State Governments: Lessons Learned from*
*   the Native American Experience*
by Steven J. Haberfeld
University of Oklahoma Press, 2022

FOR MORE THAN TWO HUNDRED YEARS, nation-to-nation relationships between Native Nations and the U.S. federal government have been fascinating, complex, and enigmatic. However, partly because these relationships are characterized by power asymmetries and are so often rife with chicanery, they have often been vexing for tribes, who spend much time and effort trying to prevent their relations with the settler state from further upending their tribal goals and aspirations.

In this highly readable and practical book, dispute-resolution specialist Steven J. Haberfeld draws upon his extensive training and half-century of experience in federal-tribal negotiations to try to help level the playing field for tribes. Haberfeld provides a wealth of knowledge, skills, and strategies to improve the chances that tribes will emerge from their diplomatic relations with federal agencies with better outcomes.

As cofounder and former executive director of the Indian Dispute Resolution Service, Inc., an organization that has long helped tribes successfully negotiate federal-tribal conflicts, the author provides valuable firsthand descriptions of many of the federal-tribal negotiations in which he was involved. These stories are among the strongest parts of the book, as Haberfeld's detailed accounts and insightful analyses illuminate numerous aspects of the high-level, international diplomatic encounters in which tribes participate. Chapter 7, arguably the book's most important chapter, tells the riveting story of the Timbisha Shoshone Tribe's successful, hard-fought efforts from 1995–98 to partially restore its land base. It is fascinating that as many as four federal agencies joined the Tribe and Haberfeld at the negotiating table: the National Park Service, the Bureau of Land Management, the Bureau of Reclamation, and the Bureau of Indian Affairs. Haberfeld drives home the complexities of the problems and issues tribes face, how intense federal-tribal diplomacy can be, and how difficult it can be simply to address (much less solve) the twenty-first-century challenges of American Indian and Alaska Native tribes.

Although almost anyone with an interest in Indigenous Peoples will find much that is valuable in this book, to Haberfeld's credit his primary audience is Native Nations, especially poorer tribes with limited histories of working with federal agencies. Haberfeld provides valuable advice in clear, accessible prose. Throughout the text, he is thoughtful and sensitive. He shows a keen appreciation of the traumas, injustices, and distinct perspectives that characterize our peoples, and his advice takes into account the reality that federal officials are often unfair, underhanded, and disrespectful to tribes.

In an early chapter, Haberfeld discusses the benefits of attending to "structure" prior to negotiations. He advises, for example, that tribal negotiation teams make time for informal interactions with the members of federal teams, develop written agreements on rules of conduct (here he provides examples of "weak language" to be avoided), and utilize tips for identifying clear objectives and strategies.

Some tribes will find at least some of Haberfeld's advice to be counterintuitive. For example, he suggests that instead of populating the tribal negotiation team with lawyers and elected or appointed tribal leaders—the norm for tribes engaging in federal-tribal negotiations—tribal leaders might appoint others: tribal citizens who are not politicians, who have different skill sets from tribal lawyers, and who represent different constituencies or interests within the tribe. The resulting diversity on the tribal team—which, he adds, is optimally five to seven persons—will allow the team to consider a fuller range of tribal views, confront potential objections to an agreement prior to its release to the tribal citizenry, and possibly achieve an agreement that more fully meets tribal goals and objectives.

Haberfeld also offers useful suggestions for navigating problems as serious as complete negotiation impasses. He advises tribes to exercise their right to meet with federal leaders higher up in the agency's hierarchy, mine the federal agency or agencies for bureaucrats who might be more sensitive to tribes, form alliances with other tribes and non-Indigenous groups, carefully craft a public narrative, and in other ways appeal to the public. This recommended book closes with appendices that offer skill-building exercises for tribes to more effectively leverage federal-tribal relations in their ongoing quest to fulfill tribal goals and objectives.

VALERIE LAMBERT (enrolled citizen, Choctaw Nation) is professor of anthropology at the University of North Carolina at Chapel Hill.

KHAL SCHNEIDER

We Are Not Animals: Indigenous Politics of Survival, Rebellion,
*   and Reconstitution in Nineteenth-Century California*
by Martin Rizzo-Martinez
University of Nebraska Press, 2022

THE TITLE OF MARTIN RIZZO-MARTINEZ'S BOOK comes from an 1812 exhortation by the Ohlone man Lino to his people to kill Mission Santa Cruz's priest Andrès Quintana. Lino was Quintana's personal assistant, and he gained firsthand perspective on the padre's sadism and the intractable problem of colonization. The Ohlone could not "run [Quintana] off"—he would return—or "take him before a judge"—the law was on his side (18, 117). Lino argued that his people were humans with souls and capable of reason, not to be goaded, whipped, and yoked like the mission herds they tended. In Rizzo-Martinez's interpretation of Lino's words (via the memory of descendant Lorenzo Asisara), Quintana died for his hypocrisy; he "overstepped his boundaries and failed to follow his own preachings" (18). Lino's assertion "we are not animals," then, was neither a "rejection of Catholicism nor an anticolonial rebellion" (121). Mission Santa Cruz's Ohlone killed the priest, but they did not overthrow Spanish colonialism. After an interlude of independence, the Spanish returned, and Indigenous Peoples continued to address immediate threats through tested methods of community action, while adapting to the colonial political order that overlaid their homelands.

Rizzo-Martinez's key theme of "Indigenous politics" is broad—it includes diverse acts of "survival, resistance, rebellion, and perseverance"—but his approach pays off in precise insights into the ways Native people undertook concerted and collective community action within the precincts of Spanish power (3). He uses the records of the Quintana assassination, for example, to discern "movement and interconnection" between mission and nonmission communities (125). The killing was an important event in the political history of Spanish colonization, but Rizzo-Martinez uses it as a lens to show that the basis of Native political action, kinship, had its own dynamics that operated independently of Spanish authority. He is appropriately attentive to the political nuances within and among the Indigenous communities that built, endured, and resisted the missions. He differentiates the positions and motivations of Awaswas and Mutsun (both Ohlone-speaking) peoples and Yokuts speakers who began to enter the missions in the 1810s and soon outnumbered Ohlone speakers. Two communities formed along linguistic lines, but a third formed from intermarriage, consisting mainly of Yokuts women and Ohlone men. Some attained "social and political status and power by working closely with Spanish or Mexican soldiers and missionaries to track down fugitives" (143). At the same time, most of the fugitives from the mission were Yokuts. Importantly, the story continues through the period of secularization and into American statehood—reorienting readers to a longer duration of Native political history within colonialism that preceded and outlasted the missions. After secularization, former mission Indians established three "Indigenous rancherias" based on extended kinship networks (185). They received plots of land and animals in 1839, although most were unable to use the colonial bureaucracy to secure the land for long, and non-Native grantees appropriated most of the land along with Native labor. Native communities survived, but American rule exacerbated the material legacies of colonization: landlessness, poverty, vulnerability to violence, and disfranchisement.

Rizzo-Martinez confines his study to Mission Santa Cruz, but his story has broader relevance. The history of this "Mission of Padre Killers" makes it a likely place to understand how Native people checked the colonial ambitions of the Spanish (109). Santa Cruz also retained excellent chancery records, which Rizzo-Martinez argues may be read as an "Indigenous archive" (4). Read with the benefit of oral histories and "archaeology, anthropology, ecology, and psychology," the "database" of "thousands of records relating to Indigenous people from Santa Cruz and neighboring communities" allows him "to follow patterns of movement, kinship, and tribal relations," tell "more complete and nuanced" family histories, and remap the mission as "a central place of Indigenous production, ingenuity, and politics" within a wider landscape of Indigenous polities (4, 5, 9, 13). His effort to identify Native voices and motives in colonial sources is not only fitting for a book on the history of Native people but also imperative for understanding a colonial institution where Native people were always in the majority. Beyond its contributions to mission historiography, in its emphasis on internally dynamic and adaptive Native politics, Rizzo-Martinez's work bridges the era of Spanish colonization with the later nineteenth century and offers a useful interpretive model for future scholarship on Native survival into the twentieth century.

KHAL SCHNEIDER is associate professor of history at Sacramento State University.

RILEY YESNO

*I Will Live for Both of Us: A History of Colonialism, Uranium Mining,
   and Inuit Resistance*
by Joan Scottie, Warren Bernauer, and Jack Hicks
University of Manitoba Press, 2022

IT IS ALWAYS INVIGORATING to find a book about Indigenous relationships with resource extraction that is firmly grounded in love and expertise gained through lived experience—*I Will Live for Both of Us* is such a book. The story is told from the first-person perspective of Joan Scottie, an Inuk woman and longtime community leader/activist, whose writing was aided by two non-Inuk researchers, Warren Bernauer and Jack Hicks. The three authors employ stories from Scottie's experiences of decades of frontline activism to provide readers with a thorough and accessible overview of community perspectives on mining in the Arctic and its relationship to settler colonialism.

Scottie begins by retelling events and lessons from her own life and that of her family in Baker Lake, Nunavut, Canada. This section is emotionally moving and helpful in adding depth to later chapters. Indeed, Scottie's stories offer readers a glimpse into Inuit ways of life and their worldviews. As the book progresses, this glimpse makes especially clear how colonial industry and governments were able to mobilize their knowledge of Inuit worldviews to try to exploit communities for mineral resources.

The remaining chapters focus on the decades of various consultation and negotiation processes between Inuit and the uranium industry/government. A particular focus is given to the tactics communities used to organize and oppose proponents of mining. Readers should anticipate that these later sections include many necessary but occasionally overwhelming details about the dozens of organizations and actors involved in the processes. In saying this, it is important to understand that this complexity is part of a lesson from the text. Put simply: if the multiple moving parts the authors traverse feel like a lot to keep track of for readers, even when laid out so plainly, one can imagine how much labor and overall diligence it took for Scottie and other Inuit leaders to keep on top of the developments over the decades. The chapters constitute a testament to the rigor and multifaceted nature of their community advocacy.

Overall, the authors have impressively and effectively included an extensive record of events, including dozens of actors over several decades. The authors' summarization skills are superb as are Scottie's recall and ability to interject feelings and memories associated with the numerous meetings and events discussed in the book. The approach keeps the reader grounded in the narrative while also providing plentiful background research.

The text offers many valuable insights into community-led consultation, the importance of grassroots Indigenous activism, and the need to protect the rights of the land, animals, and people in the Far North. The main argument addresses how ongoing efforts to mine uranium in the Arctic are a continuation of settler colonialism—with especially devastating impacts on Inuit women. The argument is solidly supported by overviews of obvious violations of inherent Inuit rights, in addition to comparisons between the contemporary moment and some of Scottie's earliest memories about the onset of colonialism in the Arctic. The parallels in colonial objectives and Inuit resistance between these two times are insightful and indisputable.

An interrelated secondary argument concerns how the current territorial government of Nunavut, often regarded as a form of Indigenous self-government by some scholars, is another form of colonial government operated by a greater number of Indigenous representatives. This argument may be particularly beneficial to those interested in Arctic governance and leaves room for more significant discussion about how Indigenous people define and operationalize self-government, and the limits of representation.

One critique to note: other than in the opening chapter (and a brief mention near the end of the book), little in-depth attention is paid to how mining has specifically impacted Inuit women. This lack of investigation was unexpected, given how this impact was stated as an objective at the outset of the text. I believe a more significant discussion in this area would have benefitted the main argument.

I Will Live for Both of Us is exemplary in balancing in-depth research and personal narrative to produce a consistently critical and intimate look at the topic. The text is altogether generous, thorough, and timely. This new work should be considered essential reading for anyone interested in the negative impacts of mining, Arctic governance, or the relationship between colonialism and resource extraction.

RILEY YESNO (Anishinaabe from Eabametoong First Nation) is a graduate student in the Department of Political Science at the University of Toronto.

JOHN N. LOW

Earthworks Rising: Mound Building in Native Literature and Arts
by Chadwick Allen
University of Minnesota Press, 2022

SINCE THEIR ARRIVAL in what is now the United States, people of European descent including settlers, journalists, politicians, anthropologists, archaeologists, historians, biographers, travelers, fiction writers, poets, and filmmakers, among others, have been telling the stories of Indigenous Peoples. Yet Native peoples were never silent. We told our stories too, using platforms such as oral histories and storytelling, song and dance, sand painting, winter counts, birch bark scrolls, weaving, pottery, beadwork, petroglyphs and pictographs, as well as monumental architecture, designated as "mounds" by settler colonists.

In his latest book, Chadwick Allen (Chickasaw ancestry), professor of English at the University of Washington, takes us along on his journey of discovery regarding these "mounds." Along the way, Allen shares insights into his own experiences and research, as well as the ways in which Native peoples of the twentieth and twenty-first centuries have reengaged with the "mounds" through, art, literature, and performance. He focuses not only on the sites themselves but also on Native peoples who connect their own creative work and energies to the "mounds." Included are Native artists and intellectuals LeAnne Howe, Allyssa Hinton, Allison Hedge Coke, Monique Mojica, Phillip Carroll Morgan, and N. Scott Momaday.

From the outset, Allen articulates the motivation behind his book: to assure the inclusion of Indigenous experiences into the literary classroom. His methodology is appropriately Indigenous and decolonizing—centered in community, conversations, debates, and performance. The book fills a glaring gap in the literature, as much is written and being written from historical and archaeological perspectives about the "mounds"; however, there is a dearth of such scholarship that connects contemporary and ancestral Indigenous Peoples and their creative work to these important places.

Contemporary Indigenous artists, writers, actors, and more continue to embrace these "mounds" not as a relic of the past, or as simply some legacy left to us by the ancestors. Rather, as Allen documents, these places are essential elements or ingredients of the creativity and creations of some Indigenous Peoples to this day. The author flips the notion that these are outdoor mummifications of a long-forgotten past. Rather, he writes of how these places of monumental architectural grandeur were (and are) places of collection and transmission of knowledge. These are places that two thousand years ago foreshadowed the world's current interest in STEAM— science, technology, engineering, art, and mathematics. Allen writes that the "mounds" represent:

> Indigenous sign making and encoding that employ "geometric regularity" and "geometric harmony" in order to record natural, human, and of course, cosmic relationships with remarkably durable structures. (19)

Allen concludes that these ancestral structures should be viewed as a form of writing with their own systems of meaning making, markers, knowledge preservation, and transmission.

The book is organized into three broad sections that correspond to many Indigenous understandings of the above, below, and surface worlds, an organization often reflected in the architecture of the "mounds" themselves. Part I is "Effigies, Crossing Worlds, Above and Below"; Part II is "Platforms // Networking Systems // Cardinal Directions"; and Part III is "Burials // Gathering Generations // Center." Each part/section is further separated into chapters that contribute to the overall through line that "mounds" are not part of a mysterious, enigmatic past but rather important places of knowledge, wisdom, and inspiration that continue to connect Indigenous Peoples to these sites and to each other.

Allen concludes with "Earthworks Uprising," an exciting chapter emphasizing that "mounds" continue to be built in Indian country across the United States and represent not only the past but our future as Indigenous Peoples. The First American Museum (FAM) near Oklahoma City is cited as an example of how Native peoples continue to use their energies to create spaces of meaning and understanding through materiality, context, alignment, and the extension of tradition.

The audience for this book is primarily college students and other scholars in the arts. It is a fun and in-depth read for those willing to commit enough time to absorbing and reflecting on the nearly four hundred pages of excellent information and insight. The book is clear, well-written, entertaining, and informative. It will be valuable to those interested in and/or teaching American Indian and Indigenous studies, literature, or any other aspect of representation, power, decolonization, art, memory, and identity.

JOHN N. LOW, J.D., Ph.D. (Pokagon Band of Potawatomi Indians) is associate professor in the Department of Comparative Studies and director of the Newark Earthworks Center at the Ohio State University, Newark.

LINDA LEGARDE GROVER

Our Bearings
by Molly McGlennen
University of Arizona Press, 2020

"I WONDER: *What would a poetic mapping of Indigenous urban space look, sound, and feel like?"* Molly McGlennen asks in her introduction to this intriguing and gorgeous collection: a poetic story portrait of several generations of her extended family and community in Minneapolis, Minnesota.

In a layering of contemporary urban Native spirit and thought over landmarks and histories (both recent and those of the distant past), McGlennen writes from the perspective of an Ojibwe/Anishinaabe woman who has grown up on traditionally Dakota lands. She examines stories and reactions among the Dakota and many other tribes, Ojibwe among them, that live in Minneapolis and the greater Twin Cities area. Points of reference—physical and experiential, past and present—loosely tether stories of the people who relocated to that place by way of federal relocation programs, job opportunities, or to be with their families who had moved to "the Cities," in that ongoing migration from reservation to urban areas. "I'm told we have circled this city for a very long time," she writes in "Development II," her story poem about her family's movement within the city west, north, south, and again west. "The directions we know to be constant with who we are. Right here. Always there."

The number four is present and significant in Anishinaabe (I use the term in its broadest sense) teachings, and *Our Bearings*, which is grounded in that worldview, is organized into four sections: "EARTH," "AIR," "WATER," and "FIRE." Many of the poems, grouped into fours, reinforce those traditions. Early in the first section, "EARTH," the series of four footbridge poems provides a physical setting with poetic interpretations of the natural and manmade terrain of Minneapolis. These are followed by the four bearings poems about McGlennen's family history and their lives in that Indigenous urban setting. This history establishes the efforts her family has made over generations to keep their bearings, a sense of rightful place, and a balanced existence in an urban setting.

"Carousel II" is a profoundly touching and riveting poem, recounting visits by the poet and her father to the Minnesota Historical Society archives, where they read letters and records of McGlennen's great-grandfather's and little sisters' lives at the orphanage in Owatonna after their mother died. Caught in the rhythm of the repeating refrain of "over and over," a father and daughter search through boxes of documents "trying to comprehend cruelty" in the handwritten letters of relatives whose pleas for help or simply news of their children were ignored or returned.

There is a deeply thoughtful quality to every piece in this collection, whether McGlennen is describing an interaction between herself and a landmark or an encounter with histories and unseen futures of those places. Against the backdrop of the past, the ever-changing present, and the fog that obscures a future about which we can only guess, is the impermanence of what is made by mankind and the permanence and solidity of the earth itself. After all our searching and wonderment—and after our endeavor to build, control, and fool ourselves that we, not Gichi-Manidoo, are doing the creating—what if, McGlennen asks (quoting Ojibwe scholar Heidi Kiiwetinepinesiik Stark), "law and policy is just another creation story along the way?"

We are reminded in the "Remains" poems that we are mortal. The last poem's final lines, "She wants to give these words all away to that person. Again and again. And with them, trace and retrace the designs embossed in her memories, the fibers that became the maps of home" are poignant and humbling in their finality and ordinariness, yet comforting: our lives will end, but the natural world is more powerful than anything built upon it— roads, bridges, cities—and its state will ultimately prevail, as will the spirit of Indigenous people, which is our collective immortality.

LINDA LEGARDE GROVER, member of the Bois Forte Band of Ojibwe, is professor emerita of American Indian studies, University of Minnesota Duluth.

NICOLAS G. ROSENTHAL

Indian Cities: Histories of Indigenous Urbanization
edited by Kent Blansett, Cathleen D. Cahill, and Andrew Needham
University of Oklahoma Press, 2022

THE TWELVE ESSAYS in this collection "highlight the work of Indigenous peoples in shaping urban places and the role that urban spaces play in shaping Indigenous communities and politics" (2). While they do not make a "methodological intervention," as the editors claim—this was done by the first wave of historical scholarship on Indigenous Peoples and urban areas, discussed at length in the introduction—they do offer "multiple perspectives on urban Indigeneity and experiences of city life across centuries" (2) and thereby make critical contributions to understanding the history of Indigenous Peoples and cities. Drawing upon recent theoretical frameworks, the essays also provide new language for conceptualizing urban Indigeneity within broader anticolonial narratives featuring Indigenous people as dynamic actors.

Collectively, the authors work from the premise that settler colonialism has depended on the "deurbanization" of Indigenous people, including both Indigenous dispossession central to the development of metropolitan regions and "narratives of dislocation" that proclaim Indigeneity antithetical to urban areas. Indigenous survivance, in contrast, has included persistence within growing urban centers, active Indigenizing of urban spaces, and histories that affirm urban Indigeneity. That tension is present in the volume's first section, "Remaking Urban Spaces in Early America," featuring Nathaniel Holly's essay on Cherokee laborers' regular use of seventeenth century Charlestown. Decentering the Anglo-Indigenous frontier, it argues the colonial British capital was "just another urban place in a world characterized by urban places," (26) where ordinary Cherokees challenged colonists seeking to exploit Indigenous labor. Similar themes of Indigenous presence run through Daniel H. Usner's contribution on early New Orleans, addressing how local Indigenous people "regularly turned the formative colonial town into their own ritual space" (51) through performances associated with diplomacy and trade, thus forging a civic culture used to negotiate relationships with French officials.

Part Two, "Imperial Cities and Dispossession in the Nineteenth Century," emphasizes that settler colonialism and urbanization were closely linked during a period of rapid industrialization. This includes Ari Kelman's essay on how the urbanization of Minnesota facilitated violence against Indigenous populations, culminating with the 1862 execution of thirty-eight Dakota men in Makato; Mishuana R. Goeman's piece exploring the ways settler fictions and urban electrification functioned to dispossess Native people and create Niagara Falls as a tourist site reinforcing heteronormative gender relations; C. Joseph Genetin-Pilawa's examination of how the cultural landscape of Washington, D.C. depicted the specter of Indigenous violence while narrating its pacification; and Maurice Crandall's history of Yavapai-Apache persistence in what became Arizona's Verde Valley. Genetin-Pilawa includes suggestions of how Native people nonetheless made the U.S. capital a "Native city," while survivance is a more defining theme for Crandall in understanding Yavapai-Apache adaptations to the urbanization of their homelands.

The chapters that make up Part Three, "Building Community in Twentieth-Century Indian Cities," cover themes most established in the scholarship on Indigenous Peoples and cities. Sasha Maria Suarez's contribution on Minneapolis and David Hugill's study of Winnipeg focus on social service organizations and community development. Douglas K. Miller works to think more broadly about Dallas as a place that has been important to Indigenous people but does not strictly define their experience nor contain their more expansive identities. Elaine Marie Nelson's essay examines the use of urban spaces, with the example of Rapid City, as a center of intertribal coalition building and broader resistance, such as challenging the tourist stories laying claim to the Black Hills. Together, the essays in this section illustrate the depth and range of urban Indigeneity, further making the case for it as a constitutive feature of modern society.

Dana E. Powell's contribution addressing the NoDAPL encampments and Jennifer Denetdale on COVID-19 and Diné peoples make up the last section of the volume, "Indigenous Urban Futures in the Twenty-First Century." Powell frames the 2016–17 encampments formed to protest the Dakota Access Pipeline as temporary, anticolonial Indigenous cities, while Denetdale argues that border towns on the Navajo Nation and other urban areas are "directly responsible for the invasion of the monster" (302) called (in Diné) Dikos Ntsaaígíí-19. Both encourage scholars to think creatively and expansively about how Indigenous Peoples and their experiences with cities contribute to a complex contemporary world. These and the other ten essays provide the types of narratives we need for continuing to counter ideologically driven tropes of Indigenous disappearance with histories of Indigenous survivance that explain our present moment.

NICOLAS G. ROSENTHAL is professor of history at Loyola Marymount University.

RITA M. PALACIOS

The Maya Art of Speaking Writing: Remediating Indigenous Orality in the Digital Age
by Tiffany D. Creegan Miller
University of Arizona Press, 2022

TIFFANY D. CREEGAN MILLER'S *The Maya Art of Speaking Writing: Remediating Indigenous Orality in the Digital Age* is a welcome new addition to the growing body of contemporary Maya cultural studies. Creegan Miller's book is an ambitious study that looks at the intersection of digital textualities, oralities, and *ts'iib* (or the author's preferred K'iche' spelling, tz'ib'), a Maya concept that extends beyond the written word and encompasses that which is recorded (weavings, paintings, sculpture, the *milpa*/cultivated field, to name a few examples). This concept has been explored by Kaqchikel anthropologist Irma Otzoy (1996), Q'anjob'al writer and intellectual Gaspar Pedro González (1997), and, most recently, settlers Paul M. Worley and Rita M. Palacios (2019). *The Maya Art of Speaking Writing* looks at orality and media studies to further explore the possibilities of tz'ib', as the author explains, to "rethink previously accepted boundaries between forms, disciplines and eras" and to look closely at "Indigenous conceptions of orality and writing (tz'ib') to media studies" (9) to ground the study.

The book is divided into four chapters, each dealing with Maya cultural expressions and uses of digital media in the twentieth and twenty-first centuries. Chapter 1 looks at the ways in which Mayas tell their own stories through tz'ib' in Q'anjob'al intellectual Víctor Montejo's *Brevísima Relación Testimonial de la continua destrucción del Mayab' (Guatemala)* (1992) and in Comalapa's murals. The chapter focuses on the stories told by images as they rewrite the history of the Guatemalan nation from a Maya perspective, which notably has complete agency and is unmediated by non-Indigenous voices. Chapter 2 examines K'iche' poet Humberto Akabal's self-translation and his treatment of orality in the onomatopoeic poem "Xalolilo lelele'." According to Creegan Miller, Ak'abal offers his public an opportunity to engage in linguistic revitalization: rather than provide a translation of the poem, the K'iche' poet invites others to challenge the supremacy of the Spanish language and participate in the dissemination and reproduction of his mother tongue. The chapter includes an interesting discussion about linguistic and digital access and reproduction of Ak'abal's performance of the poem on digital platforms, particularly by non-K'iche' speakers.

Chapter 3 focuses on the use of Kaqchikel children's songs for language teaching, noting their adaptability and specificity (some of the songs include regional variations, which note the teacher's place of origin and their own variant of the language). Creegan Miller also notes the production of materials (recordings, video) to support language learning and engage in important language activism that engages publics in Guatemala and abroad. Chapter 4 looks at Maya migration as seen through transnational family videos, an unanticipated product of the author's fieldwork on children's songs. During Creegan Miller's time in the Maya highlands recording these songs, an elderly father saw an opportunity to send a recorded message to his two sons who had migrated to the United States. The author reflects on her own participation (mediation) in the process and engages in an important discussion regarding Indigenous identity in the framework of Latinidad in the United States.

Overall, Creegan Miller's contribution to the field of Indigenous Studies is particularly noteworthy, given her ties and commitment to Maya communities, her ongoing work, her grasp of the Kaqchikel language, and her formative experiences in Guatemala as a student, teacher, and academic. *The Maya Art of Speaking Writing* offers a "Maya driven methodological approach to the role of mediation in contemporary Maya-authored literary and cultural texts" (37–38), meaning the approach privileges Maya thought above all else, which is an admirable commitment, particularly as it challenges other academics and students of Maya literature and culture to do the same. The Maya concepts related to orality (t'zij, choloj, and ch'owen) that are introduced early offer much potential for Indigenous media studies: it is my hope that the author or other scholars take up the challenge to further their study and application. *The Maya Art of Speaking Writing* is a book that will interest students and scholars of Maya cultural production and open many lines of inquiry, particularly relating to digital Indigeneities.

RITA M. PALACIOS (Guatemala-born refugee settler) is professor of interdisciplinary studies at Conestoga College.

ROBERT KEITH COLLINS

*Black Indians and Freedmen: The African Methodist Episcopal Church
and Indigenous Americans, 1816–1916*
by Christina Dickerson-Cousin
University of Illinois Press, 2021

GROUNDED IN ORAL HISTORIES and primary sources from historical church records, Christina Dickerson-Cousin challenges readers to examine the roles the African Methodist Episcopal (AME) Church played in contact between Africans and Native Americans over one hundred years. This book takes readers on a journey into the lives of ministers who struggled to create religious inclusivity in the face of discrimination and whose agency suggested that religious motivation for common unity, as fellow "people of color," played key roles in the presence of the AME Church from Oneida in the Northeast to Black Indians, Freedmen, and Native Americans of the Five Civilized Tribes in Indian Territory. The book fills three explanatory gaps found in literature relevant to Native American and Indigenous studies of African and Native American contact: (1) how the AME Church established a presence with and within Native American communities; (2) how the active roles of both Native American and African American AME ministers enabled this presence; and (3) how the intercultural interactions between former slaves of Native Americans and African American and Native American ministers of the AME Church enabled the expansion of their ministry in Indian Territory.

For Dickerson-Cousin, the notion that the AME Church has been exclusively African American is a myth. Chapter 1 interrogates this myth by discussing the lives of ministers such as Richard Allen. A former slave, Richard Allen was drawn to the Methodist movement because of its racially egalitarian message, supported by the practice of evangelizing all, regardless of race or class. Allen's early ministry as a Methodist, particularly during the American Revolution, brought him into contact with members of the Haudenosaunee (Iroquois) Confederacy. Known for preaching to customers during his salt deliveries, including "General George Washington's army encampment at Valley Forge (pg.14)," Allen may also have preached to Oneida allies that joined the encampment in May 1778. Although the historical record is not tribally specific about which Native American communities heard his preaching, what is clear is that Native American communities were active recipients of his outreach from the 1820s to the 1830s. The blended Montaukett and African American church in North Amityville, established in 1815 by Daniel Squires and Delancy H. Miller, was incorporated into the AME Church as Bethel AME Church and included prominent members such as "Elias Hunter and Fanny Hunter (née Cuffee)," whose descendants intermarried with the Montaukett, Shinnecock, and Unkechaug (19).

Chapter 2 explores the experiences and ministry of Thomas Sunrise (Oneida), the first Native American ordained as an AME minister, and John Hall (Ojibwa), the first Native American AME Deacon, who referred to his African American congregations as "brother-cousins" (45). Sunrise's ministry, like that of Hall's, centered on equality. Often wearing traditional Oneida regalia when preaching to African Americans, Sunrise's message highlighted shared experiences with displacement that he observed between fugitive slaves and Oneida coping with removal. Despite occasional negative African American stereotypes about Native Americans, his commitment to the denomination did not wane. In the 1870s he was appointed AME "missionary to the Indians of Canada" (40), and he continued to advocate for African American and Native American equality until his death in 1891.

The intriguing analyses in chapters 3 and 4 provide a foundation for understanding the nature of African Methodists Migration (AMM) into Indian Territory. These discussions center on the invitation extended by Chickasaw Freedwoman, Annie Keel, AME member responses to suffering experienced by Indian Freedmen, intermarriage between African American men and Black Indian women, and the creation of "All Black Towns" that led to the establishment of approximately seventeen AME congregations by 1878. The following year, the Indian Mission Annual Conference (IMAC) was created, an organization devoted to evangelism in Indian Territory. Chapter 5 discusses the agency and diversity of IMAC ministers, such as African Creek, Peter Stidham, who was among the first AME ministers from the Creek Nation, and Robert Grayson, who advocated for educational opportunities in the Creek Nation. The final chapters offer readers an understanding of how the AME Church created an infrastructure in Indian Territory and advanced the rights of Indian Freedmen.

Dickerson-Cousin has created a resource that scholars and students of Native American and Indigenous studies, as well as anthropology, American studies, African American studies, Ethnic studies, history, and sociology, should find useful for understanding the active roles, motivations, and avenues of contact between African Americans and Native Americans forged by AME Church members. The breadth of primary sources brings back to life the histories embodied and struggles engaged by AME ministers promoting religious inclusion together.

ROBERT KEITH COLLINS is associate professor in the American Indian Studies Department at San Francisco State University.

SAM McKEGNEY

Written by the Body: Gender Expansiveness and Indigenous
Non-Cis Masculinities
by Lisa Tatonetti
University of Minnesota Press, 2021

THE UTILITY OF INDIGENOUS MASCULINITIES as rubrics of study has been a tough sell in recent years. Breaches of trust by prominent writers and the persistence of toxic masculinities in a field ostensibly oriented toward heteropatriarchy's elimination have led scholars like Dene theorist Glen Coulthard to insist that "critical indigenous masculinities should vacate not occupy space that indigenous feminist, queer and trans voices should occupy" (@denerevenge January 27, 2016). In *Written by the Body: Gender Expansiveness and Indigenous Non-Cis Masculinities,* settler scholar Lisa Tatonetti does not simply tend to as-yet-unstudied materials and thereby resuscitate Indigenous masculinities studies; rather, by untethering Indigenous masculinities from the cis-male body and examining the masculinities experienced, imagined, and performed by Indigenous female-identified, gender-variant, and/or Two-Spirit persons, Tatonetti alters the terms of engagement altogether. She reaches to the very voices Coulthard champions to reconsider what masculinities can (and ought to) mean. *Written by the Body* pursues gender knowledges that complicate and expand the meaning of masculinities. In so doing, Tatonetti challenges Indigenous masculinities studies to do better, arguing along with the artists and activists at the center of her study that "if there is to be masculinity, let it arise from the reciprocal relationships inherent in an erotics of responsibility" (225).

Written by the Body engages with representations of gender-nonconforming visioners that cut across centuries, territories, and cultural traditions, analyzing historical archives, early novels, contemporary fantasy, full-length films, documentary shorts, memoirs, interviews, poetry, and activism. One worries the enterprise might prove unwieldy. However, the ethic of care with which Tatonetti approaches the voices she analyzes ensures they are woven into an argumentative fabric of integrity. The book's most unique chapter, concerning the life and legacy of Ojibwe HIV/AIDS activist Carole LaFavor, provides an illustrative example. Unlike other chapters, which offer comparative discussions of themes like warriorhood, embodiment, and erotics, this chapter presents an intimate case study of a single historical figure. Despite such structural divergence, the chapter remains captivating and relevant to the others in the monograph. Tatonetti traces LaFavor's struggles for queer liberation, HIV rights, and Indigenous health sovereignty, in the process illuminating how Indigenous gender-nonconforming activists threaten settler power while continuing to inhabit Indigenous ways of knowing. Here Tatonetti reaches for methods that exceed her disciplinary training in literary studies, interviewing LaFavor's daughter, coworkers, and fellow activists because that's what needs to be done to assemble a multidimensional understanding of this extraordinary figure whose voice rightfully belongs at the heart of conversations about Indigenous gender, sovereignty, and continuance. LaFavor's voice appears boldly in *Written by the Body,* as in her refusal to accept Indigenous exclusion at the 1989 International AIDS conference in Montreal: "How many Indian people does it take for them to be counted?" she asks. "A hundred? A thousand? How many Indian people make up one white person?" (qtd. 149).

Unlike settler knowledges of gender, which are conditioned to fix and constrain, the Indigenous gender knowledges raised up in *Written by the Body* are multiple and expansive. They circulate, Tatonetti insists, via the affective circuitry among Indigenous bodies. When Tatonetti reads against the settler archive to retrieve representations of Indigenous warrior women, she does so not to identify a fixed archetype to which she can return in later chapters but rather to consider the ethical and embodied teachings of "female-identified and gender-variant warriors" whose "masculinities . . . center kinship narratives that privilege familial and tribal responsibilities" (26). In other words, she is less concerned with who these warriors *are* than with what their actions tell us about ways of being in the world. As such, Tatonetti's cadence that the body is "a somatic archive of Indigenous knowledges" (17, 20, 100, 148, 221) is not designed, as one might misinterpret, to fix bodies as stable knowledge containers. Tatonetti's point is that bodies generate knowledge, share emotional intelligence, and engage in the intergenerational transmission of both trauma and joy. As Tatonetti writes, "*When we envision the body as a somatic archive, we are not talking about a static entity . . . but instead about the body holding active, shifting, enfleshed processes of memory and history*" (99). The teachings Tatonetti curates in this much-needed book enact and demand more rigorous, mobile, and expansive understandings of gender in which masculinities evoke not cis-male bodies but responsibility, kinship, and sovereignty.

SAM MCKEGNEY is a white settler scholar of Indigenous literatures and head of the English Department at Queen's University, which occupies lands of the Haudenosaunee and Anishinaabe Peoples.

JAIME HOOGESTEGER

Pachamama Politics: Campesino Water Defenders and the Anti-Mining
   Movement in Andean Ecuador
by Teresa A. Velásquez
University of Arizona Press, 2022

PACHAMAMA POLITICS IS AN ENGAGED ANALYSIS of peasant struggles against the Quimsacocha mining project in the province of Azuay in the southern Andes of Ecuador. It is informed by a very rich body of ethnographic material covering a period of almost fifteen years when the author carried out the research and accompanied many of the analyzed people and processes. This period was politically interesting, as it encompassed the rise, demise, and aftermath of the leftist-inspired Ecuadorian Citizens Revolution (2007–2017).

The book begins by analyzing the rise of the antimining movement in the communities of Victoria del Portete and Tarqui in the province of Azuay. In these communities, water became a central issue in the antimining movement that locally united peasants of different social classes. This movement was organized around disputes about water quality studies and the interpretation of the results after a mining company had started explorations in the area and a watershed protection program was initiated. Starting from this local resistance to mining activities in the upper watershed, the resistance unfolded into broader issues and merged with regional and national antimining and for-water and autonomy movements, most notably the Indigenous Ecuadorian Movement.

Velásquez foregrounds some interesting notions. She shows that water has become a mobilizing resource through which many other demands and struggles are channeled and through which networks and movements are linked. In this sense, water is linked to broader territorial development plans; to autonomy in water management; and importantly also forms a strong link to Indigenous Andean cosmovisions. The latter include among others the protection of the Pachamama, the plurinational state, the revalorization of the Indigenous symbol, and the related transformation of individual and community identity. As part of this process the Indigenous symbol "lo nuestro" ("that which is ours") has emerged as a strong emblem of local campesino struggles.

The research shows the intrinsic contradictions of the Ecuadorian *Citizens Revolution* through the eyes of the analyzed water defenders. On the one hand, the *Citizens Revolution* recognized progressive proposals in Ecuador's 2008 Constitution, such as the recognition of the Rights of Nature, the plurinational state, community-based resource management, prior consent, and participative governance. On the other hand, it built its economy and political project on the development and revenues of extractive industries, the repression of social and most notably Indigenous and environmentalist movements and protests, the waving away of local struggles as nonrepresentative: the Revolution framed its programs and the development of mining in the name of the advancement of the greater good of the Ecuadorian citizens.

In this context Teresa Velásquez analyzes how communities—especially the women—united in the Women Defenders of the Mother Earth organization, which engaged with the national Indigenous movement and its efforts to negotiate substantial changes to the proposed Water Law through (among other strategies) street protests and road blockades that were harshly repressed. Velásquez shows how as part of this broader movement Indigenous and campesino communities united with city dwellers in the defense-of-life movement that had a very clear antimining agenda. The movement was closely related to the Indigenous movement and reappropriated Indigenous symbols, language, and identities. These were expressed through the appropriation of notions of water as life and as an ethical entity that combined with Catholicism resulting in waterside masses both in the city as well as in the rural areas, pampamesas, and the related reappropriation of Indigenous identities, symbolisms, and practices.

The reappropriation of the Indigenous symbol, related identities, and shared struggles also served as a means through which race, gender, and mestizaje are reconsidered in and among campesino communities as well as in the city of Cuenca. In this process the highly stigmatized indio is negotiated, making room for the adoption of the Indigenous identity; albeit especially among men with greater access to education and urban experiences, while women mainly struggle to free themselves from being treated and identified as indias.

This is a highly recommended read for scholars interested in understanding the Indigenous movement of Ecuador, antimining protests, struggles for communitarian autonomy, and the renegotiation of "the Indigenous" as a powerful unifying force that does not always have straightforward relations to identities of race, gender, and mestizaje in Ecuador, the Andes, and beyond.

JAIME HOOGESTEGER is associate professor of water commons and collectives at Wageningen University, the Netherlands.

MAY-BRITT ÖHMAN

Indigenous Research Methodologies in Sámi and Global Contexts
edited by Pirjo Kristiina Virtanen, Pigga Keskitalo, and Torjer Olsen
Brill, 2021

INDIGENOUS RESEARCH METHODOLOGIES *in Sámi and Global Contexts* is a collection by non-Sámi and Sámi (primarily North Sámi) scholars who discuss Sámi methodologies in relation to Indigenous methodologies. The anthology makes two important contributions: discussing what Sámi methodologies might be and doing so in English to engage a global audience for further exchange. Sámi scholars and authors have a long tradition of both doing research and contributing to European research and philosophy, extending over the last millennium. Most of this work is not available in English. Sámi authors have published in Swedish, Finnish, Norwegian, and the different Sámi languages as well as other European languages. Much has been written by and about the Sámi, but there is surprisingly little acknowledged on an international level—even within the settler-colonial states crisscrossing Sámi territories.

The Sámi people, originating in and living in the Fennoscandinavian peninsula—Norway, Sweden, Finland, and northwestern Russia of today, are commonly referred to as the sole recognized Indigenous people within the European Union. Nine Sámi languages remain in use, and while the most well-known traditional livelihood is reindeer herding, Sámi have always held different trades and expertise on all societal levels. Sámi have been pushed aside through time. During the last 150 years Sámi have been increasingly subject to racism and discrimination as the states have stolen Sámi land, turning it into state property or into non-Sámi private ownership, facilitating industrial exploitation such as mining, forestry, and power production.

As noted in two chapters, one by Virtanen et al, and the other by Porsanger and Seurujärvi-Kari, Sámi authors and scholars, many educated as vicars, have actively contributed to the development of scientific thought. The last three decades have witnessed an extensive list of Sámi scholarly publications, a majority published in Swedish, Sámi, Norwegian, and Finnish languages. Many discuss what Sámi and Indigenous methodologies are or should be. Hence, this volume builds on a longtime ongoing development of Sámi scholarship, which several of the authors are part of.

The articles focus mainly on Northern Sámi contexts. The majority of authors are scholars, while one is a journalist and another is a Sámi politician and activist. The majority live in the north of Norway and Finland, and one, also of North Sámi origin, works at a university on the Swedish side of Sápmi. Two chapters discuss places and Indigenous Peoples in the Global South: Namibia and southwestern Amazonia.

The reader has to work to identify the authors' Sámi or non-Sámi status, which is frustrating when discussing Sámi and Indigenous methodologies. As a (Lule and Forest) Sámi scholar, I wish to understand the position the authors are speaking from, what lived experiences they have, and what Sámi community they belong to. However, being discreet about Sámi ethnicity is a marker of the continued discrimination and racism directed toward Sámi in Fenno-Scandinavian settler-colonial academia and society at large.

The introductory chapter makes some unfortunate misleading statements regarding the number of Sámi, as well as the geographic range of Sámi peoples. Contrary to what is stated, despite assimilation and deportations since the establishment of the modern settler-colonial states, Sámi have always lived all across the Fenno-Scandinavian region, and there are currently highly active Sámi associations with numerous members in the Nordic capitals of Helsinki, Stockholm, and Oslo. The number of Sámi is likely to be far higher than the figures presented for Sweden, which are based on narrow estimations made in the 1970s.

The chapters deal with issues of decolonial authorship and Indigenous methodologies and theories; they aim to identify specific (North) Sámi methodologies, while referring to North Sámi cultural practices and language, while as mentioned above, tracing the several-centuries-long history of Sámi authorship (see especially chapter 1 by Virtanen et al. and chapter 2 by Porsanger and Seurujärvi-Kari). Other chapters more specifically deal with language revitalization and literacy, such as the work aimed at bolstering Aanaar (Inari) Sámi authorship (by Olthuis et al.) and Sámi literacy research (by Outakoski). The chapter by Porsanger et al. thoughtfully discusses Sámi feminist methodologies and women's leadership.

The volume is a thought-provoking contribution to Sámi and Indigenous methodologies for a global audience and should be considered highly recommended reading.

MAY-BRITT ÖHMAN (Lule and Forest Sámi of the Lule River Valley, with Tornedalian heritage) is at the Centre for Multidisciplinary Studies on Racism, CEMFOR, at Uppsala University.

CHADWICK ALLEN

The Lost River: Anompolichi II
by Phillip Carroll Morgan
White Dog Press, 2022

WITH SO MUCH ATTENTION devoted to imagining Indigenous futures, it is easy to overlook recent works of scholarship, art, and literature that evoke the complex lives and brilliant achievements of Indigenous Peoples of the past, perhaps especially of the distant past: those individuals, families, bands, nations, and confederacies that lived centuries or millennia prior to the disruptions brought by European and European American colonialisms. *The Lost River,* Chickasaw and Choctaw writer Phillip Carroll Morgan's much-anticipated sequel to his 2014 historical novel *Anompolichi: The Wordmaster,* is one of these works with the power to immerse readers in the remarkable vibrancy of past Indigenous worlds.

The year is 1399, one of the known zeniths of the mound-building cultures that developed for thousands of years across the eastern half of the North American continent, from the Atlantic and Gulf coasts to the Mississippi Valley, the Great Lakes, and beyond. *The Lost River* picks up where Morgan's *Anompolichi* ends, with our small band of heroes—Iskifa Ahalopa, the experienced, visionary, multilingual wordmaster of the first novel's title; Taloa Kinta, his younger female apprentice translator and diplomat, whose repertoire of languages includes, unexpectedly, English; and Robert Williams, the shipwrecked Scottish sea captain the wordmasters have rescued and befriended—fleeing the great mound city of Tochina on the Misha' Sipokni', the River Beyond All Ages, seat of the expanding Allahashi confederacy (modeled after the great Mississippian mound city known as Cahokia in what is now southern Illinois). They must outwit their enemies so that they may safely return to their homelands within the rival Yukpan confederacy in the Southeast. Our heroes carry news of Allahashi treachery and of a mysterious disease afflicting the Allahashi that is quickly becoming a deadly pandemic. Their Yukpan relatives and allies will need to prepare for both if they are to survive.

Beyond the pleasures of well-developed characters and a heart-racing adventure plot, it is this worlding that makes *Anompolichi* and now *The Lost River* so engaging—and that makes both novels particularly important as works of contemporary Indigenous literature. Morgan's well-researched imagining of the complexity and sophistication of mound-building civilizations counters the more typical depictions of the distant Indigenous past produced by non-Native archaeologists, anthropologists, and historians, on the one hand and, on the other, by non-Native writers of popular mythologies and fictions. Eschewing the limited vocabularies that have cemented over centuries of European and European American assertions of backward and degraded "prehistoric" North American cultures, Morgan bypasses the stale stereotypes that have become associated with dominant representations of "primitive" peoples and technologies. He imagines, instead, the full humanity and resourceful creativity of Indigenous ancestors, heroes and villains alike, showcasing their abilities to organize, build, and adapt.

As I discuss in my analysis of *Anompolichi* in *Earthworks Rising: Mound Building in Native Literature and Arts* (University of Minnesota Press, 2022), Morgan imagines a complex and changing Indigenous world in which multiple mound-building cultures coexist along the rivers, creeks, and other waterways that connect the eastern half of the North American continent into a networked system for transportation and exchange. Moreover, through his narrative's juxtaposition of Native and non-Native points of view, Morgan teaches contemporary readers how to perceive the massive scale of mound-based villages, towns, and cities, and how to understand their multiple civic and sacred functions. This complexity and interconnectedness is developed even further in *The Lost River,* where Morgan reveals a trans-Indigenous internationalism that includes not only diverse peoples living across North America and multiple shipwrecked Europeans from the British Isles but also knowledge of peoples from Africa and encounters with peoples from Mexico and Central America. Indeed, *The Lost River* culminates in a dramatic battle fought on the waters of the Bay of Mabila, part of the Southern Ocean (which readers will recognize as the Gulf of Mexico), where the Yukpan and their shipwrecked Scottish allies must contend with both Allahashi warriors who arrive from the north by river and Mexica warriors who arrive from the south by sea.

Morgan's new novel is part of a growing catalog of Indigenous self-representation published by White Dog Press, an imprint of the Chickasaw Press based in Ada, Oklahoma. In line with the Press's mission to promote Chickasaw sovereignty through multiple genres, Morgan has again created prose that is appropriate for both adult and young adult (YA) audiences, ensuring that *The Lost River,* like its predecessor *Anompolichi,* will be accessible to a wide range of Native and non-Native readers and that it will work well in a wide range of K—12, university, and community classrooms.

CHADWICK ALLEN is associate vice provost for faculty advancement and professor in the Department of English at the University of Washington.

JAMES MACKAY

Conversations with LeAnne Howe
edited by Kirsten L. Squint
University Press of Mississippi, 2022

AS LEANNE HOWE REMARKS several times in the fourteen interviews that make up this fascinating volume, American Indians are often pushed to the margins in U.S. literary discourse: discussed in the past tense as haunting ghosts, asked to fit with tired (and tiresome) stereotypes, made out to be the solemn validators of the colonizer's identity. Perhaps for that reason, there are still far too few monographs dedicated to individual Native American writers. Books of published interviews centered on one writer are even rarer: as far as I can tell, the only examples are the previous volumes, also put out by University Press of Mississippi, centered on Louise Erdrich and Michael Dorris, N. Scott Momaday, and Leslie Marmon Silko. One could also count the volume *Postindian Conversations*, coedited by A. Robert Lee and Gerald Vizenor.

LeAnne Howe more than justifies such treatment. Choctaw by birth, adopted into an unstable and precarious situation with her Cherokee family, Howe has in the past decade increasingly been recognized as one of the foremost contemporary American Indian intellectuals. Her concept of tribalography, with its emphasis on the unification of genres rather than taxonomic division, stressing the central importance and power of tribal stories in the American narrative, has become a significant term of art in Native American literary studies. True to this mixed-genre sensibility—in one interview, she delights in Nathan Scott McNamara's description of her as a "genre chemist" (138)—she has created major interventions in multiple forms. One strand that runs through the interviews in the volume under review is the restlessness of her imagination, with multiple projects always on the go, always looking to overturn Euro-Western preconceptions and prioritize Native understandings, frequently in collaboration with others.

Kirstin L. Squint is one of those frequent collaborators, and we can see that collaboration deepening across the four interviews she has conducted with Howe. All of these are included in this book, but the 2019 interview really makes this collection essential reading. While Howe is never less than engaged, and frequently very funny, in the earlier interviews the reader definitely gets the sense that both interviewer and subject are meeting on quite professional terms: the questions are centered on theme and opinion, while the answers are somewhat guardedly professional, moving between academic discussion and activism. While a useful resource, then, these earlier interviews make for a slightly dry read. Certainly, reading through them, I had no particular impulse to take notes, trusting that the extensive index would help me find what I was looking for if I needed it. By contrast, the second half of my edition is bursting with bookmarks, as Howe begins to open up on a more personal level. My bookmark on Squint's final interview, previously unpublished, in which Howe talks about her childhood and its links to her work, reads "LeAnne. Pseudonym. Abuse. Autism spectrum. Family histories!" Even for people familiar with many of the facts from the work, this conversation is essential, even revelatory.

As Howe says in her discussion with Rebecca Macklin included here, her writing is "a form of activism [. . .] a story changes the world" (94). The stories that have taken hold of her imagination are notably ones of American Indian agency and intervention: the Choctaw gift to Ireland, the spectral "Savage Indian" who appeared to Mary Todd Lincoln, Native missionaries in the Middle East, the Native origins of baseball, and—always central in her imagination—Nanih Waiya and the other Choctaw mounds. One interview that really stands out here is with C. A. Conrad for the *Occult Poetry Radio* podcast, where Howe goes into great detail about the supernatural and occult nature of her inspiration, discussing moments when she has seen and interacted with otherworldly entities: ghosts, spirits, animals, and visions such as the image of one of the nooses used in Lincoln's murderous "execution" of the Dakota 38, which floated toward her in a Las Vegas hotel bathroom before becoming a character in *Savage Conversations*. In the theater-focused conversation with Jen Shook that ends this volume, Howe calls this "[being] in touch with the marvelous" (141), which seems exactly right as a description for her work, though it does not do justice to the many moments of humor that make this collection such an excellent read.

JAMES MACKAY is assistant professor of British and American Literatures at European University Cyprus.

DANIEL USNER

Louisiana Creole Peoplehood: Afro-Indigeneity and Community
edited by Rain Prud'homme-Cranford, Darryl Barthé, and
    Andrew J. Jolivétte
University of Washington Press, 2022

STUDENTS OF LOUISIANA HISTORY AND CULTURE know full well that the word "Creole" has never been a static or stable referent to identity. Use of the term in that part of the western hemisphere over time has been as fluid as the waterways and wetlands that characterize the region's geography. Beginning as an adjective applied to colonial persons both free and enslaved to distinguish them from Europeans and Africans newly entering the colony, "Creole" became a form of self-identity and external perception determined at times by language and ethnic difference and at others by class and racial difference. All the while, by the way, its reference to New Orleans cuisine and to food plants grown on local soil became ubiquitous. When the U.S. Civil War ended, white New Orleanians of French or Spanish descent—insisting that Creole identity should apply only to themselves—launched a rhetorical war against African Americans who were using "Creole" to designate their own heritage as free people of color during slavery times. Evolving usage since then continued to occur, for example, as African Americans in southwest Louisiana distinguished themselves from neighboring Cajuns and also as Louisianians of African descent carried their identity as far away as California. With publication of *Louisiana Creole Peoplehood,* readers are now introduced to another application of the term.

This anthology, coedited by Rain Prud'homme-Cranford, Darryl Barthé, and Andrew J. Jolivétte, creatively puts writings by scholars into conversation with community responders. Its contents include an array of essays, poems, and interviews intended, as the editors state, to reflect the "shared Peoplehood" of Louisiana Creole experiences. In this case, "Louisiana Creoles" are defined as "a post-contact Indigenous group" having "historic ties to specific tribal communities/histories, narratives, landbases, and practices within Louisiana terrains" (8). This anthology focuses in particular on Indigenous people also of African descent. Disenfranchisement and erasure of Afro-Indigenous people, driven by an "anti-Blackness . . . central to settler-colonial projects" (7), have not—as testified in the voices assembled in this book—halted their own pursuit of recognition. Although they do not seek the same form of recognition possessed by sovereign Indigenous nations, the contributors to *Louisiana Creole Peoplehood* do hope that those nations with whom they are kin, as put by Prud'homme-Cranford, "will support the issues faced by unrecognized post-contact Afro-Indigenous communities and peoples" (31).

The scope of themes encompassed in this book—language, food, health, gender, and ceremony—is impressive. So is the occupational and geographical range of its contributors—whether they be poets, educators, and activists working inside Louisiana or scholars teaching diverse disciplines at distant universities. The chapters, community responses, and testimonials comprising *Louisiana Creole Peoplehood* are too numerous to summarize here, so a sample must suffice. Jeffery Darensbourg critically scrutinizes the so-called founding of New Orleans and reclaims the Indigenous history of Bulbancha (the Choctaw name meaning "place of foreign tongues") by tracing Native people's relationship to the city from precolonial times to the present. Leila Blackbird's response underscores two devastating impacts of settler colonialism there, the enslavement of Indigenous people by early colonizers and the present-day hazards suffered along the petrochemical-industrial corridor between New Orleans and Baton Rouge. The background to and current phase of a movement to recover Kouri-Vini, a language with French, Native American, and African influences, are featured in an essay by Darryl Barthé and Joseph Dunn and also one by Oliver Mayeux. In results drawn from his participant-observer research, Andrew Jolivétte captures the struggles among gay and bisexual men for inclusion in their Louisiana Creole communities. Other parts of the book include writings by Tracy Colson Antee and Robert Caldwell about Antee's father, John Oswald Colson, a celebrated maker of filé (powdered sassafras leaves, which are a basic ingredient in the region's cuisine), and Carolyn Dunn's account of her life as a Louisiana Creole growing up in Los Angeles.

What unites all of this book's contributors, as expressed resoundingly across chapters, is how they think about and act upon their shared identity. Although readers will learn plenty about experiences and memories still uniquely grounded in that place now called "Louisiana," there is little doubt that they will also relate Louisiana Creoles' claims to Indigeneity with fraught interactions between African Americans and Native Americans in other areas. But this is something the editors actually wish for. "It is our hope and intention," they write in the conclusion, "that this book will inspire more conversations about the everyday realities of race, gender, class, and equity among people of mixed Afro-Indigenous descent in the Americas" (260).

DANIEL USNER is professor of history at Vanderbilt University.

HEIDI KIIWETINEPINESIIK STARK

A Short History of the Blockade: Giant Beavers, Diplomacy,
    and Regeneration in Nishnaabewin
by Leanne Betasamosake Simpson
University of Alberta Press, 2021

A SHORT HISTORY OF THE BLOCKADE: Giant Beavers, Diplomacy, and Regeneration in Nishnaabewin is a powerful reframing of blockades and Indigenous resistance to settler colonialism. This beautiful piece of prose immediately captures the audience. Initially delivered as a public talk for the Canadian Literature Centre's (CLC) Kreisel Lectures, a literary forum that brings great thinkers to the fore to consider the challenges and subjects that concern us all, this book both details the importance of story and demonstrates its powerful impacts on our understanding of the world. Refusing the narrative that non-state-sanctioned forms of activism are merely or exclusively negations, Simpson beautifully weaves together four stories of Amik the beaver to think through blockades as sites of negation and affirmation, both a disavowal of settler colonialism's attempts to devastate our territories for capitalist gain and an avowal of our long-standing relationships in and of place.

Simpson's attention to the beaver as a worldmaker beautifully centers Anishinaabe thought that understands life as continual, reciprocal, and reflective; as "a persistent world-building process" (4). She reminds us that colonial mindsets frame the beaver as "Nature's engineer," recognizing Amik as having a greater impact on the environment than any other species—aside from humans. Understood as a keystone species, beavers dramatically transform landscapes while also creating sustaining habitats. Amik reminds us that engaging with our place in transformative ways can be generative. Indeed, as Simpson shows us, by examining the beaver and their work in building blockades we can see the important distinction between impacts as forms of negation versus forms of affirmation. In these distinctions we can understand beaver as a worldmaker. Through the stories of beaver and an understanding of Amik's relational impacts, the reader is challenged to think through Indigenous forms of resistance as not just refusals of the state or capitalist extraction but also as affirmations of alternative ways of being and living with one another. The blockade, then, can be understood as not just stopping the flow of something but also ensuring the pooling of an alternative. The blockade enables regeneration.

Throughout *A Short History of the Blockade,* Simpson weaves together different forms of knowledge and ways of knowing, capturing the complexity of settler colonialism's impacts on Indigenous nations while letting Indigenous knowledge and visions for living in this place we call Turtle Island drive the narrative. Simpson somehow escapes speaking to her audience in reactionary frames. While there are clear applications to the political conditions we face today as Indigenous nations, her beautiful words are also timeless, a visionary declaration of how to understand what it means to live in a relational world. Though this book is short in terms of page count, it is expansive in the gifts it offers the reader. Just as the beaver's dam transforms the landscape, this provocative framing of beaver stories and blockades provides substantively different ways of thinking about diplomacy and regeneration.

I will never again be able to consider the work of blockades without thinking about my relatives, the beaver, and the formidable forms of worldmaking they carry forward with every nibble and placement of a log or stick. Simpson has given the reader a powerful language for thinking about both the generative aspects of Indigenous resistance and the importance of the everyday work of worldmaking. She reminds us that this assiduous work can be tiring and that we can feel as though it will be dismantled the moment we finish building a single, small dam; but in the activation of this work, worldmaking occurs. In these spaces we are both able to imagine alternative worlds and begin bringing them into form.

HEIDI KIIWETINEPINESIIK STARK (Turtle Mountain Ojibwe) is associate professor in Indigenous governance at the University of Victoria.

PHILIP STEVENS

The Apache Diaspora: Four Centuries of Displacement and Survival
by Paul Conrad
University of Pennsylvania Press, 2021

WRITTEN THINGS OF INTIMATE UNDERSTANDINGS are always a curious affair; either the passage of time mutes the veracity of the written observation, or the ignorance of the writer about the reader hinders the message. As an Apache reviewer of this book, I understand that there is a "looseness" in the Apache language that can be infuriatingly imprecise to Eurocentric ontologies. This "looseness" is a feature exacerbated in print but subdued in voice. Apache conversation is a mutual endeavor where the information shared by the speaker is built upon by the hearer. In effect conversations are custom puzzle pieces that fit together. If the speaker or hearer notices an imprecise fit, new parts are fashioned until there is a mutual understanding. While not an issue exclusive to the Apache language, the written form of Apache accentuates the looseness, as there is no hearer but only a reader. Literacy is a kind of prison; a static attempt to capture the vibrancy of conversation.

Having acknowledged books as prisons for Apache identity, Paul Conrad's *The Apache Diaspora: Four Centuries of Displacement and Survival* is an excellent example of scholarship that allows a fuller understanding of Apache people. Conrad's shaping of the term "diaspora" to fit Apache history and identity allows the reader to include so much more than the savage "Reaver" monsters of Joss Whedon's space western series *Firefly*. Diaspora allows the intimacy and love of kin and place, central tenets of Apache identity, to elucidate Apache resistance and perseverance in the face of European erasure.

In Part 1, Conrad researches Spanish archival sources to show burgeoning colonial identification of Apache as Other: apostates to the Spanish realm. Apache, thy name is legion, as Spain saw "nearly all mobile Indigenous people" as demons—termed "Apaches"—fit for subjugation or slavery (18). So began an imprecise Apache identity in a colonial system that craves precision. However, alongside the history of Apache as enemy, Conrad's ability to show Apache perseverance despite Spanish salvation through baptism or slavery, demonstrates the importance of kin and place. Conrad demonstrates "diaspora" as an appropriate term.

Conrad's relaying of the Spanish limited understanding of Apache, as any enemy can give a dazzling effect of the varied "Apaches" of the plains, the west, and the south. As each Apache group has their own creation and history that is continually passed down in voice, Spanish edicts that attempted to simplify the Apache identity as simply anti-Christian gave rise to static understandings of all Apaches. Conrad allows us to witness the gross simplification of Apaches against the backdrop of Spanish economic drives under the mantle of Christianity.

In Part 2, Conrad documents the European shift from religious economy toward religious imperial conquest. Here begins the thirst for land and displacement. A divide-and-conquer policy requires defining your enemies. Historic animosities between tribes were utilized to capture and enslave Apache apostates to be dispersed throughout the Americas. This dispersal/displacement of Apache people continued through the Spanish, Mexican, and American imperial designs. Apaches, as legion, occupied so much territory in the minds of Europeans. As exclusivity of land became part of the bartering for the reunification of family in enslavement, Conrad's use of a well-researched lens of diaspora as "migration, collective memory of an ancestral home, a continued connection to that home, a sustained group consciousness, and a sense of kinship with group members living in different places" becomes fully realized (2–3).

Conrad attempts to incorporate Apache voices throughout the book. However, as he notes, "As an outsider, I will never understand what it means to be Apache in America" (2). I applaud Conrad's recognition of the limitation. However, as the poet Wordsworth noted of cloistered nuns, so do academics rarely venture outside their domain; the written word. As a member of an Apache family who persisted through the diasporic dynamics recounted by Conrad, I find it interesting to relay the value of this book in a system that continually undermines the agency of Apache voices. Just as I find Keith Basso's work on Apache communities to be quite useful, I am aware that the written word is like a funhouse mirror. While I can never say that the reflection is not of my people, I can point out the distortions. In consideration of this prison or convent in which I am writing this review, unknown reader, I believe that Conrad's work is exemplary. I believe this book to be extremely useful to scholars, students, and popular audiences.

PHILIP STEVENS is associate professor of anthropology and the director of American Indian studies at the University of Idaho.

KRISTINA FAGAN BIDWELL

Exactly What I Said: Translating Words and Worlds
by Elizabeth Yeoman
University of Manitoba Press, 2022

AS PART OF MY RESEARCH on Indigenous-led collaboration, I have been interviewing scholars about their collaborative work. Many have said that despite having extensive collaborative experience, they have never thought in a systematic way about *how* they collaborate. By contrast, Elizabeth Yeoman's *Exactly What I Said: Translating Words and Worlds* is a deep, extended reflection on a specific collaboration. In 2019, Innu elder Tshaukuesh Elizabeth Penashue published a translation of her diaries, originally written in Innu-aimun, under the title, *Nitinikiau Innusi: I Keep the Land Alive.* While this book has Penashue's name on the cover, it was the product of an intensive collaborative process. Yeoman and Penashue worked closely together for over a decade to translate, explain, organize, edit, and illustrate the diaries. Now, with *Exactly What I Said,* Yeoman describes and reflects on that process.

Despite the title, this is not a work of translation studies in a traditional sense. Yeoman is, she freely admits, a beginning learner of Innu-aimun. Penashue orally translated her own writing into English, while Yeoman worked with her to transcribe the translations and then to edit them into a form that would be accessible to a wide English-reading audience. Yeoman describes her struggles to express Penashue's voice on paper, both her dialect of Innu-aimun and her eloquent form of English, giving examples of words that she struggled to translate, such as the Innu word nutshimit ("the land") where "something fundamental is missing in all of the attempts to convey its meaning in English or French" (134).

However, Yeoman is less concerned with translating words with translating *worlds,* that is, with the challenge of making Penashue's Innu culture, forms of expression, lands, and experiences meaningful to outside readers. Yeoman asks, "How do you convey exactly what someone said across sometimes radically different languages, cultures, and histories?" (13). In response to this question, the book's chapters are organized around various modes through which worlds are transmitted—maps, stories, images, voices, signs, texts, songs, and physical experiences. Each chapter focuses on a single mode, narrating Yeoman's experiences working with Penashue within that mode, reflecting on its potential and limitations, and then contextualizing their work within a wide range of scholarship, art, and activism.

Rather than putting forward a centralized argument, this book is story-based, exploratory, and self-reflective. Yeoman's approach could be described in terms of what Métis literary scholar Warren Cariou has called "critical humility"—an approach to academic work that is relationship-based, personal, accessible, and humble (1—12).[1] Instead of presenting herself as an authority on Innu language and culture, Yeoman emphasizes her lack of expertise and her learning process. She argues that her lack of knowledge actually became an asset in working with Penashue because it necessitated a lengthy, in-person, and open process of listening. Yeoman is critical of the ways in which federal research granting agencies work in opposition to such openness, for example, by requiring that Yeoman be the applicant rather than Penashue, that the application be in English or French, and that the project fit within the "often simplistic rules and formulas" of ethics review (163). In contrast with such institutional formulas, Yeoman's book is primarily interested in the ways in which her and Penashue's work moved outside of such boundaries: "Working together can also help us think beyond binary oppositions such as teller and recorder or oral and written as we try to understand each other" (130).

In her conclusion, Yeoman reflects on how she and Penashue, through their work together, both arrived as a place of "amazement at what we experienced in worlds outside our own when we had the courage to venture into them" (210). From this personal example of transformation, she looks toward the possibility for wider human change as we face the immense challenges of climate change. *Exactly What I Said* is thus not just a reflection on how to collaborate but also on how collaboration and translation can teach us how to live.

KRISTINA FAGAN BIDWELL is Tier 2 Canada Research Chair in Indigenous Storytelling and professor in the Department of English at the University of Saskatchewan.

Note

1. Warren Cariou, "On Critical Humility." Studies in American Indian Literatures 32, no. 3—4 (Fall—Winter 2020): 1—12.

VANESSA ANTHONY-STEVENS

Transforming Diné Education: Innovations in Pedagogies and Practice
edited by Pedro Vallejo and Vincent Werito
University of Arizona Press, 2022

I RECENTLY HAD THE PRIVILEGE to attend an educator showcase of culturally responsive pedagogical design with the Institute for Native Educators (INE) at Northern Arizona University. Roy Tracy, a representative of the Navajo Nation Department of Diné Education (DODE) and member of the DINÉ External Advisory Team with a lifetime of experience in public education, shared the following thoughts with the Indigenous and Indigenous-serving teacher audience:

> Words like culturally responsive education or Tribal Critical Race Theory, they are not things we have to teach ourselves. We live these concepts. Our ways of teaching and learning are grounded in our language, our ceremonies, and our lands. But knowing how to apply these concepts helps us to deal with colonization in our fight to continue being who we are. (Paraphrased, December 9, 2022)

Reading the collection of philosophical approaches, research studies, and case examples of Diné education within Transforming Diné Education brought me back to the words of this veteran Tribal leader. A critical question in Indian Country raised by the remarks above is, "How might explicit application of Indigenous pedagogies transform schooling practices?" Addressing that question is a direct challenge to a colonial school system that, in the words of editors Vallejo and Werito, was always designed to erase, assimilate, homogenize, and essentially "kill off the resistant Indigenous nations or tribes" (5). The authors, the vast majority of whom are Diné, advance what it means to be informed by and to enact Diné-centered pedagogy and praxis in the fight to perpetuate the Diné lifeway.

Across the chapters, themes of language and land as teacher, language as knowledge, ceremonies as the heart of Diné philosophy, and place of origin as a relational grounding in the earth (e.g., where we come from), frame a place-based and culturally specific approach and understanding of what is needed to create an educational system that works for Diné children in the here and now. Undoubtedly, the variety of places and interactions where Diné children learn, in-school, beyond-school, home, and community, required editors to carefully select chapters that reflect a unified essence of Diné pedagogy while allowing for multiple voices, institutional contexts, and professional lenses to speak to what it can mean to center the hogan (traditional Diné home) and Dinétah (the people's land) as the voice of education instead of the colonial state (chapter 13).

Divided into three sections, the book highlights different aspects of education: Part I, "School Site and Community-based Programs," includes chapters on culture-based math programs, special education, language revitalization, and wellness. Part II, "Tribal/District Level and University Programs," has chapters on Tribal sovereignty and self-determination in education and university/Tribal/community partnerships. Part III, "Perspectives of Diné Educational Sovereignty across Generations," outlines philosophical tenets and guidance for future directions in Diné educational sovereignty. While some chapters delve deeply into philosophical, methodological, and epistemological questions of Diné cosmology and education (i.e., knowledge seeking), such as Kelsey's personal and familial journey to transform research and instruction in higher education by asking, "What does it mean to be educated?" (chapter 7), other chapters infuse Diné values and symbols into current contexts of standards-driven, accountability-bound public K—12 classrooms, such as Fowler's hogan mathematics, a curricular innovation using Diné representation as a bridge between Navajo culture and school culture in the math classroom (chapter 2). Speaking to educational leaders, Secatero (chapter 8) offers a holistic framework for leadership practices that cultivate spiritual, mental, physical, and social well-being, the Corn Pollen Path (At'aa da'diin baa Hane), an approach to education connecting people and place through the literal and symbolic lifecycle of corn.

Editors Vallejo and Werito carefully curate a message throughout: the value of education is about making connections, not separations. Readers are engaged in a world where Diné knowledge is a complete standalone knowledge system and where Diné-centered pedagogy is a decolonizing educational force "intrinsically informed by Diné ways of thinking, living, learning, and being" (191). As a dialogue that grapples with the interface of Diné and Western knowledge systems, this collection provides insight into how Diné people are choosing to navigate colonization in their struggle to continue "being who we are."

This book is a valuable example of Indigenous educational philosophies in tune with relationships with land, other-than and more-than human beings, and traditional economies and healing practices. Transforming Diné Education should be read by educators and ought to be of special interest to those invested in furthering decolonial schooling in the twenty-first century.

VANESSA ANTHONY-STEVENS is associate professor of social and cultural studies in the Department of Curriculum and Instruction at the University of Idaho.

IGNACIO CARVAJAL

Trickster Academy
by Jenny L. Davis
University of Arizona Press, 2022

JENNY L. DAVIS'S *TRICKSTER ACADEMY* is a collection of poems that centers on the experience of being Native in academia. The collection brings humor, wit, cleverness, celebration of place and Chickasaw tradition, and ultimately a poignant and piercing depiction of violences within the walls of institutions of higher education.

In the first section, "Land Acknowledgement Statement," Davis addresses the paradoxical relationship between institutional recognition and the grounding that home and tradition provide. In one poem, a hypothetical administrator begs an "Officially Nondenominational Deity" to "Please let me say these names right, or at least pretty close./ Why are there so many syllables?/ And so many tribes?" (4). The poems in this section both portray the ridicule of cheap gestures of inclusion and affirm that they are ultimately needless: "These are the lands/ we have brought into being and these/ are the lands we will reclaim,/ whether or not/ you acknowledge us" (7). Davis anchors these recognitions to a notion of home in the "most beautiful place in the world," which "is a grove of trees in the hills/of northeast Oklahoma"—a place of both departure and return. From this notion of home the collection explores, for example, the experiences of queer members of the community, sometimes in a solemn way but often humorously: "We leave home because there are only three other/ queer people in this town and two of them/ are dating each other" (16). The poems create an intimate recognition of place and grounding that a land acknowledgment could hardly achieve.

The second section, "What Kind of Trickster Are You?," centers ideas of defense and survival. The poem "Chickasaw Word for *Trickster*" declares (30): "Our language is a trickster./ It let everyone think/ it was dying . . ." as a means of refusal by the speakers, protecting themselves from violent affronts when speaking it. In a recurring metaphor of a turtle's shell as a means of defense, "How Turtle Got Her Shell" tells the reader she didn't always have one but instead: "She grew it/ to keep the world/ from crushing her . . ." (34). The final poem in this section, "Academic Sideshow Woman," presents two versions of a letter to the speaker's mother. The speaker has run away to join either the circus or the academy and beckons the reader to come and be amazed and shocked (40):

by the bearded woman!	by the working-class professor!
the tattooed lady!	the two-spirit scholar!
a savage on display!"	an Indian in academe!"

At the circus they'll be lucky to "see my kind in person," whereas in the academy they'll be glad to "add my numbers to diversity tallies" (40).

The humor, irony, and tenderness of the first two sections give way to a wrenching set of poems in the final section, "Trickster Academy." On the one hand, rewarded as an accomplishment and recognition, "making it" into prestigious institutions is considered a triumph. The voice of the poems, however, reveals the contradictions and harms of the space: the internal fights for merit raises; the lack of funding for or elimination of Indigenous studies programs; the competition to be the "first" or "only"; the fact that "Dead Indians/ outnumber the living here/ five to one" (56); the caricatures of Native people on students' T-shirts; the struggle and betrayal of finding "A Seat at the Trickster's Table" (45). They all coalesce around one of the most pressing contradictions about learning spaces in higher education: the continued and normalized holding of Ancestor remains in museums, displays, laboratories, and (even worse) closets and storage rooms. "Room 119," one of several poems that address this dynamic, opens (63):

I am formatting a fifteen-page bibliography
while the Ancestors sit in boxes down the hall
and I swear I can hear them singing

Across Turtle Island, the non-Native public (and especially worried administrators) are increasingly made aware of issues like the safety of Indigenous students, staff, and faculty; the colonial realities of the institutions; the obstacles and meaningful work undertaken by Indigenous scholars therein; and the violent treatment of Ancestral lands and remains. These public discussions are accompanied by institutional gestures—with varying degrees of effect and/or exacerbation—amid which Indigenous students, staff, and faculty face new responses to old and ongoing violences. In *Trickster Academy* Davis portrays these affronts but humorously and tenderly affirms that the poems are also "always leaning home" (13).

IGNACIO CARVAJAL is a non-Native poet, scholar, translator, and assistant professor in the Department of Literature at the University of California San Diego.

ADELE PERRY

Life in the City of Dirty Water: A Memoir of Healing
by Clayton Thomas-Müller
Penguin Random House Canada, 2021

IN *LIFE IN THE CITY OF DIRTY WATER: A Memoir of Healing,* Clayton Thomas-Müller writes as "an Indigenous man, as an activist, as someone seeking the correct spiritual paths through a landscape pocked and pitted by traps, many of them centuries old, some as old as the world, some of my own creation" (213–14). The result is a powerful, compelling story and a call to action.

The title of Thomas-Müller's 240-page memoir evokes the particular space of Winnipeg, the middling Canadian prairie city that Thomas-Müller and more than seventy thousand other Indigenous people currently call home. So do I, as a settler. *Life in the City of Dirty Water* has a lot to say about Winnipeg. But Thomas-Müller also ranges well beyond this particular urban geography, tracing his teenage life in northern British Columbia, his time on his family's trapline in northern Manitoba's Inninew or Swampy Cree territories, and a career devoted to global climate justice advocacy in the United States, Latin America, and beyond. The result is a highly readable discussion of what it means to be a Cree man in contemporary Canada and an argument for environmental action and decolonization.

The memoir is a fluid and at times rollicking read. It begins with a short preface from Thomas-Müller's mother, Gail Pelltier, who offers her "full support and permission to share his story" (n.p.). Five parts follow, each with titles in Inninewmowin, English, and syllabics: *tapasîwin* (or "flight") tells the story of Thomas-Müller's immediate origins, his birth in 1977, and his early years. This includes time on the family trapline in Treaty 6 territory, in juvenile detention in British Columbia, and in Indigenous street gangs in Winnipeg. Nōtinikêwiyiniw or "warrior" documents Thomas-Müller's coming to Indigenous community organizing in 1990s Winnipeg, to global Indigenous resistance while on a solidarity trip to Chiapas in 1997, and to the U.S.-based Indigenous Environmental Network as a staff member. "You can't be an Indian and not be political," explains Thomas-Müller (77).

In the first part, *nîpîy* (or "water"), Thomas-Müller narrates a series of linked returns: to Indigenous spirituality, and the particular practices of sweat lodge and sun dance, to his marriage to Koren Thomas-Müller, and to the city of Winnipeg. *Nanâtawihowin* (or "healing") speaks of Indigenous masculinities through Thomas-Müller's stories of club and rave scenes and the birth of his two sons. It ends with Thomas-Müller joining 350.org, a well-resourced NGO organization, and his work with antipipeline campaigns. "Some mainstream environmentalists might ask what fighting a pipeline has to do with LGBTQ rights," Thomas-Müller concludes, "but I know that everything is connected" (208).

The final and shortest part of *Life in the City of Dirty Water* is *iskotêw* (or "fire"). Here Thomas-Müller connects his own life with wider struggles and argues that environmental justice and Indigenous rights are necessarily connected. "In 250 years of industrialization, colonizers have almost destroyed our ability to live on Mother Earth," Thomas-Müller explains. "Integrated, holistic governance of our nations, or cities, and the relationship that they have with the land and resources are how we are going to do it" (221).

Thomas-Müller's book was published by Penguin in 2021, two years after a short documentary of the same title as the book (https://lifeinthecityofdirtywater.com/). In book form, *Life in the City of Dirty Water* reads like a life story told in parts. It has been received well in mainstream Canadian circles, a national best-seller, shortlisted for three major awards, and featured on the annual *Canada Reads* show on Canadian Broadcasting Corporation's radio.

Life in the City of Dirty Water is a testament to Indigenous dispossession in what is now Canada, the corrosive and ongoing effects of residential schooling, the flooding of northern lands for southern hydroelectric power, and poverty. *Life in the City of Dirty Water* also testifies to the power of Indigenous resurgence in the face of colonialism. Thomas-Müller's book reminds us how poorly the brittle binaries cherished by settler discourse—bush versus city, traditional versus modern, traumatized versus healed—serve the history of Indigenous Peoples in modern Canada. In compelling prose and narrative, *Life in the City of Dirty Water* demands that we think outside those binaries and work toward both Indigenous sovereignty and environmental justice.

ADELE PERRY is Distinguished Professor of History and Women's and Gender Studies and Director, Centre for Human Rights Research at the University of Manitoba.

WARREN BERNAUER

Serpent River Resurgence: Confronting Uranium Mining at Elliot Lake
by Leanne Leddy
University of Toronto Press, 2022

IN THE SECOND HALF OF THE TWENTIETH CENTURY, a series of uranium mines in the Elliot Lake area in Canada played important roles in facilitating the United States' nuclear weapons program and the (closely related) development of "civilian" nuclear power programs in North America. Leanne Leddy's *Serpent River Resurgence* provides a unique and critically important history of uranium mining in the Elliot Lake area from the perspective of the Serpent River First Nation (SRFN), an Anishinaabe nation in Northern Ontario upon whose territory the settler town of Elliot Lake is situated. Based on a combination of oral history and archival research, *Serpent River Resurgence* makes critically important contributions to the Indigenous studies literature about uranium mining, settler colonialism, and Indigenous resurgence.

Leanne Leddy is a member of the SRFN who grew up in Elliot Lake and is currently an associate professor in Indigenous studies at Wilfred Laurier University. Leddy's meticulous empirical research, combined with insights and analysis reflecting her membership in SRFN, resulted in a rich case study of one Indigenous nation's experiences with colonial dispossession and Indigenous resistance. *Serpent River Resurgence* contains compelling arguments about the colonial implications of the Cold War nuclear arms race for the Serpent River Anishinaabe, as well as the power of Indigenous resistance and resurgence to challenge colonial relationships and processes. It includes chapters examining the history of SRFN before 1950, the establishment of the settler community of Elliot Lake and associated uranium mines, the construction and operation of a sulfuric acid plant on reserve land, and Anishinaabe resistance.

Serpent River Resurgence clearly articulates the profound loss the Serpent River Anishinaabe experienced as a result of centuries of colonial incursions, especially those related to uranium mining. Leddy shows how the establishment of a uranium mining industry on SRFN territory led to an influx of settlers and left a legacy of radioactive tailings and acid waste. The operation of the acid plant on reserve land—which supplied sulfuric acid to the uranium industry—similarly left a legacy of contamination that seriously disrupted the Anishinaabe land-based economy. The fact that the Serpent River Anishinaabe were excluded from important decisions about the uranium industry undermined their traditional role as stewards of the land.

At the same time, Leddy shows that the Serpent River Anishinaabe were not simply passive victims of settler colonialism and the nuclear industry. As the title suggests, her book uses a conceptual framework of Indigenous resurgence and celebrates SFRN's long history of resistance to colonialism: "Whether it was to question rapid and extensive expansion of uranium production at Elliot Lake, to attend meetings in Toronto or Ottawa, or to threaten to block the highway if [the Department of Indian Affairs] continued to impede a clean-up process of the acid site, SRFN community members resorted to creative and consistent means of asserting Indigenous rights" (139). According to Leddy, these strategic interventions led to an important process of Indigenous resurgence, insofar as they resulted in the Serpent River Anishinaabe reestablishing their traditional role in land stewardship.

Serpent River Resurgence will be of interest to scholars working in Indigenous studies and beyond, especially those whose teaching and research interests include Indigenous resurgence, settler colonialism, the nuclear industry, Anishinaabe history, and the politics of the Cold War. It will be a useful reading for senior undergraduate and graduate courses in Indigenous studies, political ecology, and environmental studies. The fact that Anishinaabe communities in northern Ontario are currently facing proposals for a repository for Canada's high-level nuclear waste makes Leddy's work timely and relevant to broader public debates about the future of the nuclear industry in the region.

WARREN BERNAUER is a postdoctoral fellow in the Department of Environment and Geography and the Natural Resources Institute, University of Manitoba.

Yale UNIVERSITY PRESS

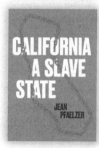

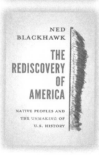

Violent Appetites
Hunger in the Early Northeast
Carla Cevasco

Talking Back
Native Women and the Making of the Early South
Alejandra Dubcovsky

THE HENRY ROE CLOUD SERIES ON AMERICAN INDIANS AND MODERNITY

The Makings and Unmakings of Americans
Indians and Immigrants in American Literature and Culture, 1879-1924
Cristina Stanciu

Indigenous London
Native Travelers at the Heart of Empire
Coll Thrush

Assembled for Use
Indigenous Compilation and the Archives of Early Native American Literatures
Kelly Wisecup

The Rediscovery of America
Native Peoples and the Unmaking of U.S. History
Ned Blackhawk

Vaudeville Indians on Global Circuits, 1880s-1930s
Christine Bold

Indigenous Visions
Rediscovering the World of Franz Boas
Edited by Ned Blackhawk and Isaiah Lorado Wilner

A Journey to Freedom
Richard Oakes, Alcatraz, and the Red Power Movement
Kent Blansett

The Sea Is My Country
The Maritime World of the Makahs
Joshua L. Reid

Ecology of Dakota Landscapes
Past, Present, and Future
W. Carter Johnson and Dennis H. Knight

THE LAMAR SERIES IN WESTERN HISTORY

California, a Slave State
Jean Pfaelzer

Lakota America
A New History of Indigenous Power
Pekka Hämäläinen

AVAILABLE IN PAPERBACK

Playing Indian
Philip J. Deloria
With a New Preface
Yale Historical Publications Series

Surviving Genocide
Native Nations and the United States from the American Revolution to Bleeding Kansas
Jeffrey Ostler

yalebooks.com

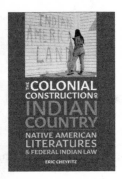

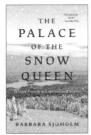